Adobe®

Illustrator® CC

CLASSROOM IN A BOOK®

The official training workbook from Adobe Systems

D0598576

Adobe® Illustrator® CC Classroom in a Book®

Adobe Press books are published by Peachpit, a division of Pearson Education located in San Francisco, California. For the latest on Adobe Press books, go to www.adobepress.com. To report errors, please send a note to errata@peachpit.com. For information on getting permission for reprints and excerpts, contact permissions@peachpit.com.

Printed and bound in the United States of America

ISBN-13: 978-0-321-92949-5
ISBN-10:   0-321-92949-7

9 8 7 6 5 4 3 2 1

WHERE ARE THE LESSON FILES?

Purchasing this Classroom in a Book gives you access to the lesson files that you'll need to complete the exercises in the book, as well as other content to help you learn more about Adobe software and use it with greater efficiency and ease. The diagram below represents the contents of the lesson files directory, which should help you locate the files you need. Please see the Getting Started section for full download instructions.

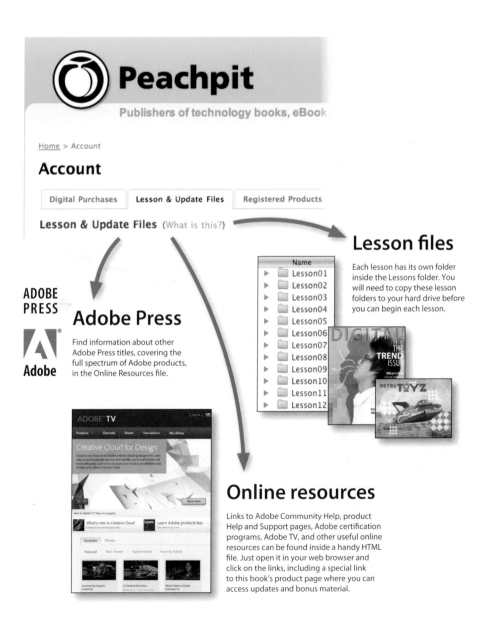

Lesson files

Each lesson has its own folder inside the Lessons folder. You will need to copy these lesson folders to your hard drive before you can begin each lesson.

Adobe Press

Find information about other Adobe Press titles, covering the full spectrum of Adobe products, in the Online Resources file.

Online resources

Links to Adobe Community Help, product Help and Support pages, Adobe certification programs, Adobe TV, and other useful online resources can be found inside a handy HTML file. Just open it in your web browser and click on the links, including a special link to this book's product page where you can access updates and bonus material.

CONTENTS

GETTING STARTED

Adobe® Illustrator® CC is the industry-standard illustration application for print, multimedia, and online graphics. Whether you are a designer or a technical illustrator producing artwork for print publishing, an artist producing multimedia graphics, or a creator of web pages or online content, Adobe Illustrator offers you the tools you need to get professional-quality results.

About Classroom in a Book

Adobe Illustrator CC Classroom in a Book® is part of the official training series for Adobe graphics and publishing software developed with the support of Adobe product experts.

The lessons are designed so that you can learn at your own pace. If you're new to Adobe Illustrator, you'll learn the fundamentals you need to master to put the application to work. If you are an experienced user, you'll find that *Classroom in a Book* teaches many advanced features, including tips and techniques for using the latest version of Adobe Illustrator.

Although each lesson provides step-by-step instructions for creating a specific project, there's room for exploration and experimentation. You can follow the book from start to finish, or do only the lessons that correspond to your interests and needs. Each lesson concludes with a review section summarizing what you've covered.

Prerequisites

Before beginning to use *Adobe Illustrator CC Classroom in a Book*, you should have working knowledge of your computer and its operating system. Make sure that you know how to use the mouse and standard menus and commands, and also how to open, save, and close files. If you need to review these techniques, see the printed or online documentation for your Windows or Mac OS.

● **Note:** When instructions differ by platform, Windows commands appear first, and then the Mac OS commands, with the platform noted in parentheses. For example, "press the Alt (Windows) or Option (Mac OS) key and click away from the artwork." In some instances, common commands may be abbreviated with the Windows commands first, followed by a slash and the Mac OS commands, without any parenthetical reference. For example, "press Alt/ Option" or "press Ctrl/Command+click."

Installing the program

Before you begin using *Adobe Illustrator CC Classroom in a Book*, make sure that your system is set up correctly and that you've installed the required software and hardware.

You must purchase the Adobe Illustrator CC software separately. For complete instructions on installing the software, visit www.adobe.com/support. Illustrator and Bridge use separate installers. You must install these applications from Adobe Creative Cloud onto your hard disk. Follow the onscreen instructions.

Fonts used in this book

The Classroom in a Book lesson files use the fonts that come with Adobe Illustrator CC and install with the product for your convenience. These fonts are installed in the following locations:

- Windows: [startup drive]\Windows\Fonts\
- Mac OS X: [startup drive]/Library/Fonts/

For more information about fonts and installation, see the Adobe Illustrator CC Read Me file on the web at www.adobe.com/support.

Accessing the Classroom in a Book files

In order to work through the projects in this book, you will need to download the lesson files from peachpit.com. You can download the files for individual lessons, or download them all in a single file. Although each lesson stands alone, some lessons use files from other lessons, so you'll need to keep the entire collection of lesson assets on your computer as you work through the book.

To access the Classroom in a Book files:

1 On a Mac or PC, go to www.peachpit.com/redeem and enter the code found at the back of your book.

2 If you do not have a Peachpit.com account, you will be prompted to create one.

3 The downloadable files will be listed under Lesson & Update Files tab on your Account page.

4 Click the lesson file links to download them to your computer.

Restoring default preferences

The preferences file controls how command settings appear on your screen when you open the Adobe Illustrator program. Each time you quit Adobe Illustrator, the position of the panels and certain command settings are recorded in different preference files. If you want to restore the tools and settings to their original default settings, you can delete the current Adobe Illustrator CC preferences file. Adobe Illustrator creates a new preferences file, if one doesn't already exist, the next time you start the program and save a file.

You must restore the default preferences for Illustrator before you begin each lesson. This ensures that the tools and panels function as described in this book. When you have finished the book, you can restore your saved settings, if you like.

To delete or save the current Illustrator preferences file

1 Exit Adobe Illustrator CC.

2 Locate the **Adobe Illustrator Prefs** file as follows:

- (Windows 7 [Service Pack 1], or Windows 8) The Adobe Illustrator Prefs file is located in the folder [startup drive]\Users\[username]\AppData\Roaming\Adobe\Adobe Illustrator 17 Settings\en_US*\x86 or x64.

- (Mac OS 10.6.8, 10.7, and 10.8**) The Adobe Illustrator Prefs file is located in the folder [startup drive]/Users/[username]/Library/Preferences/Adobe Illustrator 17 Settings/en_US*.

*Folder name may be different depending on the language version you have installed.
On Mac OS 10.7 (Lion) and Mac OS 10.8 (Mountain Lion) the Library folder is hidden by default. To access this folder, in Finder, choose Go > Go To Folder. Type **~/Library in the Go To Folder dialog box and then click OK.

● **Note:** If you cannot locate the preferences file, try using your operating system's Find command, and search for "Adobe Illustrator Prefs."

If you can't find the file, you either haven't started Adobe Illustrator CC yet or you have moved the preferences file. The preferences file is created after you quit the program the first time and is updated thereafter.

3 Copy the file and save it to another folder on your hard disk (if you wish to restore those preferences) or Delete it.

4 Start Adobe Illustrator CC.

To restore saved preferences after completing the lessons

1 Exit Adobe Illustrator CC.

2 Delete the current preferences file. Find the original preferences file that you saved and move it to the Adobe Illustrator 17 Settings folder.

● **Note:** In Windows 7, the AppData folder is hidden by default. To make it visible, open Folder Options in Control Panel and click the View tab. In the Advanced Settings pane, find Hidden Files and folders and select Show Hidden Files and Folders or Show hidden files, folders, or drives.

▶ **Tip:** To quickly locate and delete the Adobe Illustrator preferences file each time you begin a new lesson, create a shortcut (Windows) or an alias (Mac OS) to the Adobe Illustrator 17 Settings folder.

● **Note:** You can move the original preferences file rather than renaming it.

Additional resources

Adobe Illustrator CC Classroom in a Book is not meant to replace documentation that comes with the program or to be a comprehensive reference for every feature. Only the commands and options used in the lessons are explained in this book. For comprehensive information about program features and tutorials, please refer to these resources:

Adobe Illustrator Help and Support: www.adobe.com/support/illustrator is where you can find and browse Help and Support content on adobe.com.

Adobe Creative Cloud Learning: for inspiration, key techniques, cross-product workflows, and updates on new features go to the Creative Cloud Learn page https://helpx.adobe.com/creative-cloud/tutorials.html. Available only to Creative Cloud members.

Adobe Forums: forums.adobe.com lets you tap into peer-to-peer discussions, questions and answers on Adobe products.

Adobe TV: tv.adobe.com is an online video resource for expert instruction and inspiration about Adobe products, including a How To channel to get you started with your product.

Adobe Design Center: www.adobe.com/designcenter offers thoughtful articles on design and design issues, a gallery showcasing the work of top-notch designers, tutorials, and more.

Resources for educators: www.adobe.com/education and http://edex.adobe.com offer a treasure trove of information for instructors who teach classes on Adobe software. Find solutions for education at all levels, including free curricula that use an integrated approach to teaching Adobe software and can be used to prepare for the Adobe Certified Associate exams.

Also check out these useful links:

Adobe Illustrator CC product home page: www.adobe.com/products/illustrator

Adobe Labs: http://labs.adobe.com gives you access to early builds of cutting-edge technology, as well as forums where you can interact with both the Adobe development teams building that technology and other like-minded members of the community.

Adobe certification

The Adobe training and certification programs are designed to help Adobe customers improve and promote their product-proficiency skills. There are four levels of certification:

* Adobe Certified Associate (ACA)
* Adobe Certified Expert (ACE)
* Adobe Certified Instructor (ACI)
* Adobe Authorized Training Center (AATC)

The Adobe Certified Associate (ACA) credential certifies that individuals have the entry-level skills to plan, design, build, and maintain effective communications using different forms of digital media.

The Adobe Certified Expert program is a way for expert users to upgrade their credentials. You can use Adobe certification as a catalyst for getting a raise, finding a job, or promoting your expertise.

If you are an ACE-level instructor, the Adobe Certified Instructor program takes your skills to the next level and gives you access to a wide range of Adobe resources.

Adobe Authorized Training Centers offer instructor-led courses and training on Adobe products, employing only Adobe Certified Instructors. A directory of AATCs is available at http://partners.adobe.com.

For information on the Adobe Certified programs, visit www.adobe.com/support/certification/main.html.

Sync settings using Adobe Creative Cloud

When you work on multiple machines, managing and syncing preferences, presets, and libraries among the machines can be time-consuming, complex, and prone to error. The Sync Settings feature enables individual users to sync their preferences, presets, and libraries to the Creative Cloud. This means that if you use two machines, say one at home and the other at work, the Sync Settings feature makes it easy for you to keep those settings synchronized across two machines. Also, if you have replaced your old machine with a new one and have re-installed Illustrator, this feature will let you bring back all those settings on the new machine.

Syncing happens via your Adobe Creative Cloud account. All the settings are uploaded to your Creative Cloud account and then are downloaded and applied on another machine. In order to sync, you need the following:

Note: You need to initiate the sync manually; it does not happen automatically and it cannot be scheduled.

- The machine to be synced is connected to the Internet.
- Be signed in to your Adobe Creative Cloud account.

First launch of Adobe Illustrator CC

Note: This figure is from Illustrator CC on Mac OS, after logging in with an Adobe ID and launching Illustrator CC.

When you launch Adobe Illustrator CC for the first time, with no previous sync information available, you will see a prompt asking whether you want to start the sync. You have the options to sync the settings, disable the syncing, or go to preferences to set what is synced by clicking the Advanced button.

- Click Sync Settings Now to initiate the sync if you wish to sync your settings.

Sync settings on first launch if prior sync information is available

Note: This figure is from Illustrator CC on Windows, after logging in with the same Adobe ID as the Mac OS machine and launching Illustrator CC.

When you launch Adobe Illustrator CC with prior sync information available, say on another machine that is signed into your Adobe Creative Cloud account, you will see a prompt asking whether you would you like to use the settings from the cloud. To initiate the sync, click Sync Settings Now.

Illustrator may need to be restarted, or there could be a conflict with your existing settings. If Illustrator needs to be restarted for the settings to take effect, a sync

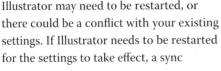

status message asking to restart Illustrator appears in the lower-left corner of the Document window. You can also click the sync status button () in the lower-left corner of the document window.

Syncing conflicts

The ideal workflow is to sync settings on one machine (say your work machine), and then sync settings on your second machine (home computer). Sometimes this doesn't happen, though. The settings in the cloud and the settings on one of your computers can become out of sync. If you try to sync when this is the case, you will see a conflict prompt in the lower-left corner of the Document window. Here's what each option means:

- **Sync Local:** sync local settings on this computer to the cloud; overwrite the cloud version with the local version of settings.

- **Sync Cloud:** sync from the cloud to this local computer; ignore changes made to the local settings and replace them with the settings in the cloud.

- **Keep Latest File:** keep the latest settings based on the timestamp.

The settings are downloaded to your local machine and are updated in the application. Subsequently, if you make changes to preferences, presets, and libraries, you should initiate sync before you close the application. You can see the sync status in the left-bottom corner of the document status bar.

Setting sync options

You can easily manage your account, change what gets synchronized with Adobe Creative Cloud, and what to do in case of a conflict.

- Choose Edit > Preferences > Sync Settings (Windows) or Illustrator > Preferences > Sync Settings (Mac OS) and set options in the Preferences dialog box that appears.

▶ **Tip:** You can also choose Edit > [username] > Manage Sync Settings (Windows) or Illustrator > [username] > Manage Sync Settings (Mac OS).

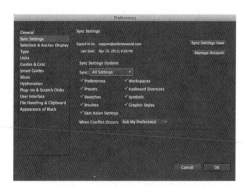

● **Note:** To sync your settings successfully, you must make changes to the settings only from within the application. The sync does not identify any manual changes done in these locations. This also applies to any libraries (swatches, symbols, etc.) copied and pasted into preferences folders.

WHAT'S NEW IN ADOBE ILLUSTRATOR CC

Adobe® Illustrator® CC is packed with new and innovative features to help you produce artwork more efficiently for print, web, and digital video publication. In this section, you'll learn about many of these new features—how they function and how you can use them in your work.

Adobe Illustrator and Adobe Creative Cloud

With all-new Adobe Illustrator CC , you always have the latest version, because access to every future release is built right in. Cloud-enabled features, like Sync Fonts, Sync Colors, and Sync Settings, turn any workspace into your workspace.

Touch Type tool

Design with type in a powerful new way. Characters can now be manipulated like individual objects. Experiment with moving, scaling, and rotating, knowing that you can edit or change the font at any time. And you can now use multitouch devices, as well as a mouse or stylus.

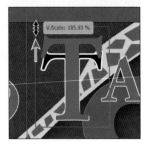

Images in brushes

Paint with a brush made from a photo. Art, Pattern, and Scatter brushes can contain raster images, so you can create complex organic designs quickly—with simple brush strokes. As with all Illustrator brushes, your strokes can be reshaped and modified at will.

Text improvements

Find the perfect font—fast. In the Character panel, type a style, such as **bold** or **italic**, a font family, or any other part of a font name. You'll get a filtered view that lets you see just the fonts that match your criteria. Work faster with type, even in your most complicated, type-intensive designs. Text that wraps around objects and type that is set in multiple connected text frames now refresh quickly when you make a change. Instantly switch between area type and point type. Text object conversion is now instantaneous so you can design freely in your text layouts. And you can work just as easily with imported type, switching formats at any time.

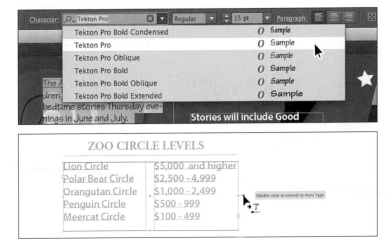

Image enhancements

Import multiple files into your Illustrator layout at the same time and with new control. Now you can define the location and scale of your files—images, graphics, and text—and use new thumbnail views to see where each file will go and how big it will be. Easily unembed images that have been placed and embedded in an Illustrator file. You can quickly make images available for editing or extract files embedded in artwork you received from someone  else. Links to the image files are created automatically. Get more complete information about any placed file in the Links panel. All of your placed elements—images, graphics, and text—appear in the Links panel, where you can track them with greater control than ever before.

CSS extraction

Hand-coding web elements, such as icons and patterns, can be frustrating. Now create websites faster by letting Illustrator generate Cascading Style Sheet (CSS) code for you, even for a complete logo that includes gradients. Copy and paste the code right into your web editor, or export the styling to a CSS file.

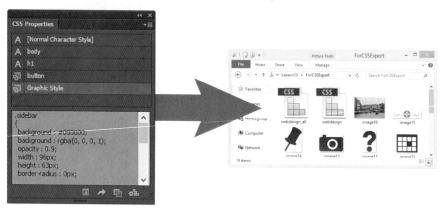

On-art Free Transform

Get hands-on with the power of the Free Transform tool. Move, scale, and rotate objects directly using a touchscreen device. Or use a mouse or other pointer right on the artboard to transform objects in a more immediate and intuitive way.

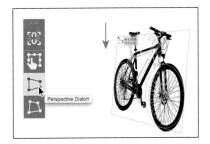

Package files

File packaging automatically gathers and saves the necessary fonts, linked graphics, and a package report into a single folder. Efficiently hand off Illustrator files to production, or keep your working files organized by packaging up your project.

Other enhancements

- Kuler for color syncing—Capture color themes out in the world with the Adobe Kuler® iPhone® app. Share your themes and explore thousands of others available on the Kuler website. Sync your favorite themes with Adobe Creative Cloud™, and they'll be accessible immediately in Illustrator.

- White Overprint—Suppress objects with White Overprint in Print and PDF.

- Separations Preview—Make the most of the improved Separations Preview panel (with Show Used Spot Colors Only selected in the panel).

- Improved find in the Swatches panel, swatch libraries, and the Color Picker dialog box.

- Auto corners for pattern brushes—Get the corners you want without extra steps. Create pattern brushes swiftly with auto-generated corners that perfectly match the rest of the stroke. No need to tediously create special corners for your sharp angles.

Although this list touches on just a few of the new and enhanced features of Illustrator CC, it exemplifies Adobe's commitment to providing the best tools possible for your publishing needs. We hope you enjoy working with Illustrator CC as much as we do.

—The Adobe Illustrator CC Classroom in a Book Team

A QUICK TOUR OF ADOBE® ILLUSTRATOR® CC

Lesson overview

In this interactive demonstration of Adobe Illustrator CC, you'll get an overview of the application while you use a few of the exciting new features.

 This lesson takes approximately an hour to complete.

Download the project files for this lesson from the Lesson & Update Files tab on your Account page at www.peachpit.com and store them on your computer in a convenient location, as described in the Getting Started section of this book.

Your Accounts page is also where you'll find any updates to the chapters or to the lesson files. Look on the Lesson & Update Files tab to access the most current content.

In this demonstration of Adobe Illustrator CC,
you will be introduced to new and exciting
application features, like the Touch Type tool and
type selection, as well as some key fundamentals for
working in the application.

Getting started

For the first lesson of this book, you will get a quick tour of the tools and features in Adobe Illustrator CC, offering a sense of the many possibilities. Along the way, you will create a flyer for a pizza restaurant.

1   To ensure that the tools and panels function exactly as described in this lesson, delete or deactivate (by renaming) the Adobe Illustrator CC preferences file. See "Restoring default preferences," on page 3.

2   Start Adobe Illustrator CC.

● **Note:** If you have not already downloaded the project files for this lesson to your computer from your Account page, make sure to do so now. See "Getting Started" at the beginning of the book.

Sync settings using Adobe Creative Cloud™

When you launch Adobe Illustrator CC for the first time, with no previous sync information available, you will see a prompt asking whether you want to start a sync with Adobe Creative Cloud. For more information on syncing with the Creative Cloud, see "Sync settings using Adobe Creative Cloud" on page 6.

• If you are launching Adobe Illustrator for the first time or if you see a dialog box appear, click Disable Sync Settings or Sync Settings Now.

Creating a new document

An Illustrator document can contain up to 100 artboards (*artboards* are similar to *pages* in a program like Adobe InDesign®). Next, you will create a document with two artboards.

● **Note:** If you don't see "Reset Essentials" in the Workspace menu, choose Window > Workspace > Essentials before choosing Window > Workspace > Reset Essentials.

1   Choose Window > Workspace > Reset Essentials.

2   Choose File > New.

3   In the New Document dialog box, change only the following options (leaving the rest at their default settings):

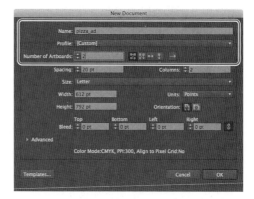

• Name: **pizza_ad**

• Number Of Artboards: **2**

• Size: **Letter**
  (the default setting)

Click OK. A new blank document appears.

4   Choose File > Save As. In the Save As dialog box, leave the name as pizza_ad.ai and navigate to the Lesson00 folder. Leave the Save As Type option set to Adobe Illustrator (*.AI) (Windows) or the Format option set to Adobe Illustrator (ai) (Mac OS), and click Save. In the Illustrator Options dialog box, leave the Illustrator options at their default settings and then click OK.

5   Choose View > Rulers > Show Rulers to show rulers in the Document window.

6   Select the Artboard
     tool (⊞) in the Tools panel
     on the left. Click the center of
     the white artboard with the
     02 - Artboard 2 label in the
     upper-left corner, to select it.

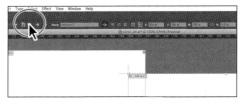

● **Note:** Learn
more about creating
new documents in
Lesson 3, "Creating and
Editing Shapes." Learn
more about editing
artboards in Lesson 4,
"Transforming Objects."

     In the Control panel, above the artboards, click the Landscape button (▣).

7   Position the pointer over the
     selected artboard, and drag it
     to the right until there is a gray
     gap between the two artboards.

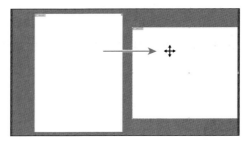

     Illustrator allows you to have
     artboards of differing sizes
     and orientations.

8   Select the Selection tool (▶) in
     the Tools panel to stop editing the artboards. Click the artboard on the right (the
     landscape, or horizontal, artboard) to make it the active artboard.

9   Choose View > Fit Artboard In Window.

Drawing shapes

Drawing shapes is the cornerstone of Illustrator, and you will create many of them
in the coming lessons. Next, you will create several shapes.

● **Note:** Learn more
about creating and
editing shapes in
Lesson 3, "Creating and
Editing Shapes."

1   Select the Rectangle tool (▢) in the
     Tools panel. Position the pointer in
     the upper-left corner of the artboard
     (see the red X in the figure). When the
     word "intersect" appears next to the
     pointer, click and drag down and to the
     right edge of the white artboard. When

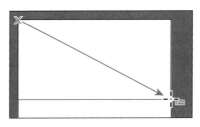

     the gray measurement label shows a width of 792 pt and a height of
     400 pt, release the mouse button. It does not have to be exact.

2   Click and hold down on the Rectangle tool in the Tools panel. Click to select the
     Polygon tool (⬡).

3   Click roughly in the center of the
     artboard to open the Polygon dialog
     box. Change the Radius to **200 pt** and
     the Sides value to **3** by typing in the
     values. Click OK to create a triangle
     that will become a slice of pizza.

Applying color

● **Note:** Learn more about creating and applying color in Lesson 6, "Color and Painting."

Applying colors to artwork is a common Illustrator task. Experimenting and applying color is easy using the Color panel, Swatches panel, Color Guide panel, and Edit Colors/Recolor Artwork dialog box.

1   Select the Selection tool (↖) in the Tools panel on the left, and click anywhere in the rectangle you drew, to select it.

2   Click the Fill color in the Control panel to reveal the Swatches panel (circled in the figure). Position the pointer over the black swatch (in the top row of colors). When the tool tip appears that shows "Black," click to apply the black swatch to the fill. Press the Escape key to hide the Swatches panel.

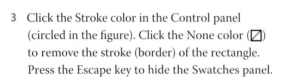

3   Click the Stroke color in the Control panel (circled in the figure). Click the None color (◨) to remove the stroke (border) of the rectangle. Press the Escape key to hide the Swatches panel.

4   Click anywhere inside of the white triangle you created, to select it.

5   Double-click the white Fill box located near the bottom of the Tools panel. In the Color Picker dialog box, change the CMYK values to C=**5**, M=**70**, Y=**100**, K=**25**. Click OK to create a new color that is applied to the fill of the triangle.

Double-click the Fill box.   Edit the color in the Color Picker dialog box.

● **Note:** The stroke is currently very small, so you may not see the color change on the stroke yet.

6   Click the Stroke color in the Control panel. Click the light orange color with the tool tip "C=0 M=35 Y=85 K=0" to paint the stroke of the triangle.

7   Choose File > Save, and leave the triangle selected for the next section.

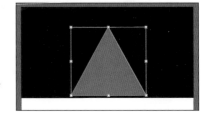

Editing strokes

In addition to changing the color of strokes, you can also format them in many other ways. That's what you'll do next with the triangle.

● **Note:** Learn more about working with strokes in Lesson 3, "Creating and Editing Shapes."

1 With the triangle still selected, click the underlined word "Stroke" in the Control panel above the document, to open the Stroke panel. Change the Stroke Weight to **3 pt** in the Stroke panel that appears. Press the Escape key to hide the Stroke panel.

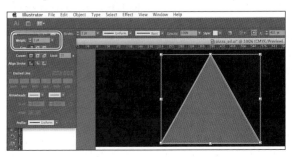

2 With the Selection tool (▸), Shift-click the black rectangle to select it, too. Choose Object > Hide > Selection to temporarily hide the rectangle and the triangle.

Creating shapes using the Shape Builder tool

The Shape Builder tool is an interactive tool for creating complex shapes by merging and erasing simpler shapes. Next, you will finish a city skyline created using the Shape Builder tool.

● **Note:** Learn more about working with the Shape Builder tool in Lesson 3, "Creating and Editing Shapes."

1 Choose File > Open, and open the city.ai file in the Lesson00 folder in the Lessons folder on your hard disk.

The city.ai file contains a series of simple shapes that were merged to create a single city shape. You'll finish the shape by adding another building and creating some windows using the Shape Builder tool.

2 Choose View > Fit Artboard In Window.

3 With the Selection tool (▸) selected, click the single building on the far right. Drag it to the left. As you drag, press the Shift key to constrain its movement. When the left edge of the building "snaps" to the right edge of the city shape, release the mouse button and then release the Shift key.

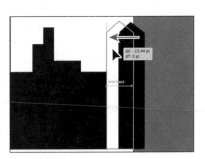

4   Choose Select > All On Active Artboard to select the city shapes.

The larger city shape and the individual building are selected, but also notice the three rectangles on one of the buildings that will become windows.

5   Select the Shape Builder tool (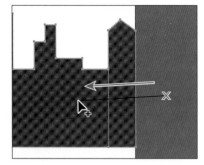) in the Tools panel. Position the pointer to the right of all of the selected shapes (see the red X in the figure), and drag to the left into the larger city shape. Release the mouse button.

This combines those two shapes into one.

6   Position the pointer over one of the smaller rectangles (where the red circle is in the figure below). Holding down the Alt (Windows) or Option (Mac OS) key, when you see the mesh pattern appear in the fill of the object (*not* a red stroke), click to subtract the highlighted shape from the city shape. Still pressing the Alt (Windows) or Option (Mac OS) key, click inside of the remaining two window shapes.

Position the pointer.

Click to remove the path.

Notice the final result.

7   Select the Selection tool (➤) in the Tools panel on the left, and make sure that the city shape is still selected. Choose Edit > Copy.

8   Choose File > Close to close the file without saving.

9   Choose Edit > Paste, back in the pizza_ad.ai file, to paste the shape in the center of the Document window.

10 With the Selection tool, click and drag the shape up toward the top of the artboard. Keep the shape in the horizontal center of the artboard (as best you can), and stop short of the top of the artboard.

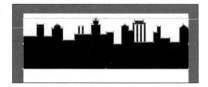

As you drag, you will see green alignment guides and a gray measurement label. These are a part of the Smart Guides feature you will learn about in a later lesson.

Creating and editing gradients

Gradients are color blends of two or more colors that you can apply to the fill or stroke of artwork. Next, you will apply a gradient to the city shape.

Note: Learn more about working with gradients in Lesson 10, "Blending Colors and Shapes."

1 Choose View > Fit Artboard In Window.

2 With the city shape still selected, choose Window > Gradient to show the Gradient panel on the right side of the workspace.

3 In the Gradient panel, change the following options:

- Click the black Fill box (circled in the figure), if it's not already selected, so that you can apply the gradient to the fill of the city shape.
- Click the Gradient menu button (⬛) to the left of the word "Type," and choose White, Black from the menu.
- Choose **90** from the Angle menu.

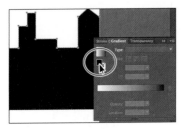
Select the Fill box.

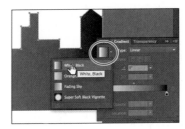
Apply the White, Black gradient.

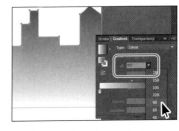
Adjust the angle of the gradient.

4 Click the white color stop in the Gradient panel (circled in the figure below), and click the arrow to the right of the Opacity value below it. Choose 0%.

5 Double-click the black color stop on the right side of the gradient slider in the Gradient panel (circled in the figure below). In the panel that appears, change the Opacity value to **20%** by clicking the arrow to the right of the Opacity value and choosing 20%. Click the Color button (⬛), and click the white color box to apply a white color. Press the Escape key to hide the Color panel.

Note: In the Color panel that appears, you may only see a K (black) slider, and that's okay.

6 Choose Object > Show All to show the triangle and rectangle again.

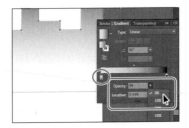
Edit the white color opacity.

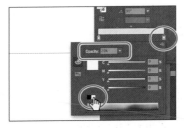
Edit the black color.

Notice the result.

7 Choose Select > Deselect, and then choose File > Save.

Working with layers

● **Note:** Learn more about working with layers and the Layers panel in Lesson 8, "Working with Layers."

Layers allow you to organize and more easily select artwork. Next, using the Layers panel, you will organize your artwork.

1   Choose Window > Layers to show the Layers panel in the workspace.

2   Double-click directly on Layer 1 (the layer name) in the Layers panel. Type **Background**, and press Enter or Return to change the layer name. Naming layers can be helpful when organizing content. Currently, all artwork is on this layer.

3   Click the Create New Layer button (▤) at the bottom of the Layers panel. Double-click Layer 2 (the new layer name), and type **Content**. Press Enter or Return.

Rename Layer 1.

Create a new layer.

Rename the new layer.

4   With the Selection tool (▸), click to select the triangle (make sure not to select the city shape that's on top of it). Choose Edit > Cut.

5   Click the eye icon (👁) to the left of the Background layer name to temporarily hide the contents of the layer on the artboard. Layers can make it easier to hide and lock content temporarily so you can focus on other artwork.

6   Click once on the layer named Content to select it in the Layers panel. New artwork is added to the selected layer.

7   Choose Edit > Paste, to paste the triangle on the selected layer (Content).

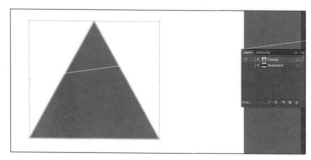

8   Leave the triangle selected for the next section, and then choose File > Save.

Working with the Width tool

The Width tool allows you to create a variable width stroke and to save the width as a profile that can be applied to other objects. Next, you'll make the stroke of the triangle look like pizza crust.

● **Note:** Learn more about the Width tool in Lesson 3, "Creating and Editing Shapes."

1   Select the Width tool (🌢) in the Tools panel. Position the pointer over the bottom edge of the triangle, close to the left end (circled in the figure). When the pointer shows a plus sign (+) next to it, drag down, away from the center of the triangle. When the gray measurement label next to the pointer shows a Width of approximately 40 pt, release the mouse button.

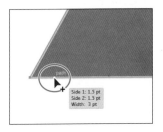 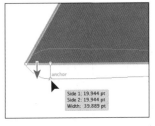 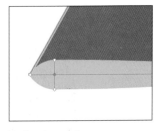

Position the pointer.   Drag away from the stroke center.   Notice the result.

2   Position the pointer a little to the right of where you just dragged the stroke. Starting at the bottom edge of the stroke (circled below), click and drag up, toward the center of the triangle. When the gray measurement label shows a Width of approximately 27 pt, release the mouse button.

▶ **Tip:** You can always choose Edit > Undo Width Point Change to remove the last point and try again.

3   Continue along the same pizza edge, adding a few more width points, alternating between dragging toward the center of the pizza and away from the center. Stop at the end of the stroke on that edge, as shown in the figure.

 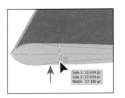 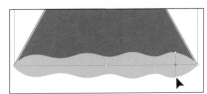

Position the pointer.   Drag to edit the width.   Notice the final result.

Creating a pattern

In addition to colors, the Swatches panel can also contain patterns. Illustrator provides sample swatches of each type, in the default Swatches panel, and lets you create your own patterns. In this section, you'll create a topping for the pizza using a pattern.

● **Note:** Learn more about patterns in Lesson 6, "Color and Painting."

1   Click and hold down on the Polygon tool (⬢) in the Tools panel. Click to select the Ellipse tool (⬤). In a blank area below the triangle, click. In the Ellipse dialog box, change the Width and Height values to **4 pt**. Click OK.

2   Select the Zoom tool (🔍) in the Tools panel. Click four times, *slowly*, directly on the new circle to zoom in.

3   Select the Selection tool (▶), and with the circle still selected, choose Edit > Copy, and then choose Edit > Paste. Paste (Edit > Paste) three more times to create five circles. All of the circle copies are on top of each other. Drag each from the center and position them like you see in the figure. They don't have to match exactly.

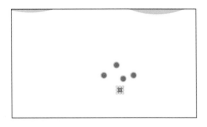

4   With the Selection tool, position the pointer in a blank area of the artboard near the circles. Click and drag across all of the circles to select them.

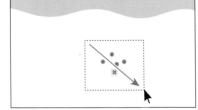

5   Choose Object > Pattern > Make. Click OK in the dialog box that appears.

6   In the Pattern Options panel, change the following options:

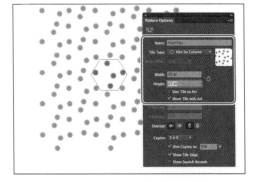

   • Name: **toppings**

   • Tile Type: **Hex By Column** (Choose from the menu.)

   • Width: **26 pt** (Type the value.)

   • Height: **22 pt** (Type the value.)

If your pattern looks different, that's okay. If the circles are overlapping too much or not enough for your taste, try making the Width and Height values in the Pattern Options panel larger or smaller.

7   Choose Select > All. Change the Stroke weight to **0**, by pressing the down arrow to the left of the stroke value until it disappears, in the Control panel above.

8   Change the Opacity value to **50%** in the Control panel by clicking the arrow to the right of the Opacity value and choosing 50% from the menu.

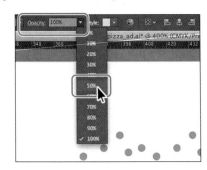

9   Change the Fill color for all of the circles to an orange color with the tool tip that shows "C=0 M=35 Y=85 K=0." Press the Escape key to hide the Swatches panel, if necessary.

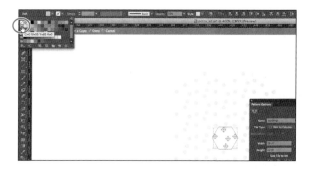

10 Choose Select > Deselect.

11 Shift-click the topmost and bottommost circles (within the hexagon shape). Change the Fill color to white in the Control panel. Press the Escape key to hide the Swatches panel.

12 Click Done in the gray bar above the artwork to finish editing the pattern.

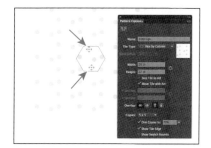

13 With the Selection tool (▶), drag across the original circles to select them. Press the Backspace or Delete key to delete them. You'll apply the pattern shortly.

Working with symbols

A *symbol* is a reusable art object stored in the Symbols panel. You will now create a symbol from artwork.

1 Select the Ellipse tool (⬭) in the Tools panel. Click in the blank area of the artboard, below the pizza. In the Ellipse dialog box, change the Width and Height values to **70 pt**. Click OK to create a circle.

2 With the circle selected, change the Stroke color to None (⬜) in the Control panel. Press the Escape key to hide the Swatches panel.

3 Double-click the Fill box near the bottom of the Tools panel. In the Color Picker dialog box that appears, change the CMYK values to C=**5**, M=**100**, Y=**90**, K=**60**. Click OK to create the color and close the Color Picker.

● **Note:** Learn more about working with symbols in Lesson 14, "Working with Symbols."

4 Choose Window > Symbols to show the Symbols panel.

5 Select the Selection tool (▶) in the Tools panel. With the circle still selected, click the New Symbol button (⬛) at the bottom of the Symbols panel.

6 In the Symbol Options dialog box, name the symbol **topping**, and click OK. The circle now appears as a saved symbol in the Symbols panel.

7 Choose View > Fit Artboard In Window.

8 Drag the original circle (that you used to make the symbol) onto the pizza shape (see the figure below for location).

● **Note:** Your topping symbol instances may be in different locations than those in the figure. That's okay.

9 From the Symbols panel, drag a symbol from the topping symbol thumbnail onto the pizza slice.
Drag five more topping symbols from the Symbols panel onto the pizza, for a total of six circles. Position them like you see in the figure (even hanging them off the edge), and don't cover the crust. Leave one of them selected on the artboard.

10 Choose Select > Same > Symbol Instance. Choose Object > Group.

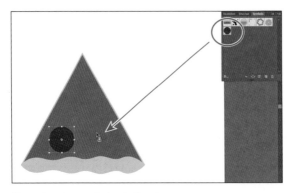

Drag a topping symbol onto the pizza.

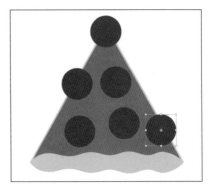

Notice the result.

Working with the Appearance panel

● **Note:** Learn more about working with the Appearance panel in Lesson 13, "Applying Appearance Attributes and Graphic Styles."

The Appearance panel allows you to control an object's attributes, such as stroke, fill, and effects. Next, you will edit the topping symbol using the Appearance panel.

1 In the Symbols panel, double-click the topping symbol thumbnail to edit the symbol artwork.

2 Choose Select > All to select the circle.

3 Choose Window > Appearance to open the panel. At the bottom of the Appearance panel, click the Add New Fill button (⬛) to add a new fill to the shape. Click the red Fill color box in the new Fill

row added. Select the toppings swatch in the Swatches panel that appears, to apply the pattern. Press the Escape key to hide the Swatches panel.

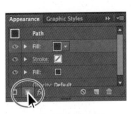 

Click the Add New Fill button.   Apply the pattern you created as a second fill.

4 Double-click a blank area of the artboard to stop editing the symbol and to update all of the topping instances on the pizza.

Creating a clipping mask

A *clipping mask* is an object which masks other artwork so that only areas that lie within its shape are visible—in effect, clipping the artwork to the shape of the mask. Next, you will copy the pizza slice and use the copy to mask the symbol instances.

● **Note:** Learn more about working with clipping masks in Lesson 15, "Combining Illustrator CC Graphics with Other Adobe Applications."

1 With the Selection tool (▸) selected, click the pizza triangle (not the symbol group).

2 Choose Edit > Copy, and then choose Edit > Paste In Front to paste a copy directly on top of the original pizza slice.

3 Choose Object > Arrange > Bring To Front to arrange the triangle on top of the symbol group.

4 Press the Shift key, and click one of the symbol instances (the large circles) that is showing from behind the pizza slice, to select the triangle and the group.

5 Choose Object > Clipping Mask > Make.

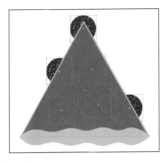   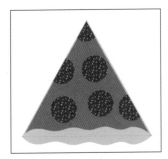

Select both objects.   Create the clipping mask.

6 Choose Select > All On Active Artboard, and then choose Object > Group.

Note: The figure shows the values after entering the Width value but before pressing Enter or Return.

7   With the group of objects selected, click the underlined X, Y, W, or H (or the word Transform) in the Control panel above the artwork to open the Transform panel. Click in the center point of the reference point locator (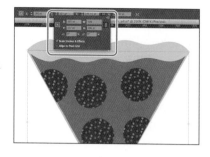), if it's not already selected, to scale the object from the center. Select Scale Strokes & Effects (located at the bottom of the panel). Change the Rotate value to **180**, and click the Constrain Width And Height Proportions button (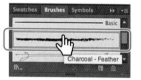). Change the W: (Width) to **500 pt**. Press Enter or Return to accept the values and close the Transform panel.

8   Choose Object > Expand Appearance, and then choose Object > Hide > Selection.

Working with brushes

Note: Learn more about working with brushes in Lesson 11, "Working with Brushes."

Brushes let you stylize the appearance of paths. You can apply brush strokes to existing paths, or you can use the Paintbrush tool to draw a path and apply a brush stroke simultaneously.

1   Choose Window > Workspace > Reset Essentials.

Note: If you don't see "Reset Essentials" in the Workspace menu, choose Window > Workspace > Essentials before choosing Window > Workspace > Reset Essentials.

2   Choose Window > Brushes to show the Brushes panel. Click the Charcoal - Feather brush.

3   Change the Fill color in the Control panel to None () and the Stroke color to a red color with the tool tip "C=0 M=90 Y=85 K=0." Press the Escape key to hide the Swatches panel.

4   Change the Stroke weight to **3 pt** in the Control panel above the artwork.

5   Select the Paintbrush tool ( ) in the Tools panel. Position the pointer on the left edge of the artboard, almost halfway down from the top (see the red X). Click and drag from left to right, to the right edge of the artboard, up and down to create a wave. See the figure for the shape to draw.

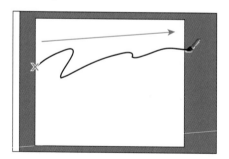

You can always choose Edit > Undo Art Stroke to try again.

6   Select the Selection tool ( ), and click the new red path to select it.

7   Choose Object > Hide > Selection to hide the path.

Working with type

Next, you will add some text to the project and apply formatting.

1 Select the Type tool (**T**) in the Tools panel, and click in the artboard. Type **City Pizza**. With the cursor in the text, choose Select > All to select it.

2 In the Control panel above the artwork, click in the Font field (to the right of the word "Character"). Type **chap**, and notice the font list that appears beneath the field. Click Chaparral Pro Bold Italic in the font list to apply it.

● **Note:** Learn more about working with type in Lesson 7, "Working with Type."

▶ **Tip:** If you don't see the Character options in the Control panel, click the word "Character" to see the Character panel.

3 Type **144** in the Font Size field (to the right of the Font Family), and press the Enter or Return key.

4 With the text still selected, change the Stroke color in the Control panel to None (☐), if necessary, and change the Fill color to white.

5 Choose Window > Layers, and click the visibility column to the left of the Background layer to show the contents of the Background layer.

● **Note:** Your Layers panel may not look the same as it is in the figure, and that's okay.

6 Select the Selection tool (▶), and drag to position the text to roughly look like the figure.

Next, you will adjust several individual letters using the Touch Type tool.

1 With the text object still selected, choose Window > Type > Character. Click the Touch Type Tool button to select the Touch Type tool.

2 Position the pointer over the "C" in "City," and click. The letter is now selected. Drag the upper-right corner point away from the center of the letter to make it larger. Stop dragging when the gray measurement label shows a width and height of approximately 135%.

3 Position the pointer over the rotation point above the box around the selected letter. Drag to the left until the measurement label that appears next to the pointer shows approximately 8°.

4 Click the letter "i" in "City" to select it. Drag it to the left until it's closer to the "C." Make sure that the gray measurement label shows 0 (it will change if you drag up or down—so drag straight across). See the figure for help.

5 Click to select the "P" in "Pizza." Drag the upper-right corner point away from the center until the gray measurement label shows a width and height of approximately 135%. Drag the letter "P" left, closer to the "y" in "City."

6 Click to select the letter "i" in "Pizza." Drag it to the left, closer to the letter "P."

7 Choose Object > Show All, and then choose Select > Deselect.

8 With the Selection tool (▸), click in the text and drag it to the center of the artboard, over the wavy red line you drew earlier (see the figure).

Drag the "P."   Drag the "i."   Position the text.

Working with perspective

● **Note:** Learn more about perspective in Lesson 9, "Working with Perspective Drawing."

You will now create a pizza box in perspective.

1 Click the First artboard button (◖◀) in the lower-left corner of the Document window to navigate to the first artboard and to fit it into the Document window.

2 Select the Perspective Grid tool (⊞) in the Tools panel to show the grid.

3 Choose View > Perspective Grid > Two Point Perspective > [2P-Normal View]. This centers the grid on the first artboard.

4 Select the Rectangle tool (▮) from the Ellipse tool (⬭) group in the Tools panel.

5 Click the Left Grid(1) in the Plane Switching Widget in the upper-left corner of the Document window to select the left grid (if it's not already selected). A tool tip will appear when you position the pointer over it.

6 Position the pointer over the bottom, center point of the grid (circled in the figure). When the word "intersect" appears next to the pointer, drag up and to the left to create a rectangle that has a height of 60 pt and a width of 570 pt (as shown in the gray measurement label next to the pointer as you draw).

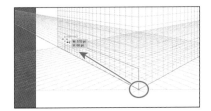

▶ **Tip:** The pointer snaps to the grid lines by default in the perspective grid to make it easier to achieve the correct size.

7 With the rectangle selected , change the Fill color to a medium gray swatch with the tool tip that displays "C=0 M=0 Y=0 K=40," and change the Stroke color to None (▨), in the Control panel. Press the Escape key to hide the Swatches panel.

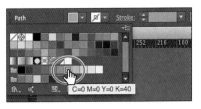

● **Note:** The rectangle may be a bit hard to see. As long as it changes color, it's okay.

8 Click the Right Grid(3) in the Plane Switching Widget in the upper-left corner of the Document window to select the right grid (see the figure below).

9 With the Rectangle tool selected, position the pointer over the origin point again (circled in the figure below). Click and drag up and to the right to create a rectangle that also has a height of 60 pt and a width of 570 pt.

10 In the Control panel, change the Fill color to a lighter gray swatch with the tool tip "C=0 M=0 Y=0 K=20." Press the Escape key to hide the Swatches panel.

11 Click Horizontal Grid(2) in the Plane Switching Widget.

12 Position the pointer over the upper-left point of the first rectangle you drew (circled in the figure below). Click and drag across, snapping the pointer to the upper-right point of the second rectangle you drew.

 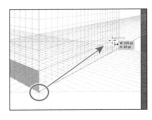  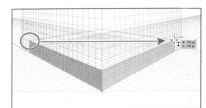

Select the Right Grid. Draw the rectangle. Select the Horizontal Grid. Draw the rectangle.

13 In the Control panel, change the Fill color to a light gray swatch with the tool tip "C=0 M=0 Y=0 K=10." Press the Escape key to hide the Swatches panel.

Now you will add artwork to the perspective grid.

1 Choose View > Fit All In Window.

2 Click and hold down on the Perspective Grid tool (▦) in the Tools panel, and select the Perspective Selection tool (▶).

Note: As you drag in this step, the pizza gets bigger and smaller in perspective. Try to center the pizza on the box top as best you can.

3 Make sure that the Horizontal grid is selected in the Plane Switching Widget (see the previous figure). Drag the pizza slice by the crust (see the red X) from the artboard on the right onto the top of the pizza box.

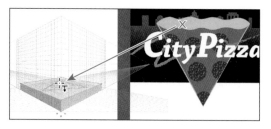

4 Choose Object > Arrange > Bring To Front to put the pizza on top of the box.

5 Although the pizza may still be selected, click it again to make the first artboard the active artboard.

6 Choose Select > All On Active Artboard. Choose Object > Group.

7 Select the Selection tool (▶), and drag the pizza group onto the right artboard. Click OK in the dialog box that appears.

8 Choose View > Perspective Grid > Hide Grid.

Placing images in Illustrator

Note: Learn more about placing images in Lesson 15, "Combining Illustrator CC Graphics with Other Adobe Applications."

In Illustrator, you can place raster images, like JPEG (jpg, jpeg, jpe) and Adobe Photoshop® (psd, pdd) files, and either link to them or embed them. Next, you will place an image of a tomato.

1 Choose File > Place. In the Place dialog box, navigate to the Lesson00 folder in the Lessons folder and select the tomato.psd file. Make sure that the Link option in the dialog box is selected, and click Place.

2 Click to place the tomato just to the right of the pizza box.

3 With the Selection tool (▶), drag the tomato so that it looks like the figure.

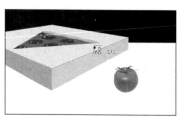

Click to place the tomato.

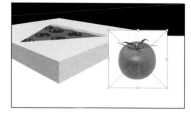

Reposition the tomato.

Using Image Trace

You can use Image Trace to convert photographs (raster images) into vector artwork. Next, you will trace the Photoshop file.

● **Note:** Learn more about Image Trace in Lesson 3, "Creating and Editing Shapes."

1 Choose View > Fit Artboard In Window.

2 Choose Window > Image Trace to open the Image Trace panel. In the panel, click the Low Color button (▦) at the top.

The image is converted to vector paths, but it is not yet editable.

3 In the Image Trace panel, click the toggle arrow to the left of Advanced. Select Ignore White near the bottom of the panel. Close the Image Trace panel.

4 With the tomato still selected, click the Expand button in the Control panel to make the object editable.

The tomato image is now a series of vector shapes that are grouped together.

5 Choose Edit > Copy, and then choose Edit > Paste. With the Selection tool, drag the copy into position next to the original tomato.

6 Choose Select > Deselect.

Working with Effects

Effects alter the appearance of an object without changing the base object. Next you will apply the Drop Shadow effect to several objects.

● **Note:** Learn more about effects in Lesson 12, "Applying Effects."

1 With the Selection tool (▶), press and hold the Shift key and then click the text "City Pizza," the pizza box, and each tomato. Release the key when you are finished selecting.

2 Choose Effect > Stylize > Drop Shadow. In the Drop Shadow dialog box, make sure that the Mode is Multiply, the Opacity is 75%, the X Offset and Y Offset are 7 pt, and the Blur is 5 pt. Select Preview, and then click OK.

3 Choose File > Save, and then choose File > Close.

1 GETTING TO KNOW THE WORK AREA

Lesson overview

In this lesson, you'll explore the workspace and learn how to do the following:

- Open an Adobe Illustrator CC file.
- Adjust the user interface brightness.
- Work with the Tools panel.
- Work with panels.
- Reset and save your workspace.
- Use viewing options to enlarge and reduce artwork.
- Navigate multiple artboards and documents.
- Explore document groups.
- Use Illustrator Help.

This lesson takes approximately 45 minutes to complete.

Download the project files for this lesson from the Lesson & Update Files tab on your Account page at www.peachpit.com and store them on your computer in a convenient location, as described in the Getting Started section of this book.

Your Accounts page is also where you'll find any updates to the chapters or to the lesson files. Look on the Lesson & Update Files tab to access the most current content.

To make the best use of the extensive drawing, painting, and editing capabilities of Adobe Illustrator CC, it's important to learn how to navigate the workspace. The workspace consists of the Application bar, menus, Tools panel, Control panel, Document window, and the default set of panels.

Getting started

You'll be working in multiple art files during this lesson, but before you begin, restore the default preferences for Adobe Illustrator CC.

1 To ensure that the tools and panels function exactly as described in this lesson, delete or deactivate (by renaming) the Adobe Illustrator CC preferences file. See "Restoring default preferences," on page 3.

2 Double-click the Adobe Illustrator CC icon to start Adobe Illustrator.

● **Note:** If you have not already downloaded the project files for this lesson to your computer from your Account page, make sure to do so now. See "Getting Started" at the beginning of the book.

3 Choose Window > Workspace > Reset Essentials to ensure that the workspace is set to the default settings.

● **Note:** If you don't see "Reset Essentials" in the Workspace menu, choose Window > Workspace > Essentials before choosing Window > Workspace > Reset Essentials.

● **Note:** Due to the differences in color settings from one system to another, a Missing Profile dialog box may appear as you open various exercise files. Click OK if you see this dialog box.

4 Choose File > Open, to open the L1start_1.ai file. In the Lesson01 folder in the Lessons folder on your hard disk, select the L1start_1.ai file and click Open.

This lesson contains a fictitious business name, address, and website address made up for the purposes of the project.

5 Choose View > Fit Artboard In Window.

This fits the active artboard into the Document window so that you can see the entire artboard.

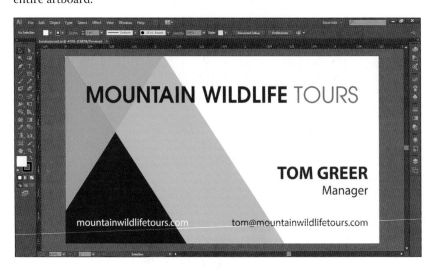

When the file is open and Illustrator is fully launched, the Application bar, menus, Tools panel, Control panel, and panel groups appear on the screen. Docked on the right side of the screen, you will see the default panels that appear as icons. Illustrator also consolidates many of your most frequently accessed options in the Control panel below the menu bar. This lets you work with fewer visible panels and gives you a larger area in which to work.

You will use the L1start_1.ai file to practice navigating, zooming, and investigating an Illustrator document and the workspace.

6 Choose File > Save As. In the Save As dialog box, name the file **businesscard.ai** and save it in the Lesson01 folder. Leave the Save As Type option set to Adobe Illustrator (*.AI) (Windows), or leave the Format option set to Adobe Illustrator (ai) (Mac OS). Click Save. If a warning dialog box appears referencing spot colors and transparency, click Continue. In the Illustrator Options dialog box, leave the options at their default settings and click OK.

● **Note:** The Illustrator Options dialog box contains options that can control how the file is saved, allow you to save to a previous version of Illustrator, and more.

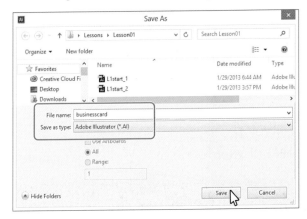

Why use Adobe Illustrator?

Vector graphics (sometimes called *vector shapes* or *vector objects*) are made up of lines and curves defined by mathematical objects called *vectors*, which describe an image according to its geometric characteristics. You'll learn more about lines and curves in Lesson 5, "Drawing with the Pen and Pencil Tools."

You can freely move or modify vector graphics without losing detail or clarity, because they are resolution-independent—they maintain crisp edges when resized, printed to a PostScript printer, saved in a PDF file, or imported into a vector-based graphics application. As a result, vector graphics are the best choice for artwork, such as logos, that will be used at various sizes and in various output media.

The vector objects you create using the drawing and shape tools in Adobe Illustrator are examples of vector graphics.

—From Illustrator Help

Understanding the workspace

● **Note:** The figures in this lesson are taken using the Windows operating system and may look slightly different from what you see, especially if you are using the Mac OS.

You create and manipulate your documents and files using various elements, such as panels, bars, and windows. Any arrangement of these elements is called a *workspace.* When you first start Illustrator, you see the default workspace, which you can customize for the tasks you perform. You can create and save multiple workspaces—one for editing and another for viewing, for example—and switch between them as you work. Below, the areas of the default workspace are described:

A. Application bar
B. Control panel

C. Panels

D. Tools panel

E. Document window

F. Status bar

A. The **Application bar** across the top contains a workspace switcher, a menu bar (Windows only, depending on screen resolution), and application controls.

● **Note:** For the Mac OS, the menu items appear above the Application bar (see below).

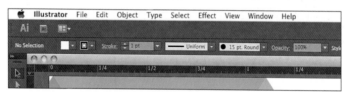

B. The **Control panel** displays options for the currently selected object.

C. **Panels** help you monitor and modify your work. Certain panels are displayed by default, but you can add any panel by choosing it from the Window menu. Many panels have menus with panel-specific options. Panels can be grouped, stacked, docked, or free-floating.

D. The **Tools panel** contains tools for creating and editing images, artwork, page elements, and more. Related tools are grouped together.

E. The **Document window** displays the file you're working on.

F. The **Status bar** appears at the lower-left edge of the Document window. It displays information, zooming, and navigation controls.

Adjusting the user interface brightness

Similar to Adobe After Effects® or Adobe Photoshop, Illustrator supports a brightness adjustment for the application user interface. This is a program preference setting that allows you to choose a brightness setting from four preset levels or to specify a custom value.

In this section, you will change the setting to see its effect and then you will change it back to the program default.

1   Choose Edit > Preferences > User Interface (Windows) or Illustrator > Preferences > User Interface (Mac OS).

2   Choose Light from the Brightness menu of the User Interface options.

You can adjust the brightness of the user interface using set options in the Brightness menu.

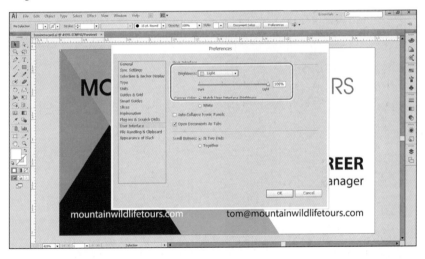

● **Note:** On Mac OS, you won't see the Scroll Buttons option, and that's okay.

3   Drag the Brightness slider to the left until you see a value of 50%.

You can drag the Brightness slider beneath the Brightness menu to the left or to the right to adjust the overall brightness using a custom value.

4   Choose Medium Dark from the Brightness menu.

5   Select White for the Canvas Color option beneath the Brightness slider.

The *canvas* is the area outside of the artboards in your document.

6   Click Cancel so as not to save the preference settings.

Working with the Tools panel

The Tools panel contains selection tools, drawing and painting tools, editing tools, viewing tools, the Fill and Stroke boxes, drawing modes, and screen modes. As you work through the lessons, you'll learn about the specific function of each tool.

● **Note:** The Tools panel shown here and throughout this lesson has two columns. You may see a single-column Tools panel, depending on your screen resolution and workspace.

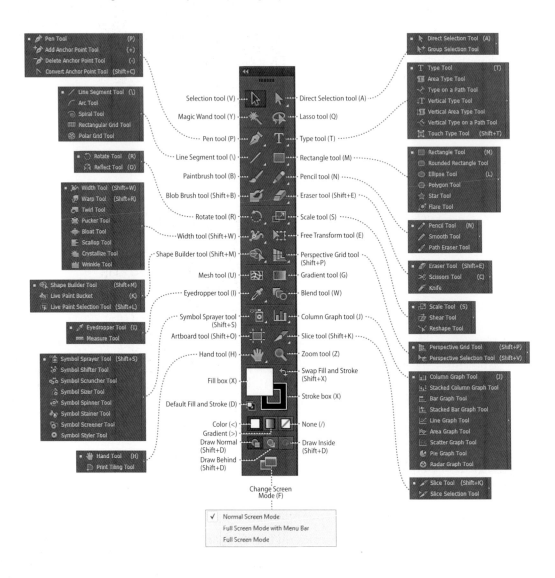

1　Position the pointer over the Selection tool (▶) in the Tools panel. Notice that the name and keyboard shortcut are displayed.

▶ **Tip:** You can turn the tool tips on or off by choosing Edit > Preferences > General (Windows) or Illustrator > Preferences > General (Mac OS) and deselecting Show Tool Tips.

2　Position the pointer over the Direct Selection tool (▷), and click and hold down the mouse button. You'll see additional selection tools. Drag to the right. Release the mouse button over an additional tool to select it.

Any tool in the Tools panel that displays a small triangle contains additional tools that can be selected in this way.

▶ **Tip:** You can also select hidden tools by pressing the Alt key (Windows) or the Option key (Mac OS) and clicking the tool in the Tools panel. Each click selects the next hidden tool in the hidden tool sequence.

3　Click and hold down the mouse button on the Rectangle tool (▭). Drag the pointer over the arrow at the right edge of the hidden tools panel, and release the mouse button. This separates the tools from the Tools panel so that you can access them at all times.

4　Click the Close button (X) in the upper-right corner (Windows) or upper-left corner (Mac OS) on the floating tool panel's title bar to close it. The tools return to the Tools panel.

Next, you'll learn how to resize and float the Tools panel.

5　Click the double arrow in the upper-left corner of the Tools panel to collapse the two columns into one column, to conserve screen space. Click the double arrow again to expand to two columns.

▶ **Tip:** Because the default keyboard shortcuts work only when you do not have a text insertion point, you can also add other keyboard shortcuts to select tools, even when you are editing text. To do this, choose Edit > Keyboard Shortcuts. For more information, see "Keyboard Shortcuts," in Illustrator Help.

▶ **Tip:** You can also collapse the floating tool panels or dock them to the workspace or each other.

● **Note:** You may see a single-column Tools panel to start with, depending on your screen resolution and workspace.

6 Click the dark gray title bar at the top of the Tools panel or the dashed line beneath the title bar, and drag the panel into the workspace. The Tools panel is now floating in the workspace.

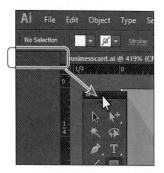 

7 With the Tools panel floating in the workspace, click the double arrow in the title bar to display the Tools panel in a single column. Click again to display the Tools panel in two columns.

 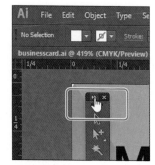 

▶ **Tip:** You can also double-click the title bar at the top of the Tools panel to switch between two columns and one column. Just be careful not to click the X.

8 To dock the Tools panel again, drag its title bar or the dashed line below it to the left side of the Application window (Windows) or screen (Mac OS). When the pointer reaches the left edge, a translucent blue border, called the *drop zone*, appears. Release the mouse button to fit the Tools panel neatly into the side of the workspace.

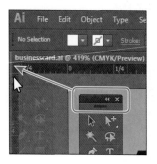 

Exploring the Control panel

The Control panel is context-sensitive, meaning that it offers quick access to options, commands, and other panels relevant to the currently selected object(s). You can click text that is underlined to display a related panel. For example, click the underlined word "Stroke" to display the Stroke panel. By default, the Control panel is docked at the top of the workspace; however, you can dock it at the bottom, float it, or hide it altogether.

1   Select the Selection tool (➤) in the Tools panel, and click in the middle of the light blue shape on the left edge of the artboard.

Notice that information for that object appears in the Control panel, including the word "Path," color options, Stroke, and more.

2   With any tool, drag the gripper bar (the dashed line along the left edge) of the Control panel into the workspace.

Once the Control panel is free-floating, you can drag the dark gray gripper bar that appears on the left edge of the Control panel to move it to the top or bottom of the workspace.

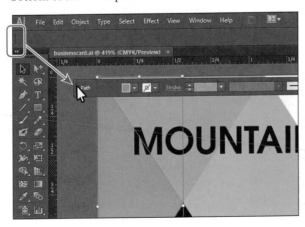

Tip: You can also dock the Control panel by choosing Dock To Top or Dock To Bottom from the Control panel menu (▼≣) on the right side of the Control panel.

3 Drag the Control panel by the dark gray gripper bar on the left edge to the bottom of the Application window (Windows) or screen (Mac OS). When the pointer (not the panel) reaches the bottom of the Application window (Windows) or screen (Mac OS), a blue line appears, indicating the drop zone in which it will be docked when you release the mouse button.

4 Drag the Control panel to the top of the Document window by the gripper bar on the left edge of the panel. When the pointer reaches the bottom of the Application bar, to the right of the Tools panel, a blue line appears indicating the drop zone. When you release the mouse button, the panel is docked.

5 Choose Select > Deselect so that the path is no longer selected.

Working with panels

Panels, which are located in the Window menu, give you quick access to many tools that make modifying artwork easier. By default, some panels are docked and appear as icons on the right side of the workspace. Next, you'll experiment with hiding, closing, and opening panels.

Tip: You can also choose Window > Workspace > Reset Essentials to reset the panels.

1 First, choose Reset Essentials from the workspace switcher in the upper-right corner of the Application bar to reset the panels to their original location.

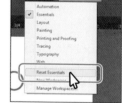

2 Click the Swatches panel icon (▦) on the right side of the workspace to expand the panel, or choose Window > Swatches. Notice that the Swatches panel appears with two other panels—the Brushes panel and the Symbols panel. They are all part of the same panel group. Click the Symbols panel tab to view the Symbols panel.

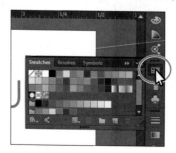 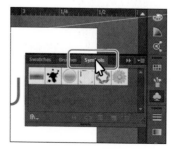

3 Now click the Color panel icon (). Notice that a new panel group appears and that the panel group that contained the Swatches panel collapses.

4 Click and drag the gripper bar at the bottom of the Color panel down to resize the panel, showing more of the color spectrum.

5 Click the Color panel icon to collapse the panel group.

> **Tip:** To find a hidden panel, choose the panel name from the Window menu. A check mark to the left of the panel name indicates that the panel is already open and in front of other panels in its panel group. If you choose a panel name that is already selected in the Window menu, the panel and its group collapses.

> **Tip:** To collapse a panel back to an icon, you can click its tab, its icon, or the double arrow in the panel title bar.

6 Click the double arrow at the top of the dock to expand the panels. Click the double arrow again to collapse the panels. Use this method to show more than one panel group at a time. Your panels may look different when expanded, and that's okay.

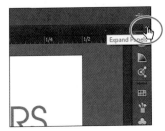
Click to expand.

Click to collapse.

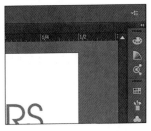
The dock collapses.

> **Tip:** To expand or collapse the panel dock, you can also double-click the panel dock title bar at the top.

7 To increase the width of all the panels in the dock, drag the left edge of the docked panels to the left until text appears. To decrease the width, click and drag the left edge of the docked panels to the right until the text disappears.

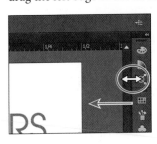
Drag to expand.

Drag to collapse.

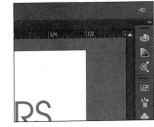
The dock collapsed.

8 Choose Window > Workspace > Reset Essentials to reset the workspace.

9 Drag the Swatches panel icon (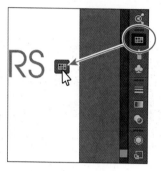) away from the dock to remove the panel from the dock and make it a free-floating panel. Notice that the panel stays collapsed as an icon when it is free-floating. Click the double arrow in the Swatches panel title bar to expand the panel so you can see its contents.

  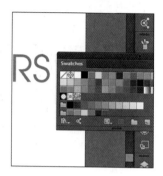

Drag the Swatches panel.   Expand the panel.   The panel expands.

You can also move panels from one panel group to another. In this way, you can create custom panel groups that contain the panels you use most often.

▶ **Tip:** To close a panel, drag the panel away from the dock and click the X in the panel title bar. You can also right-click or Ctrl-click a docked panel tab and choose Close from the menu.

10 Drag the Swatches panel by the panel tab, the panel title bar, or the area behind the panel tab onto the Brushes (�) and Symbols (▲) panel icons. Release the mouse button when you see a blue line between the panel icons and an outline around the Brushes panel group.

Next, you'll organize the panels to create more room in your workspace.

11 Choose Reset Essentials from the workspace switcher in the Application bar, to make sure that the panels are reset to their default state.

▶ **Tip:** Press Tab to hide all panels. Press Tab again to show them all again. You can hide or show all panels except for the Tools and Control panels by pressing Shift+Tab to hide and Shift+Tab to show.

12 Click the double arrow at the top of the dock to expand the panels.

13 Click the Color Guide panel tab to make sure it's selected. Double-click the panel tab to reduce the size of the panel. Double-click the tab again to minimize the panel. This can also be done when a panel is free-floating (not docked).

● **Note:** Many panels only require that you double-click the panel tab twice to return to the full-size view of the panel. If you double-click one more time, the panel fully expands.

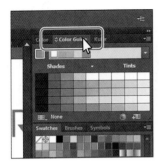
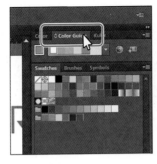
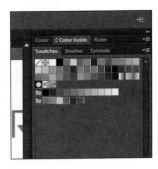

| Double-click the panel tab. | Double-click again. | The panel collapses. |

▶ **Tip:** To reduce and expand the panel size, instead of double-clicking the panel tab, you can click the small arrow icon to the left of the panel name in the panel tab, if present.

14 Click the Appearance panel tab to reveal that panel. Depending on your screen resolution, it may already be showing.

Editing panel groups

Panel groups can be docked, undocked, and arranged in either collapsed or expanded modes. Next, you will resize and reorganize panel groups, which can make it easier to see more important panels.

1 Click the Symbols panel tab. Drag the dividing line between the Symbols panel group and the Stroke panel group up to resize the group.

● **Note:** You may not be able to drag the divider very far, depending on your screen size, screen resolution, and number of panels expanded.

2 Choose Reset Essentials from the workspace switcher in the Application bar.

3 Choose Window > Align to open the Align panel group. Drag the title bar of the Align panel group (the bar above the tabs) to the docked panels on the right side of the workspace. Position the pointer below the group that the Symbols panel icon () is in so that a single blue line appears. Release the mouse button to create a new group in the dock.

Next, you will drag a panel from one group to another in the docked panels.

4 Drag the Transform panel icon (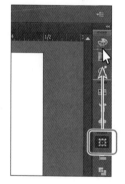) up so that the pointer is just below the Color panel icon (). A blue line appears between the Color panel icon and the Color Guide panel icon (), outlining the Color panel group in blue. Release the mouse button.

Arranging the panels in groups can help you work faster.

Resetting and saving your workspace

You can reset your Tools panel and other panels to their default positions, which you've been doing throughout this lesson. You can also save the position of panels so that you can easily access them at any time by creating a workspace. Next, you will create a workspace to access a group of commonly used panels.

1 Choose Reset Essentials from the workspace switcher in the Application bar.

2 Choose Window > Pathfinder. Click and drag the Pathfinder panel tab to the right side of the workspace. When the pointer approaches the left edge of the docked panels, a blue line appears. Release the mouse button to dock the panel.

3 Click the Close button (X) in the upper-right corner (Windows) or upper-left corner (Mac OS) to close the remaining panel group, which contains the Align and Transform panels.

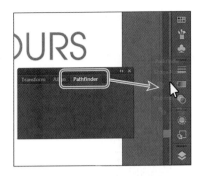

4 Choose Window > Workspace > New Workspace. Change the Name to **Navigation** in the New Workspace dialog box, and click OK. The workspace named Navigation is now saved with Illustrator until you remove it.

5 Choose Window > Workspace > Essentials, and then choose Window > Workspace > Reset Essentials. Notice that the panels return to their default positions. Choose Window > Workspace > Navigation. Toggle between the two workspaces using the Window > Workspace command, and return to the Essentials workspace before starting the next exercise.

● **Note:** To delete saved workspaces, choose Window > Workspace > Manage Workspaces. Select the workspace name, and click the Delete Workspace button.

▶ **Tip:** To change a saved workspace, reset the panels as you'd like them to appear and then choose Window > Workspace > New Workspace. In the New Workspace dialog box, name the workspace with the original name. A message appears in the dialog box warning that you will overwrite an existing workspace with the same name if you click OK. Click OK.

Using panel menus

Most panels have a panel menu in the upper-right corner. Clicking the panel menu icon (▤) gives you access to additional options for the selected panel, including changing the panel display in some cases.

Next, you will change the display of the Symbols panel using its panel menu.

1 Click the Symbols panel icon (▣) on the right side of the workspace. You can also choose Window > Symbols to display this panel.

2 Click the panel menu icon (▤) in the upper-right corner of the Symbols panel.

3 Choose Small List View from the panel menu.

This displays the symbol names, together with thumbnails. Because the options in the panel menu apply only to the active panel, only the Symbols panel view is affected.

4   Click the Symbols panel menu icon () and choose Thumbnail View, to return the symbols to their original view. Click the Symbols panel tab to hide the panel again.

In addition to the panel menus, context-sensitive menus display commands relevant to the active tool, selection, or panel.

5   Position the pointer over the Document window or a panel. Then, right-click (Windows) or Ctrl-click (Mac OS) to show a context menu with specific options.

The context-sensitive menu shown here is displayed when you right-click (Windows) or Ctrl-click (Mac OS) the artboard with nothing selected.

● **Note:** If you position the pointer over the tab or title bar for a panel, and right-click (Windows) or Ctrl-click (Mac OS), you can close a panel or a panel group in the context menu that appears.

Changing the view of artwork

When working in files, it's likely that you'll need to change the magnification level and navigate between artboards. The magnification level, which can range from 3.13% to 6400%, is displayed in the title bar (or document tab) next to the file name and in the lower-left corner of the Document window. Using any of the viewing tools and commands affects only the display of the artwork, not the actual size of the artwork.

Using the view commands

To enlarge or reduce the view of artwork using the View menu, do one of the following:

▶ **Tip:** Zoom in using the keyboard shortcut Ctrl++ (Windows) or Command++ (Mac OS). That's Ctrl *and* + (Windows) or Command *and* + (Mac OS).

• Choose View > Zoom In, to enlarge the display of the businesscard.ai artwork.

• Choose View > Zoom Out, to reduce the view of the businesscard.ai artwork.

▶ **Tip:** Zoom out using the keyboard shortcut Ctrl+– (Windows) or Command+– (Mac OS). That's Ctrl *and* – (Windows) or Command *and* – (Mac OS).

Each time you choose a Zoom option, the view of the artwork is resized to the closest preset zoom level. The preset zoom levels appear in a menu in the lower-left corner of the Document window, identified by a down arrow next to a percentage.

You can also use the View menu to fit the artwork for the active artboard to your screen, to fit all artboards into the view area, or to view artwork at actual size.

1 Choose View > Fit Artboard In Window. A reduced view of the active artboard is displayed in the Document window.

Tip: You can also double-click the Hand tool (✋) in the Tools panel to fit the active artboard in the Document window.

● **Note:** Because the canvas (the area outside the artboards) extends to 227", you can easily lose sight of your illustration. By choosing View > Fit Artboard In Window or by using the keyboard shortcuts Ctrl+0 (Windows) or Command+0 (Mac OS), artwork is centered in the viewing area.

2 Choose View > Actual Size to display the artwork at actual size.

The artwork is displayed at 100%. The actual size of your artwork determines how much of it can be viewed on-screen at 100%.

▶ **Tip:** You can also double-click the Zoom tool (🔍) in the Tools panel to display artwork at 100%.

3 Choose View > Fit All In Window.

You will see the one artboard in the document displayed in the Document window. You can learn more about navigating artboards in the section "Navigating multiple artboards," later in this lesson.

4 Choose View > Fit Artboard In Window, before continuing to the next section.

Using the Zoom tool

In addition to the View menu options, you can use the Zoom tool (🔍) to magnify and reduce the view of artwork to predefined magnification levels.

1 Select the Zoom tool (🔍) in the Tools panel, and then move the pointer into the Document window.

Notice that a plus sign (+) appears at the center of the Zoom tool pointer.

2 Position the Zoom tool over the text "TOM GREER," and click once. The artwork is displayed at a higher magnification.

Notice that where you clicked is now in the center of the Document window.

3 Click two more times on the "TOM GREER" text. The view is increased again, and you'll notice that the area you clicked is magnified.

Next, you'll reduce the view of the artwork.

4 With the Zoom tool still selected, position the pointer over the text "TOM GREER" and hold down the Alt (Windows) or Option (Mac OS) key. A minus sign (–) appears at the center of the Zoom tool pointer. With the Alt or Option key pressed, click the artwork twice to reduce the view of the artwork.

For a more controlled zoom, you can drag a marquee around a specific area of your artwork. This magnifies only the selected area.

● **Note:** The percent of the magnification is determined by the size of the marquee you draw with the Zoom tool—the smaller the marquee, the higher the level of magnification.

5 Choose View > Fit Artboard In Window.

6 With the Zoom tool still selected, click and drag a marquee around the
   "mountainwildlifetours.com" text in the lower-left corner of the artboard.
   When you see the marquee around the area you are dragging, release the mouse
   button. The marqueed area is now enlarged to fit the size of the Document
   window (as best it can).

7 Double-click the Hand tool (✋) in the Tools panel to fit the artboard in the
   Document window.

The Zoom tool is used frequently during the editing process to enlarge and reduce
the view of artwork. Because of this, Illustrator allows you to select it using the
keyboard at any time without first deselecting any other tool you may be using.

8 Select any other tool in the Tools panel, and move the pointer into the
   Document window.

9 Press Ctrl+spacebar (Windows) or Command+spacebar (Mac OS) to use the
   Zoom tool. Click or drag to zoom in on any area of the artwork, and then
   release the keys.

● **Note:** In certain versions of Mac OS, the keyboard shortcuts for the Zoom tool open Spotlight or
Finder. If you decide to use these shortcuts in Illustrator, you may want to turn off or change those
keyboard shortcuts in the Mac OS System Preferences.

10 To zoom out using the keyboard, hold down Ctrl+Alt+spacebar (Windows) or
   Command+Option+spacebar (Mac OS). Click the desired area to reduce the
   view of the artwork, and then release the keys.

11 Double-click the Hand tool in the Tools panel to fit the artboard in the
   Document window.

Scrolling through a document

You can use the Hand tool (✋) to pan to different areas of a document. Using the
Hand tool allows you to push the document around much like you would a piece of
paper on your desk.

1 Select the Hand tool (✋) in the Tools panel.

2 Drag down in the Document window. As you drag, the artwork moves with
   the hand.

As with the Zoom tool (🔍), you can select the Hand tool with a keyboard shortcut without first deselecting the active tool.

3   Click any other tool except the Type tool (T) in the Tools panel, and move the pointer into the Document window.

4   Hold down the spacebar to select the Hand tool from the keyboard, and then drag to bring the artwork back into the center of your view.

5   Double-click the Hand tool to fit the active artboard in the Document window.

● **Note:** The spacebar shortcut for the Hand tool does not work when the Type tool is active and the cursor is in text. To access the Hand tool when the cursor is in text, press the Alt (Windows) or Option (Mac OS) key.

Touch gestures

In Adobe Illustrator CC, you can use standard touch gestures (pinch and swipe) for panning and zooming. These gestures work on devices that accept touch input: a Direct touch device (a touchscreen device), or an Indirect touch device (the Trackpad on a Mac computer, touchpads, or the Wacom Intuos5 device).

- Pinch in or out, using two fingers (for example, use the thumb and forefinger), to zoom.

- Place two fingers on the document, and move the fingers together to pan within the document.

- Swipe or flick, to navigate artboards.

- In artboard editing mode, use two fingers to rotate the artboard by 90°.

Viewing artwork

To save time when working with large or complex documents, you can create your own custom views within a document so that you can quickly jump to specific areas and zoom levels. Set up the view that you want to save, and then choose View > New View. Name the view, and click OK. The view is saved with the document.

1   Choose View > Email (at the very bottom of the View menu), to zoom in to a preset area of the image.

● **Note:** Depending on the resolution of your screen, the bottom of the View menu and the menu options may be cut off. You may need to click the black arrow at the bottom of the View menu several times to see more options.

This custom view was saved with the document by the authors.

2   Choose View > Fit Artboard In Window.

When you open a file, it is automatically displayed in Preview mode, which shows how the artwork will print. When you're working with large or complex illustrations, you may want to view only the outlines, or *wireframes*, of objects in your artwork so that the screen doesn't have to redraw the artwork each time you make a change. This is called Outline mode. Outline mode can be helpful when selecting objects, as you will see in Lesson 2, "Selecting and Aligning."

3   Choose View > Outline.

Only the outlines of the objects are displayed. Use this view to find objects that might not be visible in Preview mode.

4   Choose View > Preview to see all the attributes of the artwork.

If you prefer keyboard shortcuts, use Ctrl+Y (Windows) or Command+Y (Mac OS) to toggle between Preview and Outline modes.

5   Choose View > Overprint Preview to view any lines or shapes that are set to overprint.

This view is helpful for those in the print industry who need to see how inks interact when set to overprint. You may not actually see much of a change in the logo when you change to this mode.

● **Note:** When switching between viewing modes, visual changes may not be readily apparent. Zooming in and out (View > Zoom In and View > Zoom Out) may help you see the differences more easily.

6   Choose View > Pixel Preview to see how the artwork will look when it is rasterized and viewed on-screen in a web browser. Choose View > Pixel Preview to deselect pixel preview.

Preview mode

Outline mode

Overprint mode

Pixel Preview mode

▶ **Tip:** Learn more about Outline mode in Lesson 2, "Selecting and Aligning." Learn more about Pixel Preview mode in Lesson 13, "Applying Appearance Attributes and Graphic Styles."

7   Choose View > Fit Artboard In Window, to view the entire active artboard.

Navigating multiple artboards

Illustrator allows for multiple artboards within a single file. This is a great way to create a multi-page document so that you can have collateral pieces, like a brochure, a postcard, and a business card, in the same document. You can easily share content between designs, create multi-page PDFs, and print multiple pages by creating more than one artboard. For more information on artboards, check out the sidebar, titled "Artboard overview," at the end of this section.

Multiple artboards can be added when you initially create an Illustrator document, by choosing File > New. You can also add or remove artboards after the document is created, by using the Artboard tool in the Tools panel.

Next, you will learn how to efficiently navigate a document that contains multiple artboards.

1   Choose File > Open and, in the Lesson01 folder, select the L1start_2.ai file located in the Lessons folder on your hard disk. Click Open to open the file.

2   Select the Selection tool (▶) in the Tools panel, if it is not already selected.

3   Choose View > Fit All In Window. Notice that there are two artboards in the document.

The artboards in a document can be arranged in any order, orientation, or artboard size—they can even overlap. Suppose that you want to create a four-page brochure. You can create different artboards for every page of the brochure, all with the same size and orientation. They can be arranged horizontally or vertically or in whatever way you like.

The L1start_2.ai document has two artboards which contain the designs for the front of a postcard and a business flyer.

4   Press Ctrl+ – (Windows) or Command+ – (Mac OS) until you can see the logo in the upper-left corner of the canvas, which is outside the artboards.

5   Choose View > Fit Artboard In Window.

This command fits the currently active artboard in the window. The active artboard is identified in the Artboard Navigation menu in the lower-left corner of the Document window.

6   Choose the number 2 Artboard 2 from the Artboard Navigation menu. The flyer appears in the Document window.

● **Note:** Learn how to work more with artboards in Lesson 4, "Transforming Objects."

7 Choose View > Zoom Out. Notice that zooming occurs on the currently active artboard.

Notice the arrows to the right and left of the Artboard Navigation menu. You can use these to navigate to the first (), previous (), next (), and last () artboards.

● **Note:** Since there are only two artboards in this document, you could have also clicked the First button in this step.

8 Click the Previous navigation button to view the previous artboard (Artboard 1) in the Document window.

9 Choose View > Fit Artboard In Window to make sure that the first artboard (Artboard 1) is fit in the Document window.

Another method for navigating multiple artboards is to use the Artboards panel. Next, you will open the Artboards panel and navigate the document.

10 Choose Reset Essentials from the workspace switcher in the Application bar to reset the Essentials workspace.

11 Choose Window > Artboards to expand the Artboards panel on the right side of the workspace.

The Artboards panel lists all artboards in the document. This panel allows you to navigate between artboards, rename artboards, add or delete artboards, edit artboard settings, and more.

Next, you will focus on navigating the document using this panel.

12 Double-click the number 2 in the Artboards panel. This fits Artboard 2 in the Document window.

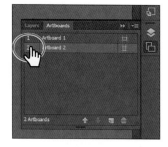

● **Note:** Double-clicking the artboard name in the Artboards panel allows you to change the name of the artboard. Clicking the artboard icon () to the right of the artboard name in the panel allows you to edit artboard options.

13 Choose View > Zoom In, to zoom in on the second artboard.

14 Double-click the number 1 to the left of Artboard 1 in the Artboards panel to show the first artboard in the Document window.

Notice that when you double-click to navigate to an artboard, that artboard is fit in the Document window.

15 Click the Artboards panel icon () in the dock to collapse the Artboards panel.

Artboard overview

Artboards represent the regions that can contain printable artwork (similar to pages in a program like Adobe InDesign). You can use artboards to crop areas for printing or placement purposes. Multiple artboards are useful for creating a variety of things such as multiple page PDFs, printed pages with different sizes or different elements, independent elements for websites, video storyboards, or individual items for animation in Adobe Flash® or Adobe After Effects.

A. **Printable area** is bounded by the innermost dotted lines and represents the portion of the page on which the selected printer can print.

B. **Nonprintable area** is between the two sets of dotted lines representing any nonprintable margin of the page. This example shows the nonprintable area of an 8.5" x 11" page for a standard laser printer.

C. **Edge of the page** is indicated by the outermost set of dotted lines.

D. **Artboard** is bounded by solid lines and represents the entire region that can contain printable artwork.

E. **Bleed area** is the amount of artwork that falls outside of the printing bounding box, or outside the crop area and trim marks.

F. **Canvas** is the area outside the artboard that extends to the edge of the 227" square window. Objects placed on the canvas are visible on-screen, but they do not print.

—From Illustrator Help

● **Note:** You can have up to 100 artboards per Illustrator document, depending on the size of the artboards. You can specify the number of artboards for a document when you create it, and you can add and remove artboards at any time while working in a document. You can create artboards of different sizes, resize them with the Artboard tool, and position them on the screen—they can even overlap each other.

Using the Navigator panel

The Navigator panel is another way to navigate a document with a single artboard or multiple artboards. This is useful when you need to see all artboards in the document in one window and to edit content in any of those artboards in a zoomed-in view.

1   Choose Window > Navigator, to open the Navigator panel. It is free-floating in the workspace.

● **Note:** You can also drag the slider in the Navigator panel to change the view of your artwork. Pause for a moment after dragging to allow the panel to catch up.

2   In the Navigator panel, type **50%** in the Zoom box in the lower-left corner of the panel and press Enter or Return, to decrease the level of magnification.

The red box in the Navigator panel, called the proxy view area, becomes larger, indicating the area of the document that is being shown. Depending on the zoom percentage, you may or may not see the proxy view area yet, but you will.

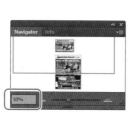

3   Click the larger mountain icon () in the lower-right corner of the Navigator panel several times to zoom in to the brochure until the percentage in the Navigator panel shows approximately 150%.

4   Position the pointer inside the proxy view area (the red box—also called the proxy preview area) of the Navigator panel. The pointer becomes a hand (🖐).

● **Note:** The percentage and proxy view area in your Navigator panel may appear differently in this section. That's okay.

5   Drag the hand in the proxy view area of the Navigator panel to pan to different parts of the artwork. Drag the proxy view area over the green star in the lower-right corner of the brochure cover.

6　In the Navigator panel, move the pointer outside of the proxy view area and click. This moves the box and displays a different area of the artwork in the Document window.

▶ **Tip:** Choosing Panel Options from the Navigator panel menu allows you to customize the Navigator panel. For example, you can change the color of the view box.

7　Choose View > Fit Artboard In Window.

8　Click the Navigator panel menu icon (▾≡) and deselect View Artboard Contents Only so that you see any artwork that is on the canvas, as well. Notice the logo on the canvas in the panel.

● **Note:** You may need to adjust the slider in the Navigator panel to see the logo in the proxy view area.

9　Close the Navigator panel group by clicking the Close button (X) in the upper-right corner (Windows) or upper-left corner (Mac OS).

Arranging multiple documents

When you open more than one Illustrator file, the Document windows are tabbed. You can arrange the open documents in other ways, such as side by side, so that you can easily compare or drag items from one document to another. You can also use the Arrange Documents window to quickly display your open documents in a variety of configurations.

You should currently have two Illustrator files open: businesscard.ai and L1start_2.ai. Each file has its own tab at the top of the Document window. These documents are considered a group of Document windows. You can create document groups to loosely associate files while they are open.

1　Click the businesscard.ai document tab, to show the businesscard.ai Document window.

2　Click and drag the businesscard.ai document tab to the right of the L1start_2.ai document tab.

● **Note:** Be careful to drag directly to the right. Otherwise, you could undock the Document window and create a new group. If that happens, choose Window > Arrange > Consolidate All Windows.

Dragging the document tabs allows you to change the order of the documents. This can be very useful if you use the document shortcuts to navigate to the next or previous document.

▶ **Tip:** You can
cycle between
open documents
by pressing Ctrl+F6
(next document),
Ctrl+Shift+F6 (previous
document) (Windows)
or Command+~
(next document),
Command+Shift+~
(previous document)
(Mac OS).

3 Drag the document tabs in the following order, from left to right: businesscard.ai, L1start_2.ai.

These two documents are marketing pieces for the same company. To see both of them at one time, you can arrange the Document windows by cascading the windows or tiling them. *Cascading* allows you to cascade (stack) different document groups. *Tiling* shows multiple Document windows at one time, in various arrangements.

Next, you will tile the open documents so that you can see them both at one time.

4 *Windows users skip to the next step.* On the Mac OS, choose Window > Application Frame. Then, click the green button (green by default) in the upper-left corner of the Application window so that it fits as well as possible.

Mac OS users can use the Application frame to group all the workspace elements in a single, integrated window, similar to working in Windows. If you move or resize the Application frame, the elements respond to each other so that they don't overlap.

5 Choose Window > Arrange > Tile.

This shows both Document windows arranged in a pattern.

● **Note:** Your
documents may be
tiled in a different order.
That's okay.

6 Click in each of the Document windows to activate the documents. Choose View > Fit Artboard In Window for each of the documents. Also, make sure that Artboard 1 is showing for each document in the Document window.

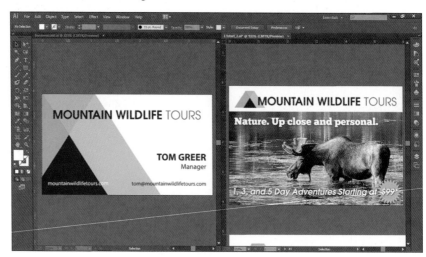

With documents tiled, you can drag the dividing line between each of the Document windows to reveal more or less of a particular document. You can also drag objects between documents to copy them from one document to another.

7 Click in the L1start_2.ai Document window. With the Selection tool (▶), drag the green starburst to the businesscard.ai Document window and release the mouse button. This copies the image from L1start_2.ai to businesscard.ai.

● **Note:** When you drag content between tiled documents, a plus sign (+) appears next to the pointer, as shown in the figure below. Depending on your operating system, the pointer may look different.

● **Note:** After dragging the content, notice that the document tab for businesscard.ai now has an asterisk to the right of the file name. This indicates that the file needs to be saved.

To change the arrangement of the tiled windows, it's possible to drag document tabs to new positions. However, it's easier to use the Arrange Documents window to quickly arrange open documents in a variety of configurations.

8 Click the Arrange Documents button (▦▾) in the Application bar to display the Arrange Documents window. Click the Consolidate All button (▭) to bring the documents back together.

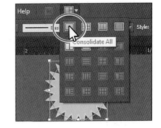

● **Note:** On the Mac OS, the menu bar is above the Application bar. Also, depending on the resolution of your screen, the Windows menus may appear in the Application bar.

9 Click the Arrange Documents button (▦▾) in the Application bar to display the Arrange Documents window again. Click the 2-Up vertical button (▥) in the Arrange Documents window.

10 Click to select the businesscard.ai tab, if it is not already selected. Then, click the Close button (X) on the businesscard.ai document tab, to close the document. If a dialog box appears asking you to save the document, click No (Windows) or Don't Save (Mac OS).

11 Click the Arrange Documents button (▦▾) in the Application bar, and click the Consolidate All button (▭) in the Arrange Documents window.

12 Choose File > Close to close the L1start_2.ai document without saving.

▶ **Tip:** You can also choose Window > Arrange > Consolidate All Windows to return the two documents to tabs in the same group.

Finding resources for using Illustrator

For complete and up-to-date information about using Illustrator panels, tools, and other application features, visit the Adobe website. By choosing Help > Illustrator Help, you'll be connected to the Adobe Community Help website, where you can search Illustrator Help and support documents, as well as other websites relevant to Illustrator users. Community Help brings together active Adobe product users, Adobe product team members, authors, and experts to give you the most useful, relevant, and up-to-date information about Adobe products.

If you choose Help > Illustrator Help, you can also download a PDF of the Illustrator Help content by clicking the download link.

Syncing with the Adobe Creative Cloud

When you work on multiple machines, managing and syncing preferences, presets, and libraries among the machines can be time-consuming, complex, and prone to error.

The new Sync Settings feature enables individual users to sync their preferences, presets, and libraries to the Adobe Creative Cloud. This means that if you use two machines, say one at home and the other at work, the Sync Settings feature makes it easy for you to keep those settings synchronized across two machines. Also, if you have replaced your old machine with a new one and have re-installed Illustrator, this friendly feature will let you bring back all those settings you took so much time to set up.

The syncing happens via your Adobe Creative Cloud account. All the settings are uploaded to your Creative Cloud account and then are downloaded and applied on the other machine.

You need to initiate the sync manually; it does not happen automatically and it cannot be scheduled. For more information on syncing, see the "Sync settings using Adobe Creative Cloud" section on page 6 in the "Getting Started" section.

3   Select the Selection tool, and then position the pointer over the edge of the red circle on the left. A word such as "path" or "anchor" may appear, because Smart Guides are turned on, by default.

Smart Guides are snap-to guides that help you align, edit, and transform objects or artboards. To learn more about Smart Guides, check out Lesson 3, "Creating and Editing Shapes."

4   Click the red circle on the left on its edge, or anywhere in its center, to select it. A bounding box with eight handles appears.

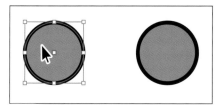

The bounding box is used when making changes to objects, such as resizing or rotating them. The bounding box also indicates that an item is selected and ready to be modified, and the color of the bounding box indicates which layer the object is on. Layers are discussed more in Lesson 8, "Working with Layers."

5   Using the Selection tool, click the red circle on the right. Notice that the left red circle is now deselected and only the right circle is selected.

6   Hold down the Shift key, and click the left red circle to add it to the selection. Both red circles are now selected, and a larger bounding box surrounds them.

● **Note:** To select an item without a fill, you can click the stroke (the edge), or drag a selection marquee across the object.

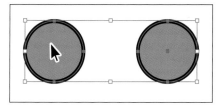

7   Reposition the circles anywhere in the document by clicking inside either selected circle (in the red area) and dragging in one motion. Because both circles are selected, they move together.

As you drag, you may notice the green lines that appear. These are called *alignment guides* and are visible because Smart Guides are turned on (View > Smart Guides). As you drag, the objects are aligned to other objects on the artboard. Also notice the measurement label (gray box) next to the pointer that shows the object's distance from its original position. Measurement labels also appear because Smart Guides are turned on.

8   Deselect the circles by clicking the artboard where there are no objects or by choosing Select > Deselect.

9 Revert to the last saved version of the document by choosing File > Revert. In the Revert dialog box, click Revert.

Using the Direct Selection tool

The Direct Selection tool (⟨⟩) selects anchor points or path segments within an object so that it can be reshaped. Next, you will become familiar with selecting anchor points and path segments, using the Direct Selection tool.

1 Choose View > Fit All In Window.

2 Select the Zoom tool (🔍) in the Tools panel, and drag a marquee around the series of orange shapes below the red circles you selected previously, to zoom in.

Tip: You can also click in the middle of a shape to select it and to see the anchor points around its edge. This can be an easy way to see where the points are, and then you can click a point to select it.

3 Select the Direct Selection tool (⟨⟩) in the Tools panel. Without clicking, position the pointer over the top edge of one of the orange shapes. Move the pointer along the top edge of the shape until the word "anchor" appears by the pointer.

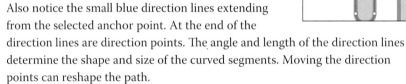

When the Direct Selection tool is over an anchor point of a path or object, the word "anchor" appears. This label is showing because Smart Guides are turned on. Also notice the small dot that appears in the center of the box to the right of the pointer. That dot indicates that the cursor is positioned over an anchor point.

4 Click to select that anchor point.

Notice that only the anchor point you selected is solid, indicating that it is selected, and the other points in the shape are hollow, indicating that they are not selected.

Also notice the small blue direction lines extending from the selected anchor point. At the end of the direction lines are direction points. The angle and length of the direction lines determine the shape and size of the curved segments. Moving the direction points can reshape the path.

Note: The gray measurement label that appears as you drag the anchor point has the values dX and dY. *dX* indicates the distance that the pointer has moved along the x axis (horizontal), and *dY* indicates the distance that the pointer has moved along the y axis (vertical).

5 With the Direct Selection tool still selected, drag the individual point up to edit the shape of the object.

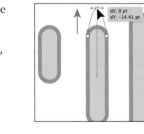

6 Try clicking another point on the edge of the shape, and notice that the previous point is deselected.

7 Revert to the last saved version of the file by choosing File > Revert. In the Revert dialog box, click Revert.

Exploring selection and anchor point preferences

Choose Edit > Preferences > Selection & Anchor Display (Windows) or Illustrator > Preferences > Selection & Anchor Display (Mac OS). You can change the size of anchor points (called *anchors* in the dialog box) or the display of the direction lines (called *handles* in the dialog box).

As you move the pointer over anchor points in your artwork, they are highlighted. You can also turn off the highlighting of anchor points as the pointer hovers over them. Highlighting anchor points makes it easier to determine which point you are about to select. You will learn more about anchor points and anchor point handles in Lesson 5, "Drawing with the Pen and Pencil Tools."

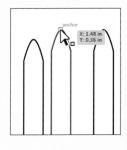

Creating selections with a marquee

Another way to make a selection is by dragging a marquee around the objects that you want to select, which is what you'll do next.

1 Choose View > Fit All In Window.

2 Select the Zoom tool (🔍) in the Tools panel, and click several times in the center of the artboard on the right, to zoom in to the red circles.

3 Select the Selection tool (▶) in the Tools panel. Position the pointer above and to the left of the leftmost red circle, and then drag downward and to the right to create a marquee that overlaps just the tops of the circles.

▶ **Tip:** When dragging with the Selection tool, you only need to encompass a small part of an object to include it in the selection.

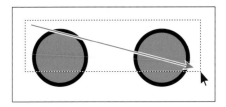
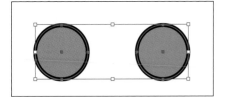

4 Choose Select > Deselect, or click where there are no objects.

5 Press the spacebar and drag the artboard up so that you can see the orange shapes beneath the red circles, if necessary.

Now, you will use the Direct Selection tool to select anchor points in multiple objects by dragging a marquee around those points.

6 Select the Direct Selection tool (⟩) in the Tools panel. Click and drag from outside the top of one of the orange shapes below the red circles, across the top edges of two of the shapes. Only the top anchor points become selected.

7 Click one of the selected anchor points, and drag to see how the anchor points reposition together. You can use this method when selecting points so that you don't have to click exactly on the anchor point that you want to select.

Note: Selecting points using this method might take some practice. You'll need to drag across only the points you want selected; otherwise, more will be selected. You can always click away from the objects to deselect them and then try again.

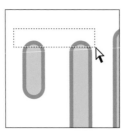 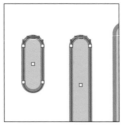 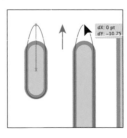

Drag to select. See the points selected. Drag the points.

8 Revert to the last saved version of the file by choosing File > Revert. In the Revert dialog box, click Revert.

Creating selections with the Magic Wand tool

You can use the Magic Wand tool (✦) to select all objects in a document that have the same attributes, like color fill. You can customize the Magic Wand tool to select objects based on options, like stroke weight, stroke color, and more, by double-clicking the Magic Wand tool in the Tools panel. You can also change the tolerances (range) used to identify similar objects.

1 Select the Selection tool (▶) and click in a blank area of the smaller artboard on the right. This makes that artboard the active artboard. Choose View > Fit Artboard In Window.

2 Select the Magic Wand tool (✦) in the Tools panel. Click one of the red circles on the right artboard, and notice that the other red circle becomes selected, as well. No bounding box (a box surrounding the two shapes) appears, because the Magic Wand tool is still selected.

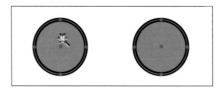

3 Holding down the Shift key, click one of the orange shapes (below the red shapes) with the Magic Wand tool and then release the key.

This adds all of the shapes filled with that same orange color to the selection.

4 With the Magic Wand tool still selected, hold down the Alt (Windows) or Option (Mac OS) key, click one of the orange shapes to deselect all of the shapes with that same fill, and then release the key. The red circles should remain selected.

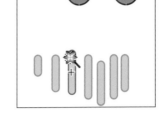

5 Choose Select > Deselect, or click where there are no objects.

Selecting similar objects

You can also select objects based on similar fill color, stroke color, stroke weight, and more, using the Select Similar Objects button or the Select > Same command.

Next, you will select several objects with the same fill and stroke applied.

1 With the Selection tool (▶), click to select one of the orange objects.

2 Click the arrow to the right of the Select Similar Objects button (⬚▾) in the Control panel to show a menu. Choose Stroke Color to select all objects on any artboard with the same stroke color (orange) as the selected object.

Notice that all of the objects with the same orange colored stroke are selected.

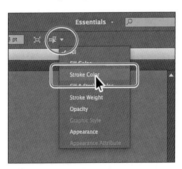

3 Choose Select > Deselect.

4 Select one of the orange shapes again, and then choose Select > Same > Fill & Stroke.

All of the orange-filled shapes have that same stroke and fill and are now selected.

5 With the selection still active, choose Select > Save Selection. Name the selection **RobotMouth** in the Save Selection dialog box, and click OK so that you'll be able to choose this selection at a later time.

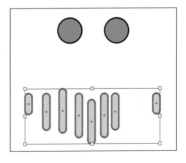

6 Choose Select > Deselect.

● **Note:** The *fill* is a color applied to the inside of an object, the *stroke* is the outline (border), and the *stroke weight* is the width of the stroke.

▶ **Tip:** It is helpful to name selections according to use or function. If you name the selection "1 pt stroke," for instance, the name may be misleading if you later change the stroke weight of the artwork.

Selecting in Outline mode

By default, Adobe Illustrator displays all artwork in color (objects show their paint attributes, like fill and stroke). However, you can choose to display artwork so that only its outlines (or paths) are visible. The next method for selecting involves viewing artwork in Outline mode and can be very useful if you want to select objects within a series of stacked objects.

1   Choose View > Fit Artboard In Window.

2   With the Selection tool (▶), click inside of the gray half circle shape to select it. This will become the robot body.

   Since the shape has a fill (a color, pattern, or gradient filling the inside an object), you can click anywhere within the bounds of the object to select it.

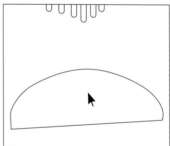

3   Choose Select > Deselect, to deselect the shape.

4   Choose View > Outline to view the artwork as outlines.

5   With the Selection tool, click inside that same half circle shape.

   Notice that you cannot select the object. Outline mode displays artwork as outlines with no fill. To select in Outline mode, you can click the edge of the object or drag a marquee across the shape to select it.

6   Click the Previous artboard button (◀) in the lower-left corner of the Document window to fit the first artboard in the window.

7   On the left artboard, with the Selection tool selected, drag a marquee across the right (smaller) ellipse that makes the robot's eye. Press the Left Arrow key several times to move the ellipse so that it almost touches the ellipse to the left.

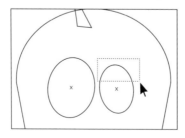 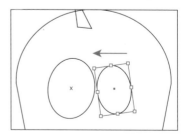

8   Choose View > Preview to see the artwork.

Aligning objects

Illustrator makes it easy to align or distribute multiple objects relative to each other, the artboard, or a key object. In this section, you will explore the options for aligning objects and aligning points, and you will learn what a key object is.

Aligning objects to each other

1   Choose Select > RobotMouth to reselect the orange shapes.

2   Click the Next artboard button (▶) in the lower-left corner of the Document window to fit the artboard with the orange and red shapes in the window.

3   Select the Zoom tool (🔍) in the Tools panel, and drag a marquee around the series of orange-filled shapes, to zoom in.

4   Choose Align To Selection from the Align To button (▦▾) in the Control panel, if it's not already selected.

This ensures that the selected objects are aligned to each other.

5   Click the Vertical Align Bottom button (▥) in the Control panel.

Notice that the bottom edges of all the orange objects move to align with the lowest orange object.

Note: The Align options may not appear in the Control panel. If you don't see the Align options, click the word "Align" in the Control panel to open the Align panel. The number of options displayed in the Control panel depends on your screen resolution.

6   Choose Edit > Undo Align to return the objects to their original positions. Leave the objects selected for the next section.

Aligning to a key object

A *key object* is an object that you want other objects to align to. You specify a key object by selecting all the objects you want to align, including the key object, and then clicking the key object again. When selected, the key object has a thick blue outline, and the Align To Key Object icon (▦▾) appears in the Control panel and the Align panel. Next, you will align the orange shapes.

1   With the orange shapes still selected, click the leftmost shape with the Selection tool (▶).

The thick blue outline indicates that the leftmost shape is the key object which other objects will align to.

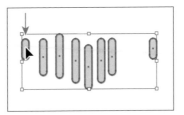

Tip: In the Align panel, you can also choose Align To Key Object from the Align To option. The object that is in front becomes the key object.

Note: To stop aligning and distributing relative to an object, click the object again to remove the blue outline, or choose Cancel Key Object from the Align panel menu.

2 In the Align options, which you can view in the Control panel or by clicking the word "Align," click the Vertical Align Top button ( ). Notice that all of the orange shapes move to align to the top edge of the key object.

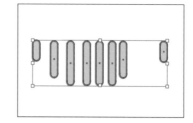

3 Choose Select > Deselect.

Aligning anchor points

Next, you'll align two anchor points to each other using the Align options. Like setting a key object in the previous section, you can also set a key anchor point with which to align other anchor points. The last selected anchor point is the key anchor.

1 Choose View > Fit Artboard In Window.

2 Select the Direct Selection tool ( ), and click the lower-left point of the gray half circle at the bottom of the artboard. Shift-click to select the lower-right point of the same gray half circle.

You select the points in a specific order because the last selected anchor point is the key anchor point. Other points align to this point.

3 Click the Vertical Align Top button ( ) in the Control panel. The first anchor point selected aligns to the second anchor point selected.

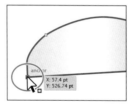
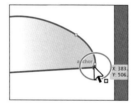
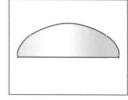

Select the first point.   Select the second point.   Align the points.

4 Choose Select > Deselect.

Distributing objects

Note: Using the Horizontal or Vertical Distribute Center buttons distributes the spacing equally between the *centers* of the objects. If the selected objects are not the same size, unexpected results may occur.

Distributing objects using the Align panel enables you to select multiple objects and to distribute the spacing between those objects equally. Next, you will make the spacing between the orange shapes even, using a distribution method.

1 Select the Selection tool ( ) in the Tools panel. Choose Select > RobotMouth, to reselect all of the orange shapes.

2 Click the Horizontal Distribute Center button ( ) in the Control panel.

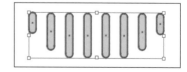

Distributing moves all of the orange shapes so that the spacing between the *center* of each of them is equal.

3   Choose Edit > Undo Align, and then choose Select > Deselect.

4   Choose View > Zoom In, twice, to zoom in to the orange shapes.

5   With the Selection tool selected, hold down the Shift key and drag the rightmost orange shape slightly to the left. Stop dragging just before the shape touches the orange shape to its left. Release the mouse button and then the key.

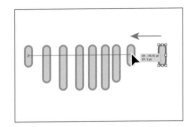

The Shift key keeps the shape aligned vertically with the other shapes.

6   Choose Select > RobotMouth to select all of the orange shapes again, and then click the Horizontal Distribute Center button ( ) again. Notice that, with the rightmost shape repositioned, the objects move to redistribute the spacing between the centers.

7   Choose Select > Deselect.

Aligning to the artboard

You can also align content to the artboard rather than to a selection or a key object. Aligning to the artboard aligns each selected object separately to the artboard. Next, you'll get the gray half circle shape on the artboard with the rest of the robot and align it to the bottom, center of the artboard.

1   With the Selection tool ( ) selected, click the gray half circle shape at the bottom of the artboard, to select it. Choose Edit > Cut.

2   Click the Previous artboard button ( ) in the lower-left corner of the Document window to navigate to the first (left) artboard in the document, which contains the robot head.

3   Choose Edit > Paste, to paste the gray half circle.

4   Click the Align To Selection button ( ), and choose Align To Artboard in the menu that appears.

5   Click the Horizontal Align Center button ( ), and then click the Vertical Align Bottom button ( ) to align the selection to the horizontal center and vertical bottom of the artboard.

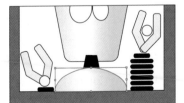

6   Choose Select > Deselect.

● **Note:** When distributing objects horizontally, make sure that the leftmost and rightmost objects are where you want them and then distribute the objects between them. For vertical distribution, position the topmost and bottommost objects and then distribute the objects between them.

● **Note:** The Align options may not appear in the Control panel but are indicated by the word "Align." The number of options displayed in the Control panel depends on your screen resolution.

Working with groups

You can combine objects in a group so that the objects are treated as a single unit. This way, you can move or transform a number of objects without affecting their individual attributes or relative positions.

Grouping items

Next, you will select multiple objects and create a group from them.

1 Choose View > Fit All In Window to see both artboards.

2 Choose Select > RobotMouth to reselect the series of orange shapes.

Tip: To select the objects in a group individually, select the group and then choose Object > Ungroup. This ungroups them permanently.

3 Choose Object > Group, and notice that the word "Group" appears on the left side of the Control panel with the shapes still selected.

4 Choose Select > Deselect.

5 With the Selection tool (➤), click one of the orange shapes in the group. Because they are grouped together, all are now selected.

6 Drag the group of orange shapes onto the robot head (below the eyes). Choose Select > Deselect.

Working in Isolation mode

Isolation mode isolates groups or sublayers so that you can easily select and edit specific objects or parts of objects without having to ungroup the objects. When in Isolation mode, all objects outside of the isolated group are locked and dimmed so that they aren't affected by the edits you make.

Next, you will edit a group using Isolation mode.

Tip: To enter Isolation mode, you can also select a group with the Selection tool and then click the Isolate Selected Object button (▣) in the Control panel.

1 With the Selection tool (➤), click the robot's hand at the end of the longer arm. You will see that it selects a group of shapes that make up the hand.

2 Double-click a shape in that hand to enter Isolation mode.

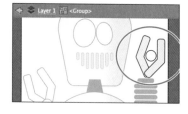

3 Choose View > Fit Artboard In Window, and notice that the rest of the content in the document appears dimmed (you can't select it).

At the top of the Document window, a gray bar appears with the words "Layer 1" and "<Group>." This indicates that you have isolated a group of objects that is on Layer 1. You will learn more about layers in Lesson 8, "Working with Layers."

4   Drag the light gray circle down to approximately match the position of the circle shape in the other hand.

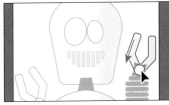

When you enter Isolation mode, groups are temporarily ungrouped. This enables you to edit objects in the group or to add new content without having to ungroup.

5   Double-click outside of the shapes within the group to exit Isolation mode.

6   Click to select the circle shape.

Notice that it is once again grouped with the rest of the shapes in the hand, and you can also select other objects.

7   Choose Select > Deselect.

▶ **Tip:** To exit Isolation mode, you can also click the gray arrow in the upper-left corner of the Document window as many times as necessary until the document is no longer in Isolation mode. Or deselect all content and click the Exit Isolation Mode button (■) in the Control panel.

Creating a nested group

Groups can also be *nested*—grouped within other objects or grouped to form larger groups. Nesting is a common technique used when designing artwork. It's a great way to keep associated content together.

In this section, you will explore how to create a nested group.

1   With the Selection tool (▶), drag a marquee across the series of black shapes below the hand that make up the longer arm of the robot.

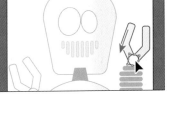

2   Choose Object > Group.

3   With the Selection tool, Shift-click the hand above the arm to select that group, as well. Choose Object > Group.

You have created a *nested group*—a group that is combined with other objects or groups to form a larger group.

4   Choose Select > Deselect.

5   With the Selection tool, click one of the grouped objects in that same arm. All objects in the group become selected.

6   Click a blank area on the artboard to deselect the objects.

Next, you will explore the Group Selection tool.

7   Hold down the Direct Selection tool () in the Tools panel, and drag to the right to access the Group Selection tool (). The Group Selection tool adds the object's parent group(s) to the current selection.

8   Click one of the shapes in the same robot hand to select it. Click again, on the same shape, to select the object's parent group (the group of hand shapes). Click once more, on that same shape, to select the group composed of the hand and arm. The Group Selection tool adds each group to the selection in the order in which it was grouped.

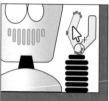

Click once.

Click twice to select the parent group.

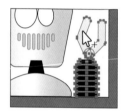

Click a third time to select all in the group.

9   Choose Select > Deselect.

<span></span>

● **Note:** To ungroup all of the selected objects, even the hand and arm shapes, choose Object > Ungroup twice.

10 With the Selection tool, click any of the objects in the nested group to select the group. Choose Object > Ungroup to ungroup the objects.

11 Choose Select > Deselect.

12 Click to select the hand. Notice that it is still a group of objects.

Exploring object arrangement

As you create objects, Illustrator stacks them in order on the artboards, beginning with the first object created. The order in which objects are stacked (called *stacking order*) determines how they display when they overlap. You can change the stacking order of objects in your artwork at any time, using either the Layers panel or Object > Arrange commands.

Arranging objects

▶ **Tip:** To learn more about objects and stacking order, see the PDF "Stack_order.pdf" in the Lesson_extras folder in the Lessons folder.

Next, you will work with the Arrange commands to change how objects are stacked.

1   Choose View > Fit All In Window to see both artboards in the document.

2   With the Selection tool () selected, click to select the black shape below the robot's head (the robot "neck").

3   Choose Object >Arrange > Send To Back to send the shape behind the robot's head and body.

4 Next, click to select either of the red circles on the right artboard.

5 Drag the selected circle on top of the smaller eye for the robot (see the figure). Release the mouse, and notice that the red circle disappears, but it's still selected.

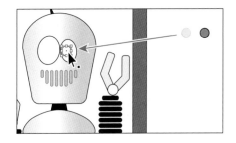

It went behind the ellipse (the eye) because it was probably created before the eye shape, which means it is lower in the stack of shapes.

6 With the red circle still selected, choose Object > Arrange > Bring to Front. This brings the red circle to the front of the stack, making it the topmost object.

Selecting objects behind

When you stack objects on top of each other, sometimes it becomes difficult to select objects that are underneath. Next, you will learn how to select an object through a stack of objects.

1 With the Selection tool (▶), select the other red circle on the right artboard, drag it onto the larger robot eye shape on the left artboard, and then release the mouse.

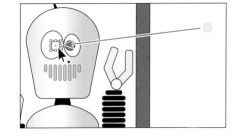

Notice that this circle disappears like the other, but is still selected. This time, you will deselect the circle and then reselect it using another method.

2 Choose Select > Deselect, and the red circle is no longer selected.

3 With the pointer still positioned over the location of the second red circle, the one behind the eye shape, hold down the Ctrl (Windows) or Command (Mac OS) key and click until the circle is selected again (this may take several clicks).

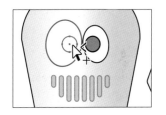

You may see an angled bracket displayed with the pointer (◁₊).

● **Note:** To select the hidden red circle, make sure that you click where the circle and the eye overlap. Otherwise, you won't be able to select the red circle.

4 Choose Object > Arrange > Bring To Front to bring the circle on top of the eye.

5 Choose Select > Deselect.

6 Choose File > Save.

Hiding and locking objects

When working on complex artwork, it may become more difficult to make selections. In this section, you'll learn how to lock and hide content to make selecting objects easier.

1 Choose View > Fit Artboard In Window.

2 Choose Object > Show All to reveal a mask over the robot's eyes. Choose Object > Arrange > Bring To Front to bring the mask to the front.

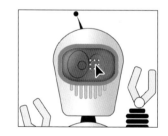

3 With the Selection tool (▶), click to attempt to select one of the eyes.

   Notice that you can't, since the mask is on top of them. In order to access the eyes, you could use one of the methods we previously discussed or use one of two other methods: hide or lock.

4 With the mask still selected, choose Object > Hide > Selection, or press Ctrl+3 (Windows) or Command+3 (Mac OS). The mask is hidden so that you can more easily select other objects. (This is how we initially hid the mask).

5 Click to select one of the red circles in the eyes, and move it.

6 Choose Object > Show All to show the mask again.

7 With the mask selected, choose Object > Lock > Selection.

   The mask is still visible, but you cannot select it.

8 With the Selection tool, click to select one of the eye shapes.

9 Choose Object > Unlock All, and then choose Object > Hide > Selection to hide the mask again.

10 Choose File > Save, to save the file, and then choose File > Close.

▶ **Tip:** To learn more selection techniques, see the PDF named Selections.pdf in the Lesson_extras folder in the Lessons folder.

Review questions

1 How can you select an object that has no fill?

2 Name two ways you can select an item in a group without choosing Object > Ungroup.

3 Of the two Selection tools (Selection [▶] and Direct Selection [▷]), which allows you to edit the individual anchor points of an object?

4 What should you do after creating a selection that you are going to use repeatedly?

5 Sometimes you are unable to select an object because it is underneath another object. Name two ways to get around this issue.

6 To align objects to the artboard, what do you need to first select in the Align panel or Control panel before you choose an alignment option?

Review answers

1 You can select an object that has no fill by clicking the stroke or by dragging a marquee across the object.

2 Using the Group Selection tool (▷⁺), you can click once to select an individual item within a group. Click again to add the next grouped items to the selection. Read Lesson 8, "Working with Layers," to see how you can use layers to make complex selections. You can also double-click the group to enter Isolation mode, edit the shapes as needed, and then exit Isolation mode by pressing the Escape key or by double-clicking outside of the group.

3 Using the Direct Selection tool (▷), you can select one or more individual anchor points and make changes to the shape of an object.

4 For any selection that you anticipate using again, choose Select > Save Selection. Name the selection so that you can reselect it at any time from the Select menu.

5 If your access to an object is blocked, you can choose Object > Hide > Selection to hide the blocking object. The object is not deleted. It is just hidden in the same position until you choose Object > Show All. You can also use the Selection tool to select behind content by pressing the Ctrl (Windows) or Command (Mac OS) key and then clicking on the overlapping objects until the object you want to select is selected.

6 To align objects to an artboard, first select the Align To Artboard option.

3 CREATING AND EDITING SHAPES

Lesson overview

In this lesson, you'll learn how to do the following:

- Create a document with multiple artboards.
- Use tools and commands to create basic shapes.
- Work with drawing modes.
- Use rulers and Smart Guides as drawing aids.
- Scale and duplicate objects.
- Join and outline objects.
- Edit strokes with the Width tool.
- Work with the Shape Builder tool.
- Work with Pathfinder commands to create shapes.
- Use Image Trace to create shapes.

This lesson takes approximately an hour and a half to complete.

Download the project files for this lesson from the Lesson & Update Files tab on your Account page at www.peachpit.com and store them on your computer in a convenient location, as described in the Getting Started section of this book.

Your Accounts page is also where you'll find any updates to the chapters or to the lesson files. Look on the Lesson & Update Files tab to access the most current content.

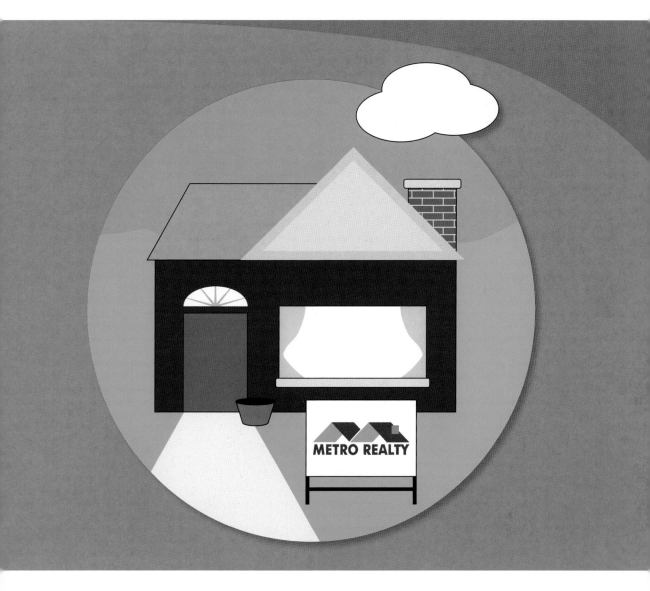

You can create documents with multiple artboards and many kinds of objects by starting with a basic shape and then editing it to create new shapes. In this lesson, you'll create a new document and then create and edit some basic shapes for an illustration.

Getting started

In this lesson, you'll create an illustration for a brochure.

1   To ensure that the tools and panels function as described in this lesson, delete or deactivate (by renaming) the Adobe Illustrator CC preferences file. See "Restoring default preferences," on page 3.

2   Start Adobe Illustrator CC.

● **Note:** If you have not already downloaded the project files for this lesson to your computer from your Account page, make sure to do so now. See "Getting Started" at the beginning of the book.

● **Note:** In Mac OS, when opening lesson files, you may need to click the round, green button in the upper-left corner of the Document window to maximize the window's size.

3   Choose File > Open. Locate the file named L3end.ai, which is in the Lesson03 folder in the Lessons folder that you copied onto your hard disk. These are the finished illustrations that you will create throughout this lesson. Choose View > Fit All In Window and leave the file open for reference, or choose File > Close.

Creating a new document

You will now create a document that will have two artboards, each with content that you will later combine.

1   Choose File > New, to open a new, untitled document. In the New Document dialog box, change the following options:

- Name: **homesale**
- Profile: Choose **Print** (the default setting).
- Number Of Artboards: **2** (to create two artboards). (When you change the number of artboards, the Profile changes to [Custom].)
- Arrange By Row (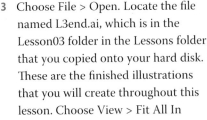): **Selected**
- Make sure that the Left To Right Layout arrow (▶) is showing.

Next, you'll jump to the units so that the rest of the changes are in inches.

- Units: **Inches**
- Spacing: **1** (The spacing value is the distance between each artboard, in inches.)
- Width: **8 in** (You don't need to type the **in** for inches, since the units are set to inches.)
- Height: **8 in**

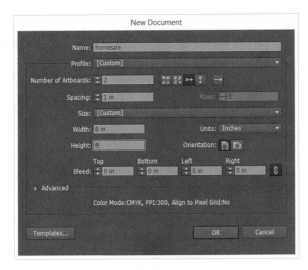

Note: You can set up a document for different kinds of output, such as print, web, video, and more, by choosing a Profile. For example, if you are designing a web page mockup, you can use a web document profile, which automatically displays the page size and units in pixels, changes the color mode to RGB, and changes the raster effects to Screen (72 ppi).

2 Click OK in the New Document dialog box.

3 Choose File > Save As. In the Save As dialog box, ensure that the name of the file is **homesale** (Windows) or **homesale.ai** (Mac OS), and choose the Lesson03 folder. Leave the Save As Type option set to Adobe Illustrator (*.AI) (Windows) or the Format option set to Adobe Illustrator (ai) (Mac OS), and click Save. In the Illustrator Options dialog box, leave the Illustrator options at their default settings and click OK.

Set up multiple artboards

Illustrator allows you to create multiple artboards. Setting up the artboards requires an understanding of the initial artboard settings in the New Document dialog box. After specifying the number of artboards for your document, you can set the order you'd like them laid out on screen. They are defined as follows:

- **Grid By Row:** Arranges multiple artboards in the specified number of rows. Choose the number of rows from the Rows menu. The default value creates the most square appearance possible with the specified number of artboards.

- **Grid By Column:** Arranges multiple artboards in the specified number of columns. Choose the number of columns from the Columns menu. The default value creates the most square appearance possible with the specified number of artboards.

- **Arrange By Row:** Arranges artboards in one straight row.

- **Arrange By Column:** Arranges artboards in one straight column.

- **Change To Right-To-Left Layout:** Arranges multiple artboards in the specified row or column format, but displays them from right to left.

—From Illustrator Help

4   Click the Document Setup button in the Control panel.

The Document Setup dialog box is where you can change the artboard size, units, bleeds, and more, after a document is created.

5   In the Bleed section of the Document Setup dialog box, change the value in the Top field to **.125 in**, either by clicking the up arrow to the left of the field once or by typing the value, and all four fields change. Click OK.

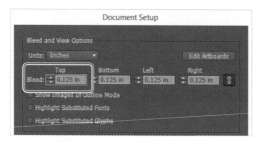

Notice the red line that appears around both artboards. The red line indicates the bleed area. Typical bleeds for printing are about 1/8 of an inch.

What is a bleed?

Bleed is the amount of artwork that falls outside of the printing bounding box, or outside the artboard. You can include bleed in your artwork as a margin of error—to ensure that the ink is still printed to the edge of the page after the page is trimmed or that an image can be stripped into a keyline in a document.

—From Illustrator Help

Working with basic shapes

In the first part of this lesson, you'll create a house using basic shapes, like rectangles, ellipses, rounded rectangles, and polygons. You'll begin this exercise by setting up the workspace.

1   Choose Window > Workspace > Essentials (if it's not already selected), and then choose Window > Workspace > Reset Essentials.

2   Choose View > Rulers > Show Rulers, or press Ctrl+R (Windows) or Command+R (Mac OS), to display rulers along the top and left side of the Document window (if they are not already showing).

The ruler units are inches because you specified them in the New Document dialog box. You can change the ruler units for all documents or for the current document only. The ruler unit applies to measuring objects, moving and transforming objects, setting grid and guide spacing, and creating shapes. It does not affect the units used in the Character, Paragraph, and Stroke panels. The units used in these panels can be changed by choosing (Edit > Preferences > Units [Windows] or Illustrator > Preferences > Units [Mac OS]).

Understanding drawing modes

Before starting to draw shapes in Illustrator, it can be helpful to understand the different drawing modes available. Notice the three drawing modes found at the bottom of the Tools panel: Draw Normal, Draw Behind, and Draw Inside.

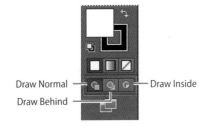

Draw Normal — Draw Inside

Draw Behind

Note: If the Tools panel you see is a single column, select a drawing mode by clicking the Drawing Modes button (🖼) at the bottom of the Tools panel and choosing a drawing mode from the menu that appears.

Drawing modes allow you to draw shapes in a different way.

- **Draw Normal mode:** You start every document by drawing shapes in Normal mode, which stacks shapes on top of each other.

- **Draw Behind mode:** This mode allows you to draw objects behind other objects without choosing layers or paying attention to the stacking order.

- **Draw Inside mode:** This mode lets you draw objects or place images inside other objects, including live text, automatically creating a clipping mask of the selected object.

▶ **Tip:** To learn more about objects and stacking order, see the PDF "Stack_order.pdf," in the Lesson_extras folder in the Lessons folder.

Note: To learn more about clipping masks, see Lesson 15, "Combining Illustrator CC Graphics with Other Adobe Applications."

As you create shapes in the following sections, you will be using the different drawing modes and learning how they affect your artwork.

Creating rectangles

First, you'll create a series of rectangles to begin the house. As you go through this section, you don't have to match the sizes of the drawn shapes exactly. They are just there as a guide.

1. Choose View > Fit Artboard In Window. Make sure that the number 1 is showing in the Artboard Navigation area in the lower-left corner of the Document window, which indicates that the first artboard is showing.

2. Choose Window > Transform to open the Transform panel.

   The Transform panel is useful for editing properties, such as the width and height of an existing shape.

3 Select the Rectangle tool (▬) in the Tools panel. Position the pointer anywhere in the artboard, and click and drag to create a small rectangle.

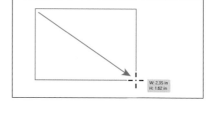

As you drag, notice the tool tip that appears as a gray box next to the cursor, indicating the width and height of the shape as you draw. This is called the *measurement label* and is a part of the Smart Guides, which will be discussed later in this lesson.

4 Choose Edit > Undo Rectangle to remove the rectangle.

▶ **Tip:** Holding down the Alt (Windows) or Option (Mac OS) key as you drag with the Rectangle, Rounded Rectangle, or Ellipse tools draws a shape from its center point rather than from its upper-left corner. Holding down the Shift key as you draw with the Rectangle, Rounded Rectangle, or Ellipse tools selected draws a shape in perfect proportion (a square, rounded corner square, or circle).

5 With the Rectangle tool still selected, position the pointer just to the left and above the center of the artboard. See the red X in the figure for where to start. Click and drag down and to the right until the rectangle is approximately 4.7 in wide and has a height of 2.3 in (as seen in the gray measurement label next to the cursor).

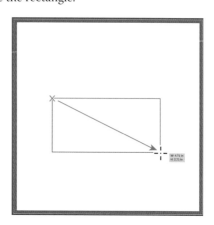

When you release the mouse button, the rectangle is selected, and its center point appears. The center point lets you drag to align the object with other elements in your artwork. Also, by default, shapes are filled with a white color and have a black stroke (border). A shape with a fill can be selected and moved by first positioning the pointer anywhere inside the shape.

6 In the Transform panel, if necessary, change the size of the selected object by typing **4.7** for the width (W:) and **2.3** for the height (H:). Typing the **in** for inches isn't necessary; it is added automatically.

7 Close the Transform panel group by clicking the Close button (X) in the upper-right corner of the group title bar (Windows) or in the upper-left corner (Mac OS).

8 With the new rectangle still selected, click the Fill color (▭▼) in the Control panel and change the fill color to a dark brown. When you position the pointer over a colors in the panel that appears, a tool tip showing the color values appears. We chose a swatch with the tool tip that shows "C=50 M=70 Y=80 K=70." Press the Escape key to hide the Swatches panel.

3 Choose View > Hide Bounding Box.

The bounding box, as you saw in previous lessons, allows you to transform the shape. If you turn the bounding box off, you can drag the shape by an edge or an anchor point without transforming it.

4 Select the Selection tool (▶) in the Tools panel. Click and drag the ellipse up by the right, middle point (see the red X in the figure). Release the mouse button when the center of the ellipse snaps to the top of the red rectangle.

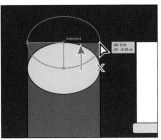

5 Choose View > Show Bounding Box.

6 Choose Window > Transform to open the Transform panel. Click the red rectangle to select it, and note the width in the Transform panel. Click the ellipse again, and see if the widths are the same in the Transform panel. If not, correct the ellipse by typing the same width value as the red rectangle and pressing Enter or Return. Close the Transform panel group.

● **Note:** If you corrected the width in the Transform panel, the ellipse may no longer be aligned with the rectangle. With the Selection tool, drag the ellipse horizontally to align it again.

7 Choose Select > Deselect, and then choose File > Save.

Creating polygons

Now, you'll create two triangles for the roof of the house, using the Polygon tool (⬡). Polygons are drawn from the center, by default, which is different than the other tools you've worked with so far.

1 Choose View > Fit Artboard In Window.

2 Click and hold down the mouse button on the Ellipse tool (⬭) in the Tools panel, and select the Polygon tool (⬡).

3 Click the Fill color in the Control panel, and make sure that the color is a light gray (with the tool tip values "C=0 M=0 Y=0 K=20").

4 Position the pointer above the brown rectangle. Drag to the right to begin drawing a polygon, but don't release the mouse button. Press the down arrow key three times to reduce the number of sides on the polygon to three (a triangle), and don't release the mouse yet. Hold down the Shift key to straighten the triangle. *Without releasing the Shift key,*

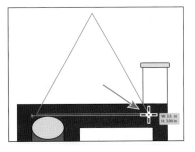

▶ **Tip:** While drawing with the Polygon tool, press the up arrow key to increase the number of sides.

drag left or right until the Smart Guides measurement label displays a width of approximately 3.5 in. Release the mouse, and then release the modifier key.

5 Select the Selection tool (↖) in the Tools panel, and drag the triangle from its center until the bottom of the triangle snaps to the top and right of the larger brown rectangle. The word "intersect" appears when it is snapped. Drag the triangle a little further to the right to hang it over the brown rectangle. See the figure for placement help.

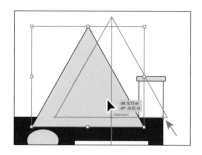

6 With the Selection tool, drag the top, middle bounding point down until the measurement label shows a height of approximately 1.7 in.

You may need to zoom out or scroll in the Document window to see the top of the triangle.

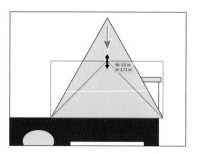

Working with Draw Behind mode

Next, you'll draw another triangle behind the one you just drew, using Draw Behind mode.

● **Note:** If the Tools panel you see is displayed as a single column, you can click the Drawing Modes button (▣) at the bottom of the Tools panel and choose Draw Behind from the menu that appears.

1 Click the Draw Behind button (▣) at the bottom of the Tools panel.

As long as this drawing mode is selected, every shape you create, using the different methods you've learned, will be created behind the other shapes on the page.

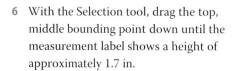

2 Select the Polygon tool (⬡) in the Tools panel. Position the pointer just to the left of the triangle you created. Click to open the Polygon dialog box. Click OK, and notice that the new triangle is behind the existing triangle on the artboard.

The values in the Polygon dialog box match the radius and number of sides of the last drawn polygon (before you modified it).

● **Note:** If your larger triangle extends a bit off the top of the artboard, don't worry. You will cut off the top of it later in the lesson.

3 Select the Selection tool (↖), and drag the new triangle from roughly in the middle, so that the bottom edge snaps to the top of the brown rectangle, as shown in the figure (the blue outline). With the triangle selected and in place, press the left or right arrow key until it hangs off the left edge of the brown rectangle a little.

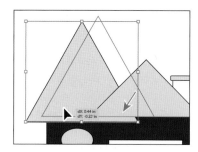

4 With the new triangle still selected, click the Fill color in the Control panel and change the fill color to a darker gray than the smaller triangle. We chose a swatch with the tool tip values "C=0 M=0 Y=0 K=50." Press the Escape key to hide the Swatches panel.

5 Click the Draw Normal button (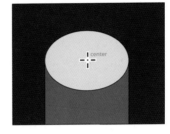) at the bottom of the Tools panel.

Creating stars

Next, you'll create a star for the window above the door, using the Star tool (⭐).

1 Select the Zoom tool (🔍) in the Tools panel, and click twice, *slowly*, on the ellipse at the top of the red door rectangle.

2 Click and hold down the mouse button on the Polygon tool (⬡) in the Tools panel, and select the Star tool (⭐). Position the pointer in the center of the gray ellipse shape. Notice that the word "center" appears.

Take the next step slowly, and reference the figure as you draw. Only release the mouse button when indicated.

● **Note:** If the Tools panel you see is displayed as a single column, you can click the Drawing Modes button (■) at the bottom of the Tools panel and choose Draw Normal from the menu that appears.

3 Click and drag slowly to the right to create a star shape. Without releasing the mouse button, press the up arrow key five times (to increase the number of points on the star to 10). Drag the mouse until you see a width of approximately .28 in and stop dragging, but don't release the mouse button yet.

Hold down the Ctrl (Windows) or Command (Mac OS) key, and continue dragging to the right. This keeps the inner radius constant. Drag until you see a width of approximately 1.3 in and stop dragging, *without releasing the mouse button*. Release the Ctrl or Command key, but not the mouse. Hold down the Shift key, and ensure that the star has a width of about 1.3 in. Release the mouse button, and then release the Shift key, and you should see a darker gray star.

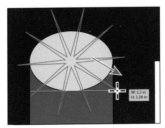
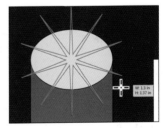

Change the number of points.   Resize the star.   Constrain the star.

4 Change the Stroke weight, to the right of the word "Stroke" in the Control panel, to **0**. Later in the lesson, you will use the ellipse and the star shape to create the window above the door.

Tips for drawing polygons, spirals, and stars

You can control the shapes of polygons, spirals, and stars by pressing certain keys as you draw the shapes. Choose any of the following options to control the shape:

- To add or subtract sides on a polygon, points on a star, or number of segments on a spiral, hold down the up arrow or down arrow key while creating the shape. This only works if the mouse button is held down. When the mouse button is released, the tool remains set to the last specified value.

- To rotate the shape, move the mouse in an arc as you draw.

- To keep a side or point at the top, hold down the Shift key while drawing.

- To keep the inner radius constant, start creating a shape and then hold down Ctrl (Windows) or Command (Mac OS).

—From Illustrator Help

Changing stroke width and alignment

Every shape, by default, is created with a 1-point stroke. You can easily change the stroke weight of an object to make it thinner or thicker. Strokes are also aligned to the center of a path edge, by default, but you can change the alignment, as well, using the Stroke panel.

1　Choose View > Fit Artboard In Window.

2　With the Selection tool (⬆), click to select the smaller light-gray triangle that makes up part of the roof.

3　Select the Zoom tool (🔍) in the Tools panel, and click that triangle once to zoom in.

● **Note:** You can also open the Stroke panel by choosing Window > Stroke.

4　Click the underlined word "Stroke" in the Control panel to open the Stroke panel. In the Stroke panel, change the Stroke weight to **10 pt**. Notice that the stroke of the triangle is centered on the edge of the shape, by default.

5　Click the Align Stroke To Inside button (⬜) in the Stroke panel. This aligns the stroke to the inside edge of the triangle.

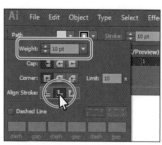

You set the stroke to the inside of the triangle so that the bottom edge still visually aligns with the bottom of the other triangle.

● **Note:** Going forward, you will find that opening a panel in the Control panel (such as the Stroke panel in this step), you will need to hide it before moving on. You can do this by pressing the Escape key.

6   With the triangle still selected, click the Stroke color in the Control panel (to the left of the word "Stroke"), and change the stroke color to a darker gray than the fill of that same triangle.

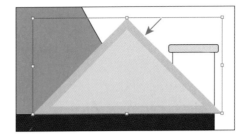

7   Choose File > Save.

About aligning strokes

If an object is a closed path (such as a square), you can select an option in the Stroke panel to align the stroke along the path to the center (default), inside, or outside:

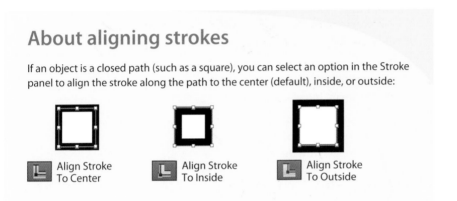

Align Stroke To Center   Align Stroke To Inside   Align Stroke To Outside

Working with line segments

Next, you'll work with straight lines and line segments, known as *open paths*, to create a flower pot. Shapes can be created in many ways in Illustrator, and the simpler way is usually better.

1   Select the Zoom tool (🔍) in the Tools panel, and click four times, slowly, below the red door to zoom in on the empty artboard space below it.

2   Choose Reset Essentials from the workspace switcher in the Application bar.

You've been working in the default Preview mode, which lets you see how objects are painted with fill and stroke colors. If paint attributes seem distracting, you can work in Outline mode, which you'll do next.

3   Choose View > Outline, to switch from Preview to Outline mode.

● **Note:** Outline mode temporarily removes all paint attributes, such as colored fills and strokes, to speed up selecting and redrawing artwork. You can't select or drag shapes by clicking in the middle of a shape, because the fill temporarily disappears.

4   Select the Ellipse tool (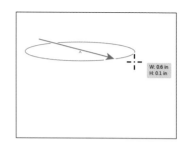) in the Tools panel. Below the house shapes, draw an ellipse that has a width of 0.6 in and a height of 0.1 in, as shown in the measurement label that appears.

Note: When you drag to select, make sure that you do not drag across the points on the left and right ends of the ellipse.

5   Select the Direct Selection tool (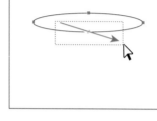) in the Tools panel. Drag across the lower part of the ellipse to select the bottom half.

6   Choose Edit > Copy, and then choose Edit > Paste In Front to create a new path that is directly on top of the original.

This copies and pastes only the bottom half of the ellipse as a single path, because that is what you selected with the Direct Selection tool.

7   Select the Selection tool (▶), and press the down arrow key about five times to move the new line down.

8   Click and drag the line straight down until you see, in the measurement label, a dY of approximately .25 in.

Make sure that you position the pointer directly on the line to select and drag it.

Note: Depending on the resolution of your screen, the Transform options may appear in the Control panel. If they do appear, you can change the W value.

9   Click the word "Transform" in the Control panel to show the Transform panel. Change the Width of the selected line to **.4 in**.

You could also open the Transform panel by choosing Window > Transform.

10 Select the Line Segment tool (/) in the Tools panel. Draw a line by clicking the left anchor point of the ellipse and dragging to the left anchor point of the new path. The anchor points are highlighted when the line snaps to them and the word "anchor" appears. Repeat this on the right side of the ellipse.

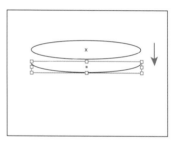
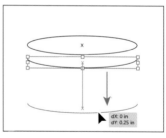
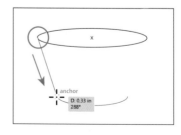
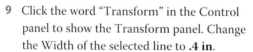

11 Choose Select > Deselect, and then choose File > Save.

Next, you will take the three line segments that make up part of the flower pot and join them together as one path.

Joining paths

When more than one open path is selected, you can join them together to create a closed path (like a circle). You can also join the endpoints of two separate paths.

Next, you will join the three paths to create a single closed path.

1 Select the Selection tool (▶) in the Tools panel. Drag a selection marquee across each of the three paths that you just created, to select them all (not the top ellipse).

2 Choose Object > Path > Join.

The three paths are converted to a single path (sort of in a "u" shape). Illustrator identifies the anchor points on the ends of each path and joins the closest points together.

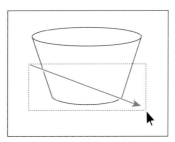

▶ **Tip:** After paths are selected, you could also join paths by pressing Ctrl+J (Windows) or Command+J (Mac OS).

3 With the path still selected, choose Object > Path > Join once more. Choose Select > Deselect to see the joined path.

This creates a closed path, connecting the two endpoints of the path. If you select a single open path and choose Object > Path > Join, Illustrator creates a path segment between the endpoints of the open path, creating a closed path.

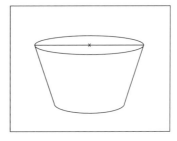

● **Note:** If you only want to fill the shape with a color, it is not necessary to join the path to make a closed path. An open path can have a color fill. It is, however, necessary to do this if you want a stroke to appear around the entire fill area.

4 With the Selection tool, drag a marquee across the two flower pot shapes to select them both. Change the Stroke weight in the Control panel to **1 pt**. Change the Stroke color to black. Change the Fill color to black.

5 Choose View > Preview.

6 Choose Select > Deselect. Click to select the bottom flower pot shape, and choose Object > Arrange > Send To Back.

7   In the Control panel, change the Fill color to
    a brown (C=35 M=60 Y=80 K=25).

● **Note:** To select a path without a fill, click the stroke or
drag across the path.

8   Hold down the Shift key and click the ellipse
    with the Selection tool, to select both flower
    pot shapes.

9   Choose Object > Group, and then choose Select > Deselect.

Open path vs. closed path

As you draw, you create a line called a *path*. A path is made up of one or more
straight or curved segments. The beginning and end of each segment are marked
by anchor points, which work like pins holding a wire in place. A path can be closed
(for example, a circle), or open, with distinct endpoints (for example, a wavy line).

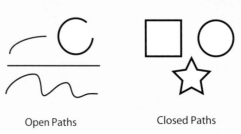

Open Paths   Closed Paths

Both open and closed paths can have fills applied to them.

—From Illustrator Help

Using the Width tool

Not only can you adjust the stroke weight and the alignment of the stroke, but
you can also alter regular stroke widths either by using the Width tool (🖊) or by
applying width profiles to the stroke. This allows you to create variations along the
stroke of a path.

Next, you will use the Width tool to create some curtains in the window.

1   Choose View > Fit Artboard In Window. Select the Zoom tool (🔍) in the Tools
    panel, and then click the white window rectangle three times, slowly, to zoom in.

2   With the Selection tool (▶), press the Shift key and click the white window
    rectangle, the gray rounded rectangle beneath it, and the brown rectangle, to
    select them all. Choose Object > Lock > Selection to temporarily lock them.

3 Select the Line Segment tool (╱) in the Tools panel, and position the pointer at the top of the white rectangle, away from the left edge. Hold down the Shift key, and drag straight down, snapping the end of the line to the bottom of the white rectangle. Release the mouse button, and then release the modifier key.

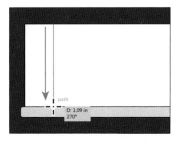

4 Make sure that in the Control panel the Stroke color of the line is black and that the Stroke weight is **1 pt**.

5 Select the Width tool (🐍) in the Tools panel. Position the pointer over the middle of the line, and notice that the pointer has a plus symbol next to it (▸₊). Drag to the right, away from the line. Notice that, as you drag, you are stretching the stroke to the left and right equally. Release the mouse when the measurement label shows Side 1 and Side 2 at approximately .25 in.

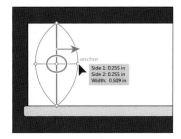

The new point on the stroke of the original line is called the *width point*. The lines extending from the width point are the handles. Width points created at a corner or at a direct-selected anchor point stick to the anchor point during basic editing of the path.

6 The width point on the stroke (circled in the figure) should still be selected. You can tell it's selected, because it's not hollow like the points at the ends of the handles. Press Delete to remove it.

Because you only created one width point on the stroke, removing that one removed the width completely.

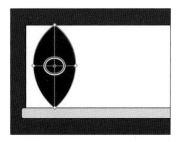

● **Note:** If you need to reselect the point, make sure that the Width tool is selected, position the pointer over the point, and then click it.

7 Position the pointer over the top anchor point of the line, and notice that the pointer has a wavy line next to it (▸～). Press the Alt (Windows) or Option (Mac OS) key, and drag to the right until you see that Side 1 is approximately 0.25 in. Release the mouse button, and then release the modifier key.

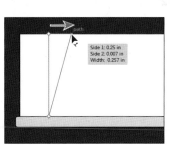

● **Note:** When you edit with the Width tool, you are only editing the stroke of the object.

The modifier key allows you to drag one side of the stroke rather than both sides, as you did previously.

8 Position the pointer over the bottom anchor point of the line. Press the Alt (Windows) or Option (Mac OS) key, and drag to the right until you see that Side 1 is approximately 0.3 in. Release the mouse button, and then release the modifier key.

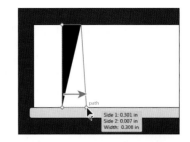

▶ **Tip:** You can use the Width Point Edit dialog box to ensure that width points are the same.

9 With the Width tool still selected, position the pointer over the top width point or handle of the line (circled in the figure). When the pointer changes (▶~), double-click to open the Width Point Edit dialog box. Change the Side 1 width to **.3 in**. Make sure that Side 2 is set to **0,** and click OK.

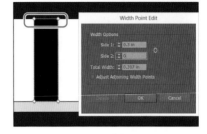

The Width Point Edit dialog box allows you to adjust the sides together or separately, using more precision. Clicking the Adjust Widths Proportionately button (▦) would link Side 1 with Side 2 so that they adjust together, in proportion. Also, if you select the Adjust Adjoining Width Points option, changes to the selected width point affect neighboring width points, as well.

10 Position the pointer over the bottom width point or handle of the line. When the pointer changes (▶~), double-click to open the Width Point Edit dialog box. Change the Side 1 width to **.3 in**. Make sure that Side 2 is set to **0 in**, and click OK.

11 Position the pointer over the middle of the line (indicated by the X in the figure). Click and drag to the right until you see a Side 1 width of approximately .06 in.

● **Note:** You don't have to position the pointer over the center of the line and drag to create another width point. You can also drag from anywhere in the stroke area.

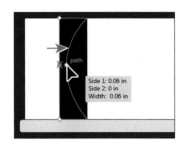

12 Position the pointer over the new width point you just created (circled in the figure) and, pressing the Alt (Windows) or Option (Mac OS) key, drag the new width point down to create a copy. Release the mouse button, and then release the key.

13 Click the new width point to select it.

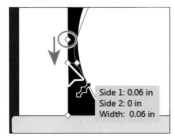

Next, you will select another width point and move them both. You may want to zoom in to the line, and take it slowly.

14 With the Width tool, press the Shift key and click the width point above the selected width point to select both. Release the Shift key. Drag the point you just selected down just a bit. Notice that the two width points move together proportionately.

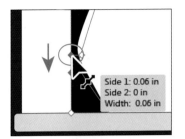

▶ **Tip:** You can drag one width point on top of another width point to create a discontinuous width point. If you double-click a discontinuous width point, the Width Point Edit dialog box allows you to edit both width points.

15 Position the pointer between the top width point and the second width point from the top. See the figure for help. Click and drag to the right until you see a Side 1 width of approximately .2 in.

16 Choose File > Save.

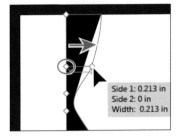

Saving width profiles

After defining the stroke width, you can save the variable width profile from the Stroke panel or the Control panel.

Width profiles can be applied to selected paths by choosing them from the Width Profile drop-down list in the Control panel or Stroke panel. When a stroke with no variable width is selected, the list displays the Uniform option. You can also select the Uniform option to remove a variable width profile from an object. To restore the default width profile set, click the Reset Profiles button at the bottom of the Profile drop-down list.

If you apply a variable width profile to a stroke, it is indicated with an asterisk (*) in the Appearance panel.

—From Illustrator Help

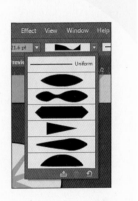

Outlining strokes

Paths, such as a line, can show a stroke color but not a fill color, by default. If you create a line in Illustrator and you want to apply both a stroke and a fill, you can outline the stroke, which converts the line into a closed shape (or compound path).

Next, you will outline the stroke of the curtain you just created.

Note: If the line initially has a color fill, a more complex group is created when you choose Outline Stroke.

1 With the line still selected, choose None (⊘) from the Fill color in the Control panel (if it is not already selected).

2 Choose Object > Path > Outline Stroke. This creates a filled shape that is a closed path.

3 With the new shape selected, click the Fill color in the Control panel and change the color to a light orange that shows "C=0 M=35 Y=85 K=0" in the tool tip. Click the Stroke color, and make sure that the color is None (⊘).

4 Select the Selection tool (▸), and begin dragging the left edge of the curtain shape to the left. As you drag, press the Shift key. When it snaps to the left edge of the white window rectangle, release the mouse button and then release the key.

5 Drag the right, middle bounding point of the curtain shape to the right to make the curtain a bit wider.

6 Press the Alt (Windows) or Option (Mac OS) key, and drag the curtain shape to the right until its right edge aligns to the right edge of the white rectangle.

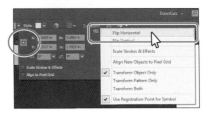

Note: Depending on the resolution of your screen, the word "Transform" may not appear in the Control panel. Click the underlined X, Y, W, or H links to open the Transform panel if you see them instead.

7 In the Control panel, click the word "Transform" to open the Transform panel (Window > Transform). Making sure that the center point of the reference point locator (▦) is selected (to flip the curtain shape around its center), choose Flip Horizontal from the Transform panel menu (▾≡).

8 Choose Object > Unlock All, and then choose Select > Deselect.

9 With the Selection tool, click to select the white window rectangle. Click the word "Stroke" in the Control panel to open the Stroke panel. Click the Align Stroke To Outside button (▣).

10 Click to select the gray rounded rectangle beneath the white window rectangle and curtain shapes. Choose Object > Arrange > Bring To Front.

11 Choose Select > Deselect, and then choose File > Save.

12 Choose View > Fit Artboard In Window.

Combining and editing shapes

In Illustrator, you can combine vector objects to create shapes in a variety of ways. The resulting paths or shapes differ depending on the method you use to combine the paths. The first method you will learn for combining shapes involves working with the Shape Builder tool. This tool allows you to visually and intuitively merge, delete, fill, and edit overlapping shapes and paths directly in the artwork.

Working with the Shape Builder tool

Using the Shape Builder tool (⊕), you'll change the appearance of the red door and create the window above it. Then, you'll make a cloud.

1 Select the Selection tool (►) in the Tools panel, and click to select the star shape. Choose Object > Hide > Selection to temporarily hide it.

2 Select the Zoom tool (🔍) in the Tools panel, and click three times on the top of the red door to zoom in.

3 Choose View > Outline so you can draw without affecting other shapes.

4 Select the Rectangle tool (▭) in the Tools panel. Position the pointer off the left edge of the door, aligned with the top. When the green alignment guide appears, click and drag down and to the right to create a rectangle with an approximate width of 1.2 in and a height of .1 in.

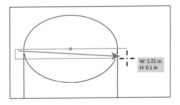

5 Choose View > Preview.

6 With the Selection tool, Shift-click the gray ellipse and the red rectangle to select all three shapes. With the shapes selected, select the Shape Builder tool (⊕) in the Tools panel.

Using the Shape Builder tool, you will now combine, delete, and paint these shapes.

7 Position the pointer over the bottom of the ellipse, indicated by the red X in the figure. Drag the pointer from the X down into the red rectangle. Release the mouse button to combine the shapes.

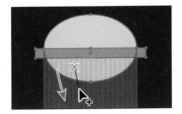

▶ **Tip:** Zooming in can help you see which shapes you are going to combine.

In order to edit shapes with the Shape Builder tool, they need to be selected. When you select the Shape Builder tool, the overlapping shapes are divided into separate objects temporarily. As you drag from one part to another, a red outline appears, showing you what the final shape outline will look like when it merges the shapes together.

8 With the shapes still selected, hold down the Alt (Windows) or Option (Mac OS) key and click the left end of the rectangle to delete it.

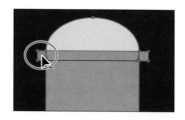

Notice that, with the modifier key held down, the pointer shows a minus sign (▶_).

Next, you will delete a series of shapes by dragging with the Shape Builder tool.

9 With the Shape Builder tool still selected, position the pointer off the left edge of the small rectangle below the ellipse, indicated by the red X in the figure. Hold down the Alt (Windows) or Option (Mac OS) key, and drag to the right to delete all of the shapes. Release the mouse button, and then release the modifier key.

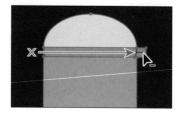

Notice that all of the shapes that will be deleted are highlighted as you drag.

10 With the shapes still selected, change the Fill color in the Control panel to red, with the tool tip showing "C=15 M=100 Y=90 K=10." Press the Escape key to hide the panel. This won't change anything on the artboard. Position the pointer over the larger rectangle that is the door, and click to apply the red color fill.

You can apply fills to any of the selected shapes with the Shape Builder tool by selecting the fill color first and then clicking the shape.

11 Choose Select > Deselect, and then choose View > Fit Artboard In Window.

12 Choose Object > Show All, to show the star shape.

Lastly, with the Shape Builder, you will build a simple cloud.

1 Select the Ellipse tool ( ) in the Tools panel, and draw an ellipse that has an approximate width of 1.4 in and an approximate height of .8 in, above the chimney on the house.

2 Select the Selection tool (▶) and, pressing the Alt (Windows) or Option (Mac OS) key, drag the ellipse twice to create two copies.

3 With the Selection tool, position the shapes like you see in the figure at right. Select all three cloud shapes.

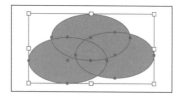

4 Select the Shape Builder tool ( ) in the Tools panel.

5   Press the Shift key and, starting at the upper-left edge of the shapes, drag a marquee across them all. Release the mouse button, and then release the key.

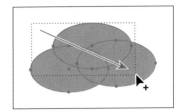

▶ **Tip:** Pressing Shift+Alt (Windows) or Shift+Option (Mac OS) and dragging a marquee across selected shapes with the Shape Builder tool selected allows you to delete a series of shapes within the marquee.

6   Select the Selection tool and, with the cloud shape selected, change the Fill color in the Control panel to white and the Stroke color to black.

7   Choose Select > Deselect, and then choose File > Save.

Shape Builder tool options

You can set up and customize various options such as gap detection, coloring source, and highlighting to get the required merging capability and better visual feedback.

Double-click the Shape Builder Tool icon in the Tools panel to set these options in the Shape Builder Tool Options dialog box.

—From Illustrator Help

▶ **Tip:** To learn more about the Shape Builder tool options, choose Help > Illustrator Help, and search for "Shape Builder tool options."

Working with Pathfinder effects in the Pathfinder panel

The bottom row of buttons in the Pathfinder panel, called *Pathfinder effects*, lets you combine shapes in many different ways to create paths or compound paths, by default. When a Pathfinder effect (such as Merge) is applied, the original objects selected are permanently transformed. If the effect results in more than one shape, they are grouped automatically.

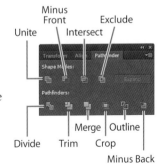

Next, you will finish the roof of the house by removing a portion of one of the gray triangles.

1   Choose View > Fit Artboard In Window. Press and hold the spacebar to access the Hand tool (🖐). Drag the artboard down a bit so that you can see the gray area above the artboard.

2   Choose Window > Pathfinder to open the Pathfinder panel group.

3 Select the Rectangle tool (■) in the Tools panel. Position the pointer above the artboard on the left edge. Click and draw a rectangle that covers the top part of the larger triangle. See the figure for guidance.

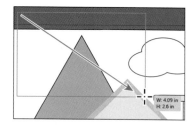

4 With the Selection tool (▶), hold down the Shift key and click the larger triangle to select it, as well.

5 With the shapes selected, in the Pathfinder panel, click the Minus Front button (▣).

With the new shape selected, notice the word "Path" on the left side of the Control panel.

6 Choose Object > Arrange > Send To Back.

7 Choose Select > Deselect, and then choose File > Save.

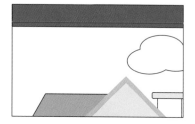

Working with shape modes in the Pathfinder panel

The buttons in the top row of the Pathfinder panel, called *shape modes*, create paths just like the Pathfinder effects, but they can also be used to create compound shapes. When several shapes are selected, clicking a shape mode while pressing the Alt (Windows) or Option (Mac OS) key creates a compound shape rather than a path. The original underlying objects of compound shapes are preserved. As a result, you can still select each original object within a compound shape. Using a shape mode to create a compound shape can be useful if you think that you may want to retrieve the original shapes at a later time.

Next, you will use shape modes to finish the window above the door.

1 Choose View > Fit Artboard In Window.

2 Select the Zoom tool (🔍), and click several times on the star above the red rectangle.

● **Note:** If the star is not showing, you can choose Object > Show All to show the star shape.

3 With the Selection tool (▶), click to select the star, hold down the Shift key, and then click the gray ellipse behind it to select both shapes. Release the Shift key, and then click the ellipse once more to make it the key object.

4 Click the Horizontal Align Center button (▤) in the Control panel.

5 With the objects selected, hold down the Alt (Windows) or Option (Mac OS) key and click the Minus Front button () in the Pathfinder panel.

This creates a compound shape that traces the outline where the two objects overlap. You will still be able to edit the star and the ellipse shape separately.

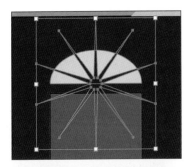

6 Choose Select > Deselect to see the final shape.

The star was removed from the ellipse shape, and the stroke is around the final window shape.

7 With the Selection tool, double-click the window shape above the door to enter Isolation mode.

8 Choose View > Outline so that you can see the two shapes (the ellipse and the star). Click the edge of the ellipse to select it, if it isn't already selected. In the Control panel, change the Fill color to white.

9 Drag the top, middle bounding point of the ellipse bounding box down to make it shorter. Drag until the measurement tool tip shows a height of approximately 0.3 in. Leave the ellipse selected.

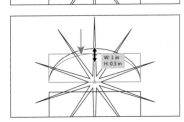

10 Choose View > Preview.

11 Choose Edit > Copy, to copy the ellipse shape. Choose Select > Deselect.

12 Press the Escape key to exit Isolation mode.

13 With the Selection tool, click to select the window shape again. Choose Edit > Paste In Back. In the Control panel, change the Fill color of the ellipse copy to a darker gray (C=0 M=0 Y=0 K=40) and make sure that the Stroke color is None.

14 Choose Select > Deselect. Click to select the window shape again (the compound shape on top). Click the Stroke panel icon (▤) on the right side of the workspace to expand the Stroke panel. Change the Stroke weight to **0** by clicking the down arrow to the left of the field or by typing in the value and pressing Enter or Return. Click the Stroke panel tab to collapse the panel. Leave the window compound shape selected.

▶ **Tip:** To edit the original shapes in a compound shape like this one, you can also select them individually with the Direct Selection tool (▸).

● **Note:** It is easier to resize a shape precisely if you zoom in. You can also change the width and height of the selected shape in the Transform panel.

You will now expand the window shape. Expanding a compound shape maintains the shape of the compound object, but you can no longer select or edit the original objects.

15 Click the Expand button in the Pathfinder panel. Close the Pathfinder panel group. Choose Select > Deselect.

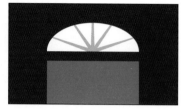

16 Choose View > Fit Artboard In Window, and then choose File > Save.

Using the Draw Inside mode

Next, you will learn how to draw a shape inside of another using the Draw Inside drawing mode. This can be useful if you wanted to hide (mask) part of artwork.

1 Select the Ellipse tool (●) in the Tools panel. Position the pointer over the upper-left corner of the artboard, and click without dragging. In the Ellipse dialog box, enter **7 in** for the Width and **7** for the Height. Click OK.

2 With the new circle selected, choose Align To Artboard from the Align To menu (⊞▾) in the Control panel. Click the Horizontal Align Center button (⊞) and the Vertical Align Center button (⊞)

3 Change the Fill color to blue (C=70 M=15 Y=0 K=0) and the Stroke weight to **0** in the Control panel.

Create the ellipse.

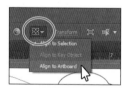

Align the ellipse.

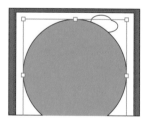

Change the Fill color.

4 Click the Draw Inside button (◙), near the bottom of the Tools panel.

This button is active when a single object is selected (path, compound path, or text), and it allows you to draw within the selected object only. Every shape you create will now be drawn inside of the selected shape (the circle). Also, notice that the blue circle has a dotted open rectangle around it, indicating that, if you draw, paste, or place content, it will be inside of the circle.

11 Choose Outlines With Source Image from the View menu in the Control panel, and take a look at the image. Choose Tracing Result from that same menu.

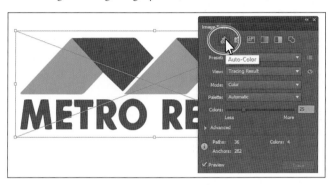

An image tracing object is made up of the original source image and the tracing result (which is the vector artwork). By default, only the tracing result is visible. However, you can change the display of both the original image and the tracing result to best suit your needs.

12 Choose Window > Image Trace to open the Image Trace panel. In the panel, click the Auto-Color button (🖼) at the top of the panel.

The buttons along the top of the Image Trace panel are saved settings for converting the image to grayscale, black and white, and more.

Tip: The Image Trace panel can also be opened with traced artwork selected, by clicking the Image Trace Panel button (≣) in the Control panel.

13 Press and hold the eye icon (👁) to the right of the View menu in the Image Trace panel to see the source image on the artboard. Release the mouse button.

14 In the Image Trace panel, click the toggle arrow to the left of the Advanced options to reveal them. Change only the following options:

- Colors: **3**
- Paths: **88%**
- Corners: **90%**
- Noise: **20 px**
- Method: Click the Overlapping button (🖼)
- Snap Curves To Lines: **Selected**

Tip: To the right of the Preset menu in the Image Trace panel, you can click the panel options and choose to save your settings as a preset, delete a preset, or rename a preset.

Note: Below the buttons at the top of the Image Trace panel, you will see the Preset and View options. These are the same as those in the Control panel. The Mode option allows you to change the color mode of resulting artwork (color, grayscale, or black and white). The Palette option is useful for limiting the color palette or for assigning colors from a color group.

▶ **Tip:** For information on Image Trace and the options in the Image Trace panel, see "Tracing artwork" in Illustrator Help (Help > Illustrator Help).

15 With the logo image tracing object still selected, click the Expand button in the Control panel. The logo is no longer an image tracing object but is composed of shapes and paths that are grouped together.

16 Close the Image Trace panel.

Cleaning up traced artwork

After tracing, you may need to clean up the resulting vector artwork.

1 Select the Selection tool (▸), and double-click the logo group to enter Isolation mode. Click the blue shape on the left, above the "M," and choose Object > Path > Simplify.

● **Note:** You will learn a lot more about working with paths and shapes in Lesson 5, "Drawing with the Pen and Pencil Tools."

2 In the Simplify dialog box, select Straight Lines and make sure that the Angle Threshold is **30** degrees. Select Preview, if it's not already selected, to see the effect. Click OK.

You can apply the Simplify command to other parts of the logo, as well. By aligning points and using other methods, you can turn the raster logo into a viable vector logo.

3 Press the Escape key to exit Isolation mode, and choose View > Fit Artboard In Window.

4 Choose Object > Show All to show the realty sign frame. With the Selection tool, click to select the logo and, pressing the Shift key, drag the top, middle bounding point down until the logo fits into the sign frame.

5 With the Selection tool, move the logo into the sign frame and visually center it.

6 Choose Select > All On Active Artboard, and then choose Object > Group. With the group selected, choose Edit > Copy.

7 Click the Previous artboard button (◀) in the status bar to show the first artboard in the Document window, and choose Edit > Paste.

8 Using the Selection tool, drag the sign and resize it, making it smaller, positioning it like you see in the figure. Drag the flower pot into position next to the right side of the door.

9 Choose File > Save, and then choose File > Close.

Review questions

1 What are the basic tools for creating shapes?

2 How do you select a shape with no fill?

3 How do you draw a square?

4 How do you change the number of sides on a polygon as you draw?

5 Name two ways you can combine several shapes into one.

6 How can you convert a raster image to editable vector shapes?

Review answers

1 There are six basic shape tools: Rectangle, Rounded Rectangle, Ellipse, Polygon, Star, and Flare. As was mentioned in Lesson 1, to tear off a group of tools from the Tools panel, position the pointer over the tool that appears in the Tools panel and hold down the mouse button until the group of tools appears. Without releasing the mouse button, drag to the triangle on the right side of the group and then release the mouse button to tear off the group.

2 Items that have no fill can be selected by clicking the stroke or by dragging a marquee across the item.

3 To draw a square, select the Rectangle tool (▣) in the Tools panel. Hold down the Shift key and drag to draw the square, or click the artboard to enter equal dimensions for the width and height in the Rectangle dialog box.

4 To change the number of sides on a polygon as you draw, select the Polygon tool (⬢) in the Tools panel. Start dragging to draw the shape, and press the down arrow key to reduce the number of sides and the up arrow key to increase the number of sides.

5 Using the Shape Builder tool (⬤), you can visually and intuitively merge, delete, fill, and edit overlapping shapes and paths directly in the artwork. You can also use the Pathfinder effects to create new shapes out of overlapping objects. You can apply Pathfinder effects by using the Effects menu or the Pathfinder panel.

6 You can convert a raster image to editable vector shapes by tracing it. To convert the tracing to paths, click Expand in the Control panel or choose Object > Image Trace > Expand. Use this method if you want to work with the components of the traced artwork as individual objects. The resulting paths are grouped.

4 TRANSFORMING OBJECTS

Lesson overview

In this lesson, you'll learn how to do the following:

- Add, edit, rename, and reorder artboards in an existing document.
- Navigate artboards.
- Work with rulers and guides.
- Move, scale, and rotate objects using a variety of methods.
- Reflect, shear, and distort objects.
- Position objects with precision.
- Position with measurement labels.
- Use the Free Transform tool to distort an object.

 This lesson takes approximately an hour to complete.

Download the project files for this lesson from the Lesson & Update Files tab on your Account page at www.peachpit.com and store them on your computer in a convenient location, as described in the Getting Started section of this book.

Your Accounts page is also where you'll find any updates to the chapters or to the lesson files. Look on the Lesson & Update Files tab to access the most current content.

You can modify objects in many ways as you create
artwork, by quickly and precisely controlling their size,
shape, and orientation. In this lesson, you'll explore
creating and editing artboards, the various Transform
commands, and specialized tools, while creating
several pieces of artwork.

Getting started

In this lesson, you'll create content and use it to create a flyer, a "save the date" card (front and back), and an envelope. Before you begin, you'll restore the default preferences for Adobe Illustrator and then open a file containing the finished artwork to see what you'll create.

1 To ensure that the tools and panels function exactly as described in this lesson, delete or deactivate (by renaming) the Adobe Illustrator CC preferences file. See "Restoring default preferences," on page 3.

2 Start Adobe Illustrator CC.

● **Note:** If you have not already downloaded the project files for this lesson to your computer from your Account page, make sure to do so now. See "Getting Started" at the beginning of the book.

3 Choose File > Open, and open the L4end.ai file in the Lesson04 folder, located in the Lessons folder on your hard disk.

This file contains the three pieces of finished artwork: a flyer, a "save the date" card (front and back), and an envelope. This lesson contains a fictitious business name, address, and website address made up for the purposes of the project.

4 Choose View > Fit All In Window, and leave the artwork onscreen as you work. If you don't want to leave the file open, choose File > Close (without saving).

To begin working, you'll open an existing art file.

● **Note:** In Mac OS, you may need to click the round, green button in the upper-left corner of the Document window to maximize the window's size.

● **Note:** If you don't see "Reset Essentials" in the Workspace menu, choose Window > Workspace > Essentials before choosing Window > Workspace > Reset Essentials.

5 Choose File > Open to open the L4start.ai file in the Lesson04 folder, located in the Lessons folder on your hard disk.

6 Choose File > Save As. In the Save As dialog box, name the file **recycle.ai**, and navigate to the Lesson04 folder. Leave the Save As Type option set to Adobe Illustrator (*.AI) (Windows) or the Format option set to Adobe Illustrator (ai) (Mac OS), and then click Save. In the Illustrator Options dialog box, leave the Illustrator options at their default settings and then click OK.

7 Choose Window > Workspace > Reset Essentials.

Working with artboards

Artboards represent the regions that can contain printable artwork, similar to pages in Adobe InDesign. You can use multiple artboards for creating a variety of things, such as multiple-page PDF files, printed pages with different sizes or different elements, independent elements for websites, or video storyboards, for instance.

Adding artboards to the document

You can add and remove artboards at any time while working in a document. You can create artboards in different sizes, resize them with the Artboard tool or Artboards panel, and position them anywhere in the Document window. All artboards are numbered and can have a unique name assigned to them.

Next, you will add more artboards to create the "save the date" card (front and back) and the envelope.

1   Choose View > Fit Artboard In Window. This is the first artboard.

2   Press the spacebar to temporarily access the Hand tool (✋). Drag the artboard to the left until you see the dark canvas off the right side of the artboard.

3   Select the Artboard tool (⊞) in the Tools panel. Position the Artboard tool pointer to the right of the existing artboard and in line with its top edge (a green alignment guide appears). Drag down and to the right to create an artboard that is 9 in (width) by 4 in (height). The measurement label indicates when the artboard is the correct size.

▶ **Tip:** If you zoom in on an artboard, the measurement label has smaller increments.

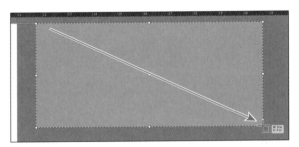

4   Click the New Artboard button (🗐) in the Control panel. This allows you to create a duplicate of the last selected artboard.

5   Position the pointer below the lower-left corner of the new artboard. When a vertical green alignment guide appears, click to create a new artboard. This is Artboard 3.

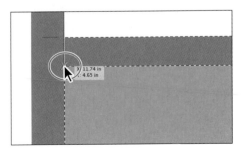

6   Select the Selection tool (▸) in the Tools panel.

7 Click the Artboards panel icon () on the right side of the workspace to expand the Artboards panel.

Notice that Artboard 3 is highlighted in the panel. The active artboard is always highlighted in this panel.

The Artboards panel allows you to see how many artboards the document currently contains. It also allows you to reorder, rename, add, and delete artboards and to choose many other options related to artboards.

Next, you will create a copy of an artboard using this panel.

8 Click the New Artboard button () at the bottom of the panel to create a copy of Artboard 3, called Artboard 4.

Notice that a copy is placed to the right of Artboard 2 in the Document window (the first artboard you created).

▶ **Tip:** With the Artboard tool (⊞), you can also copy an artboard by holding down the Alt (Windows) or Option (Mac OS) key and dragging it until the copied artboard clears the original. When creating new artboards, you can place them anywhere—you can even overlap them.

9 Click the Artboards panel icon to collapse the panel.

10 Choose View > Fit All In Window to see all of your artboards.

Resizing artboards

You can edit or delete artboards at any time by using the Artboard tool, menu commands, or the Artboards panel. Next, you will reposition and change the sizes of several of the artboards using multiple methods.

1 Select the Artboard tool (⊞) in the Tools panel, and click Artboard 4 in the Document window (the last one you made), to make sure it's selected.

Next, you will resize an artboard by entering values in the Control panel.

2   Select the upper-left point in the reference point locator (⊞) in the
    Control panel.

    This allows you to resize an artboard from the upper-left corner of the artboard.
    By default, artboards are resized from their center.

3   With the artboard named "04 – Artboard 4" selected in the Document window,
    in the Control panel, change the width to **9.5 in** and press Enter or Return.
    Make sure that the height is **4 in**.

    You can see the Constrain Width and Height Proportions icon (⊡) in the
    Control panel, between the Width and Height fields. This icon, if selected (⊡),
    allows both fields to change in proportion to each other.

Another way to resize an artboard is to do so manually, using the Artboard tool,
which is what you'll do next.

4   With Artboard 4 (04 – Artboard 4) still selected, choose View > Fit Artboard
    In Window.

5   With the Artboard tool selected, drag the bottom-center bounding point of the
    artboard down until the height is 4.15 in, as shown in the measurement label.

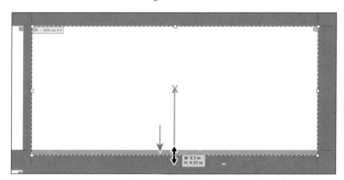

> **Tip:** To delete an artboard, select the artboard with the Artboard tool and either press Delete,
> click the Delete Artboard button (🗑) in the Control panel, or click the Delete icon (⊠) in the upper-
> right corner of an artboard. You can delete all but one artboard.

6   With Artboard 4 (04 – Artboard 4) still selected, click the Show Center
    Mark button (⊡) in the Control panel to show a center mark for the active
    artboard only. The center mark can be used for many purposes, including
    working with video content.

7   Select the Selection tool (▶), and choose View > Fit All In Window.

    Notice the subtle black outline around Artboard 4, and "4" showing in the
    Artboard Navigation menu (lower-left corner of the Document window), which
    both indicate that Artboard 4 is the currently active artboard.

● **Note:** If you don't
see the Width (W) and
Height (H) fields in the
Control panel, click
the Artboard Options
button (▦) in the
Control panel and enter
the values in the dialog
box that appears.

● **Note:** Clicking
the Artboard Options
button (▦) in the
Control panel, with the
Artboard tool selected,
also allows you to
display the center mark
for an artboard.

8 Click the Artboards panel icon (image) to show the Artboards panel (Window > Artboards). Click the name "Artboard 1" in the Artboards panel to make it the active artboard.

This is the original artboard. Notice that a dark border appears around Artboard 1 in the Document window. This indicates that it is active. There can only be one active artboard at a time. Commands such as View > Fit Artboard In Window apply to the active artboard.

Next, you will edit the active artboard size by choosing a preset value.

9 Click the Artboard Options button (image) to the right of the name "Artboard 1" in the Artboards panel. This opens the Artboard Options dialog box.

▶ **Tip:** The Artboard Options button appears to the right of the name of each artboard in the Artboards panel. It not only allows access to the artboard options for each artboard but also indicates the orientation of the artboard.

10 Find the reference point locator (image) to the left of the X and Y values, and make sure that the upper-left point is still selected. This ensures that the artboard is resized from the upper-left corner. Choose Letter from the Preset menu, and click OK.

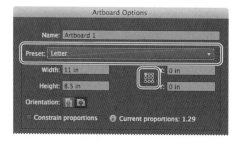

The Preset menu lets you change a selected artboard to a set size. Notice that the sizes in the Preset menu include typical print, video, tablet, and web sizes. You can also fit the artboard to the artwork bounds or the selected art, which is a great way to fit an artboard to a logo, for instance.

Editing document setup options

When working with artboards for the current document, you can change default setup options, like units of measure, bleed guides, type settings (such as language), and more in the Document Setup dialog box.

Next, you'll add bleed guides to the artboards.

1 With the Selection tool (image) still selected (but no art selected), click the Document Setup button in the Control panel (or choose File > Document Setup) to open the Document Setup dialog box.

2 In the Document Setup dialog box, change the Top Bleed option to **0.125 in** by clicking the up arrow to the left of the field. Notice that all the values change together, because Make All Settings The Same (▢) is selected. Click OK.

● **Note:** Know that all changes made in the Document Setup dialog box apply to all artboards in the current document.

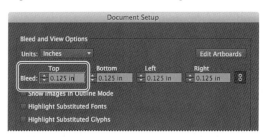

3 Select the Artboard tool (▦) in the Tools panel.

4 Click the upper-right artboard (04 – Artboard 4), and drag it below the original letter-sized artboard (01 – Artboard 1). Align the left edges of the artboards.

● **Note:** When you drag an artboard with content on it, the art moves with the artboard, by default. If you want to move an artboard but not the art on it, select the Artboard tool and then click to deselect Move/Copy Artwork With Artboard (▦).

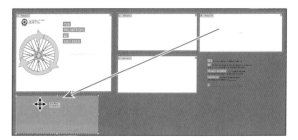

You can reposition artboards at any time and even overlap them, if necessary.

5 Select the Selection tool in the Tools panel to stop editing the artboards.

6 Choose Window > Workspace > Reset Essentials, and then choose File > Save.

Renaming artboards

By default, artboards are assigned a number and a name. When you navigate the artboards in a document, it can be helpful to name them.

Next, you are going to rename the artboards so that the names are more useful.

1 Click the Artboards panel icon (▦) to show the Artboards panel.

2 Double-click the name "Artboard 1" in the Artboards panel. Change the name to **Flyer**, and press Enter or Return.

▶ **Tip:** You can also change the name of an artboard by clicking the Artboard Options button (▦) in the Artboards panel and changing the name in the Artboard Options dialog box. Another way is to double-click the Artboard tool (▦) in the Tools panel to change the name for the currently active artboard in the Artboard Options dialog box. You can make an artboard the currently active artboard by clicking it with the Selection tool (▶).

You will now rename the rest of the artboards.

3   Double-click the name "Artboard 2" in the panel, and change the name to **Card-front**.

4   Rename the remaining two artboards, changing "Artboard 3" to **Card-back** and "Artboard 4" to **Envelope**.

5   Choose File > Save, and keep the Artboards panel showing for the next steps.

Reordering artboards

When you navigate your document, the order in which the artboards appear can be important, especially if you are navigating the document using the Next artboard and Previous artboard buttons. By default, artboards are ordered according to the order in which they are created, but you can change that order. Next, you will reorder the artboards so that the two sides of the card are in the correct order.

1   With the Artboards panel still open, click the name "Envelope" in the panel. This makes the Envelope artboard the active artboard and fits it in the Document window.

2   Choose View > Fit All In Window.

▶ **Tip:** You can also reorder the artboards by selecting an artboard in the Artboards panel and clicking the Move Up (⬆) or Move Down (⬇) button at the bottom of the panel.

3   Position the pointer over the Envelope artboard listed in the Artboards panel. Click and drag up until a line appears between the Flyer and Card-front artboards. Release the mouse button.

This moves the artboard up in order so that it becomes the second artboard in the list.

4   Double-click to the right or left of the name "Flyer" in the Artboards panel to fit that artboard in the Document window.

5   Click the Next artboard button (▶) in the lower-left corner of the Document window to navigate to the next artboard (Envelope). This fits the Envelope artboard in the Document window.

If you had not changed the order, the next artboard would have been the Card-front artboard.

6   Choose File > Save.

Now that the artboards are set up, you will concentrate on transforming artwork to create the content for your project.

Transforming content

Transforming content allows you to move, rotate, reflect, scale, shear, and either free distort or perspective distort objects. Objects can be transformed using the Transform panel, selection tools, specialized tools, Transform commands, guides, Smart Guides, and more. For the remainder of the lesson, you will transform content using a variety of methods and tools.

Working with rulers and guides

Rulers help you accurately place and measure objects. They appear at the top and left of the Document window and can be shown and hidden. *Guides* are non-printing lines that help you align objects. Next, you will create a few guides based on ruler measurements so that later you can more accurately align content.

1 In the Artboards panel, double-click to the right or left of the name "Card-front" to fit that artboard in the Document window.

2 Choose View > Rulers > Show Rulers, if you don't see the rulers.

3 Shift-drag from the left vertical ruler toward the right to create a vertical guide at 1/2 inch on the horizontal ruler. Notice, as you drag with the Shift key pressed, that the guide "snaps" to the measurements on the ruler. (The guide snaps because the Shift key is pressed.) Release the mouse button, and then release the Shift key. The guide is selected.

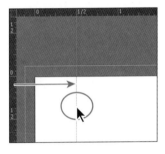

● **Note:** You may not see "1/2" in your ruler, and that's okay. You can zoom in until you see "1/2" using any method, including View > Zoom In. Zooming in to your document shows finer measurement increments in the rulers.

▶ **Tip:** To change the units for a document, you can right-click (Windows) or Ctrl-click (Mac OS) either ruler and choose the new units.

Take a look at the rulers, and notice the point where 0 appears on each ruler. The point on each ruler where the vertical 0 and the horizontal 0 appear is called the *ruler origin*. By default, the ruler origin is in the upper-left corner of the active artboard. As you can see, the 0 point on both rulers corresponds to the edges of the active artboard.

There are two types of rulers in Illustrator: *artboard rulers* and *global rulers*. Artboard rulers, which are the default rulers that you are seeing, set the ruler origin at the upper-left corner of the *active* artboard as shown, in the figure above. Global rulers set the ruler origin at the upper-left corner of the *first* artboard, no matter which artboard is active.

● **Note:** You could switch between artboard and global rulers by choosing View > Rulers > and selecting Global or Artboard, (depending on which option is currently chosen), but don't do that now.

4 Choose View > Fit All In Window.

5 With the Selection tool (▶), click each of the artboards and, as you do, look at the horizontal and vertical rulers. Notice that the 0 for each ruler is always in the upper-left corner of the active (selected) artboard.

6 In the Artboards panel, double-click to the right or left of the name "Card-front" to fit that artboard in the Document window.

7 With the Selection tool, click the guide to select it, if necessary (it will be orange in color when selected). Change the X value in the Control panel to **.25 in**, and press Enter or Return.

● **Note:** If you don't see the X value, you can click the word "Transform" or open the Transform panel (Window > Transform).

Guides are similar to drawn objects in that they can be selected like a drawn line, and they can be deleted by pressing the Backspace or Delete key.

▶ **Tip:** If you Ctrl-drag (Windows) or Command-drag (Mac OS) from the ruler intersect, you create a horizontal and vertical guide that intersects where you release the mouse button and then release the Ctrl or Command key.

8 Position the pointer in the upper-left corner of the Document window, where the rulers intersect (▓), and drag the pointer to the upper-right corner of the artboard (not to the corner of the red bleed guides). When the word "intersect" appears, release the mouse button.

As you drag, a cross hair in the window and in the rulers indicates the changing ruler origin. This sets the ruler origin (0,0) to the upper-right corner of the artboard.

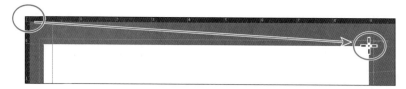

Next, you'll add a guide using a different method that can sometimes be faster.

9 Shift-double-click the horizontal ruler at the 1/4 inch mark, to the left of the 0 on the ruler. This creates a guide that crosses the right edge of the artboard.

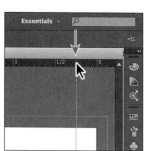

10 With the guide selected (it should be orange when selected), check the X value in the Control panel, making sure it's –0.25 in.

On the horizontal ruler, measurements to the right of 0 (zero) are positive and to the left are negative. On the vertical ruler, measurements below 0 (zero) are positive and above are negative.

11 Position the pointer in the upper-left corner of the Document window, where the rulers intersect, and double-click to reset the ruler origin.

12 Choose View > Guides > Lock Guides to prevent them from being accidentally moved. Choose View > Fit All In Window.

The guides are no longer selected and are aqua in color, by default.

Scaling objects

So far, you've scaled most content with the selection tools. In this lesson, you'll use several other methods to scale the objects. First, you'll set a preference to scale strokes and effects. Then, you'll scale a logo by using the Scale command and aligning that logo to a guide.

1   With the Selection tool (↑), click to select the large yellow/green wheel logo on the Flyer artboard.

2   Open the Transform panel by clicking the X, Y, W, or H link in the Control panel (or the word "Transform" if that appears in the Control panel). Select Scale Strokes & Effects.

By default, strokes and effects, like drop shadows, are not scaled along with objects. For instance, if you enlarge a circle with a 1 pt stroke, the stroke remains 1 pt. But by selecting Scale Strokes & Effects before you scale—and then scaling the object—that 1 pt stroke would scale (change) relative to the amount of scaling applied to the object.

3   Alt-drag (Windows) or Option-drag (Mac OS) the object to the upper-right artboard to copy the logo. Release the mouse button and then release the key, when the logo is in position.

4   Select the Zoom tool (🔍) in the Tools panel, and click twice, slowly, on the new wheel logo, to zoom in.

5   Choose View > Hide Edges.

This hides the inside edges of the shapes, not of the bounding box. It can make it easier to see the artwork.

► **Tip:** The Scale dialog box can also be accessed by choosing Object > Transform > Scale.

6 Double-click the Scale tool (⊡) in the Tools panel.

7 In the Scale dialog box, change Uniform to **50%**. Select Preview (if it's not already selected). Deselect and then select Preview to see the change in size. Click OK.

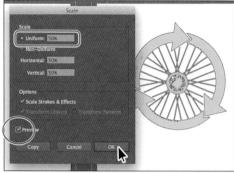

You could have also selected Scale Strokes & Effects in the Scale dialog box.

Next, you will drag the logo so that the left edge of the logo roughly aligns with the guide.

● **Note:** When snapping to a point, the snapping alignment depends on the position of the pointer, not on the edges of the dragged object. Also, you can snap points to guides because the View > Snap To Point command is selected by default.

8 Select the Selection tool (▸), and position the pointer over the left edge of the lower-left arrow head in the wheel. When you see the word "anchor" appear, drag the wheel to the left until the pointer snaps to the guide. The pointer turns white when it is snapped.

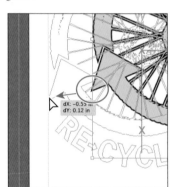

● **Note:** You may need to turn off the Smart Guides in order to snap the content to the guide (View > Smart Guides). If you do turn them off, turn them back on after you have completed the step.

9 Choose View > Fit All In Window, and then choose View > Show Edges.

10 Choose View > Outline.

11 With the Selection tool, drag a marquee across the text that starts with "YOU DONATE YOUR" and ends with "KEEP MAKING ART," on the first artboard (Flyer), to select it all. Choose Edit > Copy.

12 Choose 3 Card-front from the Artboard Navigation menu in the lower-left corner of the Document window to return to the Card-front artboard.

13 Choose Edit > Paste In Place.

This command pastes the grouped content in the same relative position on the Card-front artboard as it was on the Flyer artboard.

14 In the Control panel, click the middle-left reference point of the reference point locator (▦) to set the reference point. Click to select the Constrain Width And Height Proportions icon (⬚), located between the W and H fields. Type **75%** in the Width (W) field, and then press Enter or Return to decrease the size of the grouped text.

Enter 75% for the width.

Notice the result.

● **Note:** Depending on the resolution of your screen, the Transform options may not appear in the Control panel. If they do not appear, you can click the word "Transform" to see the Transform panel or you can choose Window > Transform.

15 Choose View > Preview, and then choose File > Save.

You will position the text, along with other content, later in the lesson.

Reflecting objects

When you *reflect* an object, Illustrator flips the object across an invisible vertical or horizontal axis. In a similar way to scaling and rotating, when you reflect an object, you either designate the reference point or use the object's center point, by default.

Next, you'll move content onto an artboard and use the Reflect tool to flip it 90° across the vertical axis and copy it.

1 Choose View > Fit All In Window. Press Ctrl+– (Windows) or Command+– (Mac OS), twice, to zoom out to see the bicycle off the left edge of the Flyer artboard.

2 With the Selection tool (▸), click on the bicycle (and not the area around it) to select it. Choose Edit > Cut.

3 Choose 4 Card-back from the Artboard Navigation menu in the lower-left corner of the Document window to return to the Card-back artboard.

4 Choose Edit > Paste, to paste the bicycle in the center of the Document window.

5   With the Selection tool, drag the bicycle down into the lower-right corner of the artboard. Try to approximately align the right side of the bicycle with the right guide, using the figure as a guide. It doesn't have to be exact.

6   With the bicycle still selected, choose Edit > Copy and Edit > Paste In Front to put a copy directly on top.

▶ **Tip:** If all you want to do is flip content in place, you can also choose Flip Horizontal or Flip Vertical from the Transform panel menu (▼≡).

7   Select the Reflect tool (🔁), which is nested within the Rotate tool (🔁) in the Tools panel. Click the left edge of the front bicycle tire (the word "anchor" or "path" may appear).

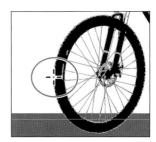

This sets the invisible axis that the shape will reflect around on the left edge of the bicycle, rather than on the center, which is the default.

▶ **Tip:** You can reflect and copy in one step. With the Reflect tool selected, Alt-click (Windows) or Option-click (Mac OS) to set a point to reflect around and to open the Reflect dialog box, in one step. Select Vertical, and then click Copy.

8   With the bicycle copy still selected, position the pointer off the left edge and drag clockwise. As you are dragging, hold down the Shift key. When the measurement label shows −90°, release the mouse button and then release the modifier key.

The Shift key constrains the rotation to 45° as it is reflected. Leave the new bicycle where it is for now. You'll move it a bit later.

Rotating objects

You rotate objects by turning them around a designated reference point. There are lots of ways to do this, including methods that range from more precise to more free-form rotation.

Next, you'll precisely rotate one of the wheels using the Rotate command.

1   Choose 1 Flyer from the Artboard Navigation menu in the lower-left corner of the Document window.

2   Select the Zoom tool (🔍), and drag a marquee across the small, black wheel logo in the upper-left corner of the Flyer artboard.

3   With the Selection tool (▶), select the small, black wheel. Choose Object > Transform > Rotate.

    By default, the wheel logo will rotate around its center.

▶ **Tip:** To access the Rotate dialog box, you can also double-click the Rotate tool (⟳) in the Tools panel. The Transform panel (Window > Transform) also has a rotate option.

4   In the Rotate dialog box, make sure that Preview is selected. Change the angle to **20**, and then click OK to rotate the wheel around the center.

▶ **Tip:** If you select an object and then select the Rotate tool, you can Alt-click (Windows) or Option-click (Mac OS) anywhere on the object (or artboard) to set a reference point and to open the Rotate dialog box in one step.

5   With the Selection tool, and with the small wheel logo selected, press the Shift key and click the text to the right of logo that begins, "THE CHILDREN'S ART CENTER," to select both.

6   Choose Edit > Cut.

7   Choose 2 Envelope from the Artboard Navigation menu, and choose Edit > Paste In Place.

8   Click the word "Transform" in the Control panel to open the Transform panel. With the middle-left point chosen in the reference point locator (▦), change the X value to **.25 in** and the Y value to **0.6 in**. Press Enter or Return to hide the panel again.

Next, you'll rotate content manually, using the Rotate tool (⟳).

9 Choose View > Fit All In Window.

10 With the Selection tool, click to select the large yellow/green wheel logo on the Flyer artboard. Choose View > Hide Edges.

11 Select the Rotate tool (⟳), which is nested within the Reflect tool (🔄) in the Tools panel. Click the approximate center of the wheel part of the logo to set the reference point (◈) (just above where the reference point, is by default). Position the pointer to the right of the wheel logo, and drag up. Notice that the movement is constrained to a circle rotating around the reference point. When the measurement label shows approximately 20°, release the mouse button.

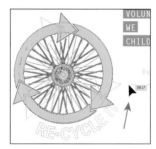

Next, you will rotate the wheel logo on the 3 Card-front artboard in the same way.

12 Choose 3 Card-front from the Artboard Navigation menu in the lower-left corner of the Document window. Select the Selection tool, and click to select the yellow/green wheel logo.

13 Select the Rotate tool, and click the approximate center of the wheel part of the logo to set the reference point (◈) (just above where the reference point is, by default). Position the pointer to the right of the wheel logo, and drag up. When the measurement label shows approximately 20°, release the mouse button.

14 Choose View > Show Edges, and then choose File > Save.

Distorting objects with effects

You can distort the original shapes of objects in different ways, using various tools. Now, you'll distort a logo shape, first using the Pucker & Bloat effect and then applying the Twist effect to twirl the shape. These are different types of transformations because they are applied as effects, which means you could ultimately edit the effect later or remove it in the Appearance panel.

● **Note:** To learn more about effects, see Lesson 12, "Applying Effects."

1 Click the First button (◀◀) in the status bar to navigate to the first artboard.

2   Click the Layers panel icon () to open the panel, and then click the visibility column (circled in figure) to the left of the Flyer Background layer name to show that content.

3   Select the Selection tool (▸), and click to select the white triangle in the lower-right corner of the Flyer artboard.

4   Choose Effect > Distort & Transform > Pucker & Bloat.

5   In the Pucker & Bloat dialog box, select Preview and drag the slider to the left to change the value to roughly **–60%**, which distorts the triangle. Click OK.

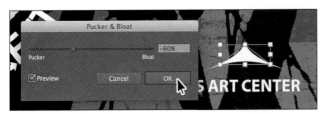

6   Choose Effect > Distort & Transform > Twist. Change the Angle to **20**, select Preview (if it's not already selected), and then click OK.

7   Choose Select > Deselect, and then choose File > Save.

Shearing objects

Shearing an object slants, or skews, the sides of the object along the axis you specify, keeping opposite sides parallel and making the object asymmetrical.

Next, you'll copy a bicycle object and apply shear to it.

1   Click the Artboards panel tab. Double-click the 4 to the left of the Card-back artboard name. Click the Artboards panel tab to collapse the panel group.

2   Select the Selection tool (▸). Click to select the bicycle shape on the left. Choose Object > Hide > Selection. Click to select the remaining bicycle shape.

3   Choose Edit > Copy, and then choose Edit > Paste In Front to paste a copy directly on top of the original.

4 Select the Shear tool (⤨), nested within the
   Scale tool (⬚) in the Tools panel. Position
   the pointer at the bottom of the bicycle shape,
   between the wheels, and click to set the
   reference point.

5 Drag from the approximate center of the bicycle
   to the left, and stop when the sheared copy looks like what you see in the figure.
   Release the mouse button.

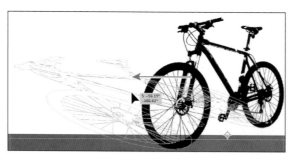

▶ **Tip:** You can also apply shear numerically in the Transform panel (Window > Transform) or in the
Shear dialog box (Object > Transform > Shear).

6 Change the Opacity value in the Control
   panel to **20%**.

7 Choose Object > Arrange > Send Backward
   to put the copy behind the original
   bicycle shape.

8 Choose Object > Show All to show and select the reflected bicycle copy you hid
   earlier. Choose Edit > Cut to cut the bicycle from the artboard.

9 Choose 2 Envelope from the Artboard Navigation menu in the lower-left corner
   of the Document window. Choose Edit > Paste.

10 Choose Select > Deselect, and then choose File > Save.

Positioning objects precisely

At times, you may want to position objects more precisely—either relative to other objects or in relation to the artboard. You can use the Smart Guides and the Transform panel to move objects to exact coordinates on the x and y axes and to control the position of objects in relation to the edge of the artboard.

Next, you'll add content to the backgrounds of both sides of the card and then position that content precisely.

1   Choose View > Fit All In Window to see all of the artboards.

2   Press Ctrl+- (Windows) or Command+- (Mac OS) (or View > Zoom Out) once to zoom out. You should see two images off the left edge of the Flyer artboard.

3   With the Selection tool (⬏), click to select the top, darker image.

4   Click the Artboards panel icon (▦), if the panel isn't showing. Click the 3 Card-front artboard name in the list, once, to make it the active artboard.

The ruler origin is now in the upper-left corner of that artboard.

5   Click the upper-left point of the reference point locator (▦) in the Control panel. Then, change the X value to **0** and the Y value to **0**.

6   Choose Object > Arrange > Send to Back, and then choose Select > Deselect.

The image should now be precisely positioned on the artboard, since it was the same size as the artboard to begin with.

● **Note:** Again, depending on the resolution of your screen, the Transform options may not appear in the Control panel. If they do not appear, you can click the word "Transform" to see the Transform panel, or you can choose Window > Transform.

7   Choose View > Fit Artboard In Window to fit the 3 Card-front artboard in the Document window.

8   With the Selection tool, hold down the Shift key and, in the text on the right, drag to the left from the word "YOU" until the right edge of the "h" in "MAY 19th" is aligned with the right guide. Release the mouse button, and then release the Shift key.

9   In the Artboards panel, click once on the name "4 Card-back" in the list to make it the active artboard. Click the Artboards panel tab to collapse the panel group.

10 Choose View > Fit All In Window to see all of the artboards.

11 Press Ctrl+– (Windows) or Command+– (Mac OS) once to zoom out.

    You should see the second, lighter image off the left edge of the Flyer artboard.

12 With the Selection tool, click to select that image.

13 With the upper-left point of the reference point locator (⊞) selected in the Control panel, change the X value to **0** and the Y value to **0**.

14 Choose Object > Arrange > Send to Back.

15 Choose View > Fit Artboard In Window to fit the 4 Card-back artboard in the Document window.

Positioning with Smart Guides

When moving objects with the Smart Guides turned on (View > Smart Guides), measurement labels appear next to the pointer and display the distance (X and Y) from the object's original location. You will use these to make sure that an object is a certain distance from the edge of the artboard.

1   Press Ctrl+– (Windows) or Command+– (Mac OS), *twice*, to zoom out. You should see the text group off the right edge of the artboard.

2   With the Selection tool (↖), click to select the text group. With the upper-left point of the reference point locator (▦) in the Control panel selected, change the X value to **0** and the Y value to **0**.

3   Choose View > Fit Artboard In Window.

4   Using the Selection tool, position the pointer over the word "YES" and drag the text group down and to the right. When the measurement label shows dX: 0.25 in and dY: 0.5 in, release the mouse button.

If you can't get the exact values, that's okay.

The dX indicates the distance moved along the x axis (horizontally), and dY indicates the distance moved along the y axis (vertically).

● **Note:** You can also choose Edit > Preferences > Smart Guides (Windows) or Illustrator > Preferences > Smart Guides (Mac OS) and deselect the Measurement Labels option to turn off just the measurement labels when Smart Guides are on.

5   With the text group still selected, choose Object > Arrange > Bring To Front, to bring the text on top of the other content on the artboard.

6   Click away from the artwork to deselect it, and then choose File > Save.

Transforming with the Free Transform tool

The Free Transform tool (⊞) is a multipurpose tool that allows you to distort an object, combining functions like moving, scaling, shearing, rotating, and distorting (perspective or free). The Free Transform tool is also touch-enabled, which means you can control transformation using touch controls on certain devices. For more information on touch controls, see the sidebar at the end of this section.

1 Choose 2 Envelope from the Artboard Navigation menu in the lower-left corner of the Document window.

2 Click to select the bicycle on the artboard with the Selection tool (▸).

● **Note:** To learn more about the Free Transform tool options, search for "Free Transform" in Adobe Help (Help > Illustrator Help).

3 Select the Free Transform tool (⊞) in the Tools panel.

After selecting the Free Transform tool, the Free Transform widget appears in the Document window. This widget, which is free-floating and can be repositioned, contains options to change how the Free Transform tool works. By default, the Free Transform tool allows you to move,

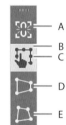

A. Constrain
B. Free Transform
C. Selected Action (light gray background)
D. Perspective Distort
E. Free Distort

shear, rotate, and scale objects. By selecting other options, like Perspective Distort, you can change how the tool transforms content.

Next, you'll use the Free Transform tool to apply multiple transformations to the selected bicycle.

4 Choose View > Hide Edges.

5 Position the pointer over the left-middle point of the bicycle bounding box, and the pointer changes its appearance (↔), indicating that you can shear or distort. Drag to the right. As you drag to the right, notice that you can't drag up or down—the movement is constrained to horizontal. When a width of approximately 2.8 in shows in the

measurement label below the widget, release the mouse button.

● **Note:** If you were to drag the side bounding point up first to distort the bicycle by shearing, the movement wouldn't be constrained and you could move in any direction.

Next, you are going to rotate the bicycle around the lower-right bounding point, so you will set the reference point before rotating.

6 Position the pointer over the upper-right bounding point. When the pointer changes (⊹), press the Shift key and drag toward the center of the bike to make it smaller. When the measurement label shows a height of 2.75 in, release the mouse and then the modifier key.

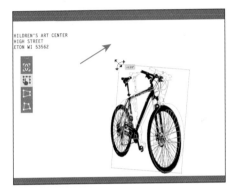

7 Position the pointer over the lower-right bounding point, and double-click when the pointer looks like this (⊹). This moves the reference point and ensures that the bicycle will rotate around it.

8 Position the pointer directly over the upper-left corner of the bicycle bounding box. The pointer changes appearance (⊹), indicating that you can rotate or scale. Click and drag in a clockwise motion until you see approximately −5° in the measurement label below the widget.

▶ **Tip:** You can also just drag the reference point to a location. The reference point is reset to the center of the object immediately after an action is performed. You can double-click the reference point to reset its position.

● **Note:** If you find that, by trying to rotate, you are instead scaling, stop dragging and choose Edit > Undo Scale and try again.

Like other transform tools, by holding down the Shift key while dragging with the Free Transform tool, you can constrain the movement for most of the transformations. If you don't want to hold down the Shift key, you can also select the Constrain option in the widget (circled at right) before transforming, to constrain movement automatically. After dragging, the Constrain option is deselected.

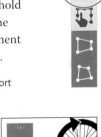

● **Note:** The Constrain option cannot be selected when the Perspective Distort option is selected.

9 With the Free Transform tool still selected, click the Perspective Distort option in the Free Transform widget (circled in the figure).

With this option selected, you can drag a corner point of the bounding box to distort the perspective.

Perspective Distort

10 Position the pointer over the upper-left corner of the bounding box, and the pointer changes in appearance (↘). Drag down until a height of approximately 2.5 in shows in the measurement label beneath the widget.

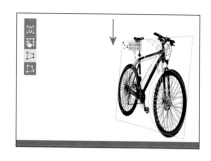

11 Select the Selection tool, and drag the bicycle until the left edge is close to the left edge of the artboard.

12 Choose View > Show Edges.

13 Change the Opacity to **20%** in the Control panel.

14 Choose File > Save, and then choose File > Close.

Applying multiple transformations

There are a lot of ways to speed up transformations in Illustrator. One of those ways is to use the Transform Each command. To learn more about this command, open the PDF file, "Multi_transforms.pdf," in the Lesson_extras folder in the Lessons folder.

The Free Transform tool and touch-enabled devices

In Illustrator CC, the Free Transform tool is touch-enabled. This means that, if you are using either a Windows 7– or 8–based touchscreen PC or a Touchscreen device, like Wacom Cintiq 24HD Touch, you can utilize certain touch-enabled features.

Here are a few noteworthy examples:

* You can touch and drag from the center of an object and move the reference point.

* Double tapping on any of the corner points moves the reference point for the object to that point.

* Double tapping on the reference point resets it to the default position (if it's not already there).

* To constrain movement, you can tap the Constrain option in the widget before transforming.

4 In the Control panel, click Fill color and choose None (⬜). Then, click the Stroke color and make sure that the black swatch is selected.

5 Make sure the Stroke weight is 1 pt in the Control panel.

When you begin drawing with the Pen tool, it's usually best to have no fill on the path you create. You can add a fill later, if necessary. Next, you'll draw a path in the work area of the artboard that looks like the zigzag path at the top of the artboard.

6 Select the Pen tool (✐) in the Tools panel. Position the pointer in the artboard area, and notice the asterisk next to the Pen icon (✎.), indicating that you are starting a path.

● **Note:** If you see a crosshair (-¦-) instead of the Pen icon (✎.), the Caps Lock key is active. Caps Lock turns tool icons into crosshairs for increased precision.

7 In the area labeled Work Area, click where the blue "start" square is, to set the first anchor point. Move the pointer to the right of the original point.

The asterisk has disappeared, indicating that you are drawing a path.

8 Position the pointer down and to the right of the original point, and click to create the next anchor point in the path.

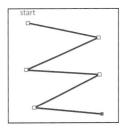

● **Note:** The first segment you draw is not visible until you click to create a second anchor point. If the path looks curved, you have accidentally dragged with the Pen tool; choose Edit > Undo Pen, and then click again.

9 Click a third anchor point beneath the initial anchor point to create a zigzag pattern. Create a zigzag that has a total of six anchor points, which means you will click the artboard three more times.

One of the many benefits of using the Pen tool is that you can create custom paths and continue to edit the anchor points that make up the path. Notice that only the last anchor point is filled (not hollow like the rest of the anchor points), indicating that it is selected.

10 Choose Select > Deselect.

Selecting paths

Next, you'll see how the Selection tools work with selecting paths.

1 Select the Selection tool (▶) in the Tools panel, and position the pointer directly over a straight line in the zigzag path. When the pointer shows a solid black box (▶.) next to it, click. This selects the path and all of the anchor points. You can tell the anchor points are selected because they become filled.

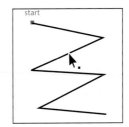

▶ **Tip:** You can also drag across a path to select it with the Selection tool.

Tip: If the Pen tool (✐) were still selected, you could Ctrl-click (Windows) or Command-click (Mac OS) in a blank area of the artboard to deselect the path. This temporarily selects a Selection tool. When you release the Ctrl or Command key, the Pen tool would again be selected.

2 Drag from one of the straight lines in the path to a new location anywhere on the artboard. All the anchor points travel together, maintaining the zigzag path.

3 Deselect the zigzag path in one of the following ways:

- With the Selection tool, click an empty area of the artboard.
- Choose Select > Deselect.

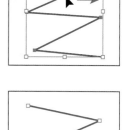

4 In the Tools panel, select the Direct Selection tool (▷) and position the pointer over any anchor point. The anchor point will become highlighted (large), and the pointer shows a small box with a dot in the center (▷.), indicating that, if you click, you will select an anchor point. Click to select the anchor point.

The selected anchor point is filled (looks solid), and the deselected anchor points are hollow.

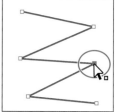

5 Drag the anchor point to the left a bit, to reposition it.

The anchor point moves, but the others remain stationary. This is one method for editing a path, like you saw in Lesson 2, "Selecting and Aligning."

6 Click in a blank area of the artboard to deselect.

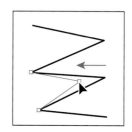

Note: If the entire zigzag path disappears, choose Edit > Undo Cut and try again.

7 Position the Direct Selection pointer over a straight line segment in the middle of the zigzag shape. When the pointer changes (▷.), click to select. Choose Edit > Cut. This cuts only the selected segment from the zigzag.

When you position the pointer over a line segment *that is not already selected*, a black, solid square appears next to the Direct Selection tool pointer, indicating that you will select a line segment.

8 Select the Pen tool (✐), and position the pointer over one of the end anchor points that was connected to the line segment that was cut. Notice that the Pen tool shows a forward slash (✐/), indicating that, if you click, you will continue drawing from that anchor point. Click the point.

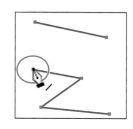

9 Position the pointer over the other anchor point that was connected to the cut line segment. The pointer now shows a merge symbol next to it (⬚), indicating that you are connecting to another path. Click the point to reconnect the paths.

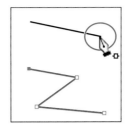

Constraining lines

In Lesson 4, "Transforming Objects," you learned that using the Shift key and Smart Guides in combination with shape tools constrains the shape of objects. The Shift key and Smart Guides also constrain the Pen tool to create paths of 45°.

Next, you will learn how to draw straight lines and constrain angles as you draw.

1 Choose 2 from the Artboard Navigation menu in the lower-left corner of the Document window.

2 Choose View > Smart Guides to select the Smart Guides, and then choose View> Fit Artboard In Window.

3 With the Pen tool (🖊) selected, in the area labeled Work Area, click where the blue "start" square is to set the first anchor point.

Don't worry if the Smart Guides are attempting to "snap" the anchor point you create to other content on the artboard, making it difficult to click directly on the "start" square.

4 Move the pointer to the right of the original anchor point approximately 1.5 in, as indicated by the measurement label. It doesn't have to be exact. A green alignment guide appears when the pointer is vertically aligned with the previous anchor point. Click to set another anchor point.

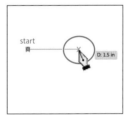

▶ **Tip:** If Smart Guides are deselected, the measurement label and alignments guides won't appear. If you don't use Smart Guides, you can press the Shift key and click to create constrained lines.

As you've learned in previous lessons, the measurement label and alignment guides are a part of the Smart Guides. When working with the Pen tool, you will learn that you can achieve finer measurements in the measurement label when you zoom in. You will also see that the Pen tool attempts to snap to other objects on the artboard, which sometimes can make using the Smart Guides difficult while drawing.

5 Click to set three more points, following the same generic shape as shown in the top half of the artboard.

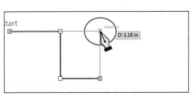

Notice the green alignment guides that appear as you draw. Sometimes they are helpful for aligning points, and sometimes they align to content that you don't necessarily want to align to.

● **Note:** The points you set don't have to be in exactly the same position as the path at the top of the artboard. Also, the measurement you see in your measurement label may not match what you see in the figure, and that's okay.

6   Press the Shift key, and move the pointer to the right and down. When the green alignment guide appears, aligning the new point with the bottom two points, and the measurement label shows 2 in, Click to set an anchor point, and then release the modifier key.

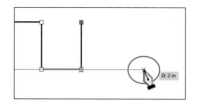

Notice that the new anchor point is not where you clicked. That's because the line has been constrained to 45°. Pressing the Shift key creates angled lines constrained to 45°.

7   Position the pointer below the last point, and click to set the last anchor point for the shape.

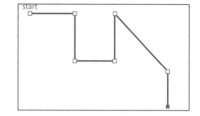

8   Choose Select > Deselect, and then choose File > Save.

Components of a path

As you draw, you create a line called a *path*. A path is made up of one or more straight or curved segments. The beginning and end of each segment are marked by *anchor points*, which work like pins holding a wire in place. A path can be closed (for example, a circle) or open, with distinct endpoints (for example, a wavy line). You change the shape of a path by dragging its anchor points, the direction points at the end of direction lines that appear at anchor points, or the path segment itself.

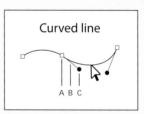

A. Anchor point
B. Direction line
C. Direction point

Paths can have two kinds of anchor points: corner points and smooth points. At a *corner point*, a path abruptly changes direction. At a *smooth point*, path segments are connected as a continuous curve.

You can draw a path using any combination of corner and smooth points. If you draw the wrong kind of point, you can always change it.

—From Illustrator Help

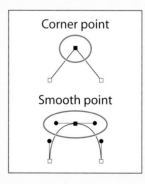

Introducing curved paths

In this part of the lesson, you'll learn how to draw smooth, curved lines with the Pen tool. In vector drawing applications, such as Illustrator, you draw a curve, called a *Bezier curve*, with anchor points and direction handles. By setting anchor points and dragging direction handles, you can define the shape of the curve. Although drawing curves this way can take some time to learn, it gives you the greatest control and flexibility in creating paths.

1 Choose View > Smart Guides to deselect them.

2 Choose 3 from the Artboard Navigation menu in the lower-left corner of the Document window. You will draw in the area labeled Practice.

3 Press Z to switch to the Zoom tool (🔍) (or select it in the Tools panel), and click *twice* in the bottom half of the artboard to zoom in.

4 Select the Pen tool (✒) in the Tools panel. In the Control panel, make sure that the Fill color is None (☐) and the Stroke color is black. Also, make sure the Stroke weight is still 1 pt in the Control panel.

5 With the Pen tool (✒), click in a blank area of the artboard to create a starting anchor point.

6 Click another location, and drag away from the point to create a curved path. Continue clicking and dragging at different locations on the artboard.

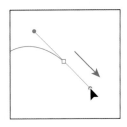

   The goal for this exercise is not to create anything specific but to get accustomed to the feel of the Bezier curve.

   Notice that, as you drag, direction handles appear. *Direction handles* consist of direction lines that end in round direction points. The angle and length of the direction handles determine the shape and size of the curve. Direction handles do not print and are not visible when the anchor point is inactive.

7 Choose Select > Deselect.

8 Select the Direct Selection tool (▷) in the Tools panel, and click the line between two anchor points (called a *line segment*) to display the direction handles. Click and drag the end of a direction handle, as you see in the figure. Moving the direction handles reshapes the curve.

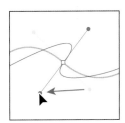

9 Choose Select > Deselect. Leave the file open for the next section.

Drawing a curve with the Pen tool

In this part of the lesson, you will learn how to adjust the direction handles to control curves. You will use the top artboard to trace a shape.

1   Press the spacebar to temporarily select the Hand tool (✋), and drag down until you see the curve at the top of the artboard (on Artboard 3).

● **Note:** The artboard may scroll as you drag. If you lose visibility of the curve, choose View > Zoom Out until you see the curve and anchor point. Pressing the spacebar allows you to use the Hand tool to reposition the artwork.

2   Select the Pen tool (✒) in the Tools panel. Click the "start" square, and drag up to create a direction line going the same direction as the arch. Release the mouse button when the pointer reaches the gold dot.

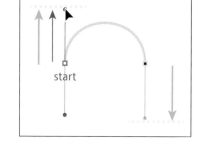

▶ **Tip:** If you make a mistake while drawing with the Pen tool, choose Edit > Undo Pen to undo the points you have set.

3   Click the black point on the right side of the arch, and drag down. Release the mouse button when the pointer reaches the gold dot, and the path you are creating follows the arch.

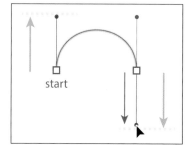

● **Note:** Pulling the direction handle longer makes a steeper slope; when the direction handle is shorter, the slope is flatter.

If the path you created is not aligned exactly with the template, use the Direct Selection tool (▷) to select the anchor points one at a time. Then, adjust the direction handles using the Direct Selection tool until your path follows the template more accurately.

4   Select the Selection tool (▶), and click the artboard in an area with no objects, or choose Select > Deselect.

Deselecting the first path allows you to create a new path. If you click somewhere on the artboard with the Pen tool while the path is still selected, the path connects to the next point you draw.

▶ **Tip:** To deselect objects, you can also press the Ctrl (Windows) or Command (Mac OS) key to temporarily switch to the Selection or Direct Selection tool, whichever was last used. Then, click the artboard where there are no objects.

5   Choose File > Save.

If you want to try drawing the curve for more practice, scroll down to the Practice area in the same artboard and trace the curve down there.

Drawing a series of curves with the Pen tool

Now that you've experimented with drawing a few curves, you will draw a shape that contains several continuous curves.

1   Choose 4 from the Artboard Navigation menu in the lower-left corner of the Document window. Select the Zoom tool (🔍), and click several times in the top half of the artboard to zoom in.

2   In the Control panel, make sure that the Fill color is None (⬜) and the Stroke color is black. Also, make sure the Stroke weight is still 1 pt in the Control panel.

3   Select the Pen tool (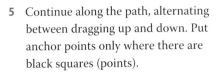). Click the blue "start" square, and drag up in the direction of the arch, stopping at the gold dot.

4   Position the pointer over the black square point to the right, click and drag down to the gold dot, adjusting the first arch with the direction handle before you release the mouse button.

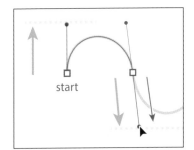

● **Note:** Don't worry if the path you draw is not exact. You can correct the line with the Direct Selection tool (𝕜) when the path is complete.

5   Continue along the path, alternating between dragging up and down. Put anchor points only where there are black squares (points).

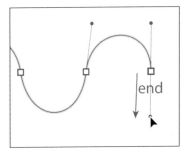

If you make a mistake as you draw, you can undo your work by choosing Edit > Undo Pen and then draw the last point again. Note that your direction lines may not match the figure at right, and that's okay.

6   When the path is complete, select the Direct Selection tool and click to select an anchor point.

When the anchor point is selected, the direction handles appear and you can readjust the curve of the path if necessary. With a curve selected, you can also change the stroke and fill of the curve. When you do this, the next line you draw will have the same attributes. For more information about these attributes, see Lesson 6, "Color and Painting."

If you want to try drawing the shape again, for more practice, scroll down to the bottom half of the same artboard (labeled Practice) and trace the shape down there.

7   Choose File > Save.

Converting smooth points to corner points

When creating curves, the direction handles help to determine the shape and size of the curved segments, as you've already heard and seen. Removing the direction lines from an anchor point can convert a smooth curve into a corner. In the next part of the lesson, you will practice converting between smooth points and corner points.

1   Choose 5 from the Artboard Navigation menu in the lower-left corner of the Document window.

On the top of the artboard, you can see the path that you will trace. You will use the top artboard as a template for the exercise, creating your paths directly on top of those. Use the Practice section at the bottom of the artboard for additional practice on your own.

2   In the top artboard, use the Zoom tool (🔍) and click several times to zoom in.

3   In the Control panel, make sure that the Fill color is None (▨) and the Stroke color is black. Also, make sure the Stroke weight is still 1 pt in the Control panel.

● **Note:** Pressing the Shift key when dragging constrains the direction lines to multiples of 45°.

4   Select the Pen tool (✏️), and, pressing the Shift key, click the blue "start" square and drag up to the gold dot. Release the mouse button, and then release the Shift key.

5   Click the next black anchor point to the right, and, pressing the Shift key, drag down to the red dot. When the curve looks correct, release the mouse button and then release the Shift key. Leave the path selected.

Now, you need the curve to switch directions. This time, the curve needs to create another arch. You will *split* the direction lines to convert a smooth point to a corner point.

▶ **Tip:** After you draw a path, you can also select single or multiple anchor points and click the Convert Selected Anchor Points To Corner button (◣) or Convert Selected Anchor Points To Smooth button (◤) in the Control panel.

6   Press the Alt (Windows) or Option (Mac OS) key, and position the pointer over either the last anchor point created or the bottom direction point. When a convert-point icon (caret) appears next to the Pen tool pointer (◣ₙ), click and drag a

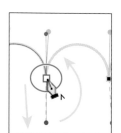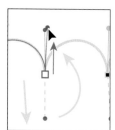

direction line up to the gold dot. Release the mouse button, and then release the modifier key. If you do not see the caret, you may create an additional loop.

● **Note:** If you don't click exactly on the anchor point or the direction point at the end of the direction line, a warning dialog box appears. Click OK, and try again.

Reflect

Axis
- Horizontal
- Vertical
- Angle: 90°

Options
- ☑ Transform Objects ☐ Transform Patterns

☐ Preview

[Copy] [OK] [Cancel]

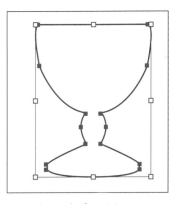

Alt or Option click the point.   Set the Reflect options.   Notice the result after joining.

12 Choose View > Smart Guides, to turn off the Smart Guides.

Editing curves

In this part of the lesson, you'll adjust curves you've drawn by dragging either anchor points or direction handles. You can also edit a curve by moving the line.

1 Choose 1 Ice Cream from the Artboard Navigation menu in the lower-left corner of the Document window.

2 Choose View > Ice Cream.

Aside from zooming in on the ice cream path, the content from the template layer should be displayed, as well, showing the guides you used to draw the path.

3 Select the Direct Selection tool (⬕), and click the edge of the ice cream path. All of the anchor points will appear.

Clicking with the Direct Selection tool displays the direction handles for the selected line segment and lets you adjust the shape of individual curved segments. Clicking with the Selection tool (▶) selects the entire path.

4 Click the anchor point (J) that is at the top of the ice cream path, to select it. Drag the point down just a bit until it roughly matches the figure.

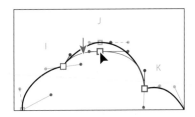

▶ **Tip:** You can also press the arrow keys to nudge an anchor point in a direction. Pressing and holding down the Shift key and then pressing an arrow key moves the point five times further than pressing the arrow key without the modifier key.

5   With the Direct Selection tool, drag a marquee selection across points G and F to select them both. See the figure.

    The points will be filled (not hollow) when selected.

6   Click the Layers panel icon (⬕) to show the Layers panel. Click the eye icon (👁) to the left of the layer named template to hide its contents. Click the Layers panel tab to hide the panel.

    With the template content hidden, notice that, when multiple points are selected, none of the direction handles for the selected points are showing.

7   In the Control panel, click Show Handles For Multiple Selected Anchor Points (🔲), to the right of the word "Handles," to see the direction handles for all of the selected points.

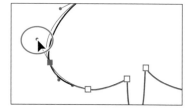

8   With the Direct Selection tool, drag the top direction point (circled in the figure) up and to the left to make the curve a little more rounded.

9   Choose Select > Deselect, and then choose File > Save.

Deleting and adding anchor points

Most of the time, the goal of drawing paths with a tool like the Pen tool is to avoid adding more anchor points than necessary. You can, however, reduce a path's complexity or change its overall shape by deleting unnecessary points (and therefore gain more control over the shape), or you can extend a path by adding points to it. Next, you will delete and add anchor points to a path.

1   Select the Selection tool (▶) in the Tools panel.

2   Choose View > Fit Artboard In Window.

3   Click the second cherry from the right (an arrow is pointing to it in the figure), choose Edit > Copy, and then choose Edit > Paste.

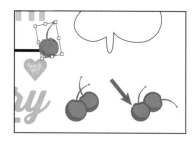

4   Drag the cherry to the top of the ice cream shape. See the next figure.

5   Choose Object > Arrange > Send To Back.

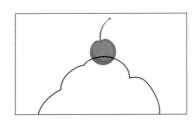

6   With the Direct Selection tool () selected, click the edge of the ice cream path.

7   Select the Zoom tool () in the Tools panel, and click three times, *slowly*, on the cherry at the top of the ice cream path to zoom in.

8   Select the Pen tool () in the Tools panel, and position the pointer over the ice cream path to the right of the anchor point you dragged down. When a plus sign (+) appears to the right of the Pen tool pointer (), click to add another point to the path.

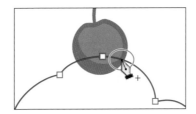

9   Select the Direct Selection tool, and drag the point up until it covers the cherry a bit.

    You're trying to make it look like the cherry was pushed into the ice cream.

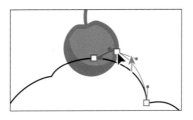

Next, you will add another point and reposition it while keeping the Pen tool selected.

10 Select the Pen tool in the Tools panel, and position the pointer over the ice cream path on the left side of the cherry. A plus sign (+) appears to the right of the Pen tool pointer (). Click to add another point to the path.

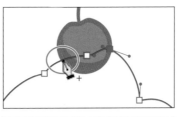

11 Press the Ctrl (Windows) or Command (Mac OS) key to temporarily select the Direct Selection tool. With the key held down, drag the new anchor point up to cover the cherry a bit (see the figure).

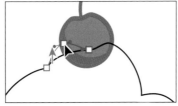

Note: When you press the Ctrl or Command key with the Pen tool selected, the last selected Selection tool (Selection or Direct Selection) is temporarily selected.

12 Press the spacebar to temporarily access the Hand tool (). Drag up in the Document window until you see the bottom of the ice cream path, and then release the spacebar.

13 With the Pen tool still selected, add points to the path on the right and left side of the bottom point of the drip.

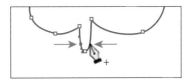

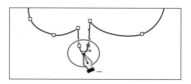

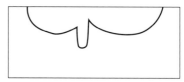

▶ Tip: With an anchor point selected, you can also click Remove Selected Anchor Points (✐) in the Control panel to delete the anchor point.

14 Position the Pen tool pointer over the bottom anchor point on that same drip. When a minus sign (–) appears next to the pointer (◐_), click to delete the anchor point.

15 Choose Select > Deselect, and then choose File > Save.

Converting between smooth points and corner points

To more precisely control the path you create, you can convert points from smooth points to corner points and from corner points to smooth points, using several methods.

1 Choose 3 Spoon from the Artboard Navigation menu in the lower-left corner of the Document window.

2 Select the Direct Selection tool (▷), and position the pointer over upper-left corner point on the spoon handle. When an open square with a dot in the center (▷₀) appears next to the pointer, click the anchor point to select it.

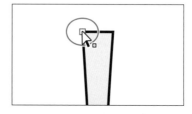

3 With the point selected, click the Convert Selected Anchor Points To Smooth button (◪) in the Control panel.

● Note: If you don't drag directly from the end of the direction line, the shape may be deselected. You can click back on the anchor point to try again.

4 Drag the direction handle that's pointing down, toward the center of the spoon. It doesn't have to match perfectly, but see the figure for roughly where to drag.

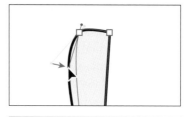

5 Repeat Steps 2–4 for the upper-right anchor point of the spoon handle.

Next, you will convert multiple points at one time to corner points.

6 Choose 2 Dish from the Artboard Navigation menu in the lower-left corner of the Document window.

7 With the Direct Selection tool, drag across the top of the dish path to select the top three anchor points.

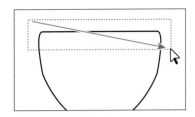

8 Click the Convert Selected Anchor Points To Corner button () in the Control panel to convert them all to corner points and to remove the direction lines.

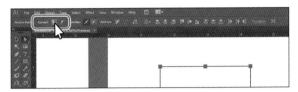

Next, you'll convert anchor points using the Convert Anchor Point tool.

9 Click the Layers panel icon () to show the Layers panel. Click the visibility column to the left of the layer named template to show its contents.

10 Position the pointer over the Pen tool (✐), click and hold down the mouse button, and select the Convert Anchor Point tool (Ν). You will also see the Add Anchor Point tool (⁺✐) and the Delete Anchor Point tool (✐), which are specifically for adding or removing anchor points.

11 With the Convert Anchor Point tool, click the D anchor points (right and left), one at a time, to convert them to corner points.

● **Note:** If you don't click directly on the anchor point, a dialog box will appear telling you that you need to use the tool on an anchor point of a path.

12 Position the pointer over the C anchor point on the left side of the path, and click and drag down. As you drag, press the Shift key. Drag until the direction point on the end of the direction handle that's pointed upward reaches point B (circled in red below). Release the mouse button, and then release the key.

13 Position the pointer over the C anchor point on the right side of the path, click and drag up. As you drag, press the Shift key. Drag to point B straight above it (on the right side). Release the mouse button and the release key.

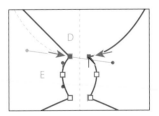
Convert the anchor points.

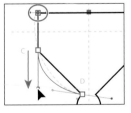
Reshape the path.

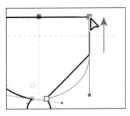
Reshape the path.

14 Choose Select > Deselect, and then choose File > Save.

Cutting with the Scissors tool

There are several tools which allow you to cut and divide shapes. The Scissors tool (✂) splits a path at an anchor point or on a line segment, and the Knife tool allows you to cut objects that become closed paths.

Next, you'll cut the ice cream dish path with the Scissors tool to reshape it.

1 Choose Select > All On Active Artboard to select the dish path.

● **Note:** If you click the stroke of a closed shape (a circle, for example) with the Scissors tool, it simply cuts the path so that it becomes open (a path with two end points).

2 With the path selected, in the Tools panel, click and hold down the Eraser tool (✎) and select the Scissors tool (✂). Position the pointer over point E, and click to cut the path at that anchor point. Go to the reflected side on the right, and click the same point. See the figure for where to click.

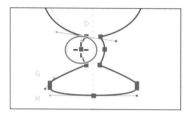
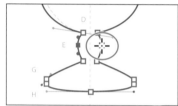

Cut the path at the first point E.   Cut the path at the second point.

If you don't click directly on the path, you will see a warning dialog box. You can simply click OK and try again. Cuts made with the Scissors tool must be on a line or a curve rather than on an endpoint. When you click with the Scissors tool, a new anchor point appears and is selected.

3 Choose Select > Deselect.

▶ **Tip:** You can press Shift + arrow key (up or down) to move the artwork further.

4 Select the Selection tool (▶), and click the bottom part of the dish path to select it. Press the down arrow key six times or so, to move the base down until you see a small gap between the two paths.

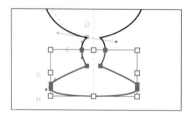
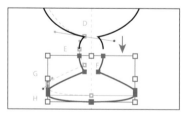

Select the bottom path.   Move the bottom path down.

5 Choose Select > All On Active Artboard to select both paths.

6 Press Ctrl+J (Windows) or Command+J (Mac OS) once, and then press Ctrl+J (Windows) or Command+J (Mac OS) *again* to join the two open paths into one closed path. There should be no longer be gaps between the cut paths.

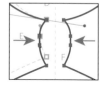

Creating a dashed line

Dashed lines apply to the stroke of an object and can be added to a closed path or an open path. Dashes are created by specifying a sequence of dash lengths and the gaps between them. Next, you'll create a line and add a dash to it.

1   Select the Zoom tool (🔍) in the Tools panel, and click twice, slowly, on the top of the cup path to zoom in.

2   Select the Line Segment tool (╱) in the Tools panel.

3   Position the pointer over the left side of the cup path, where the red horizontal dashed line is (see the red X in the figure). Click and drag to the right, and as you drag, press the Shift key. When the pointer reaches the other side of the shape, release the mouse and then release the modifier key to create a straight line.

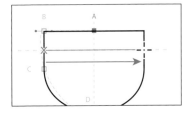

▶ **Tip:** Notice that, without the Smart Guides on, that the line isn't snapping to other shapes. It's okay if your line isn't exactly lined up, you can always adjust it later.

4   Click the word "Stroke" in the Control panel to show the Stroke panel. Change the following options in the Stroke panel:

- Weight: **40 pt**
- Dashed Line: **Selected** (By default, this creates a repeating dash pattern of 12 pt dash, 12 pt gap.)
- First Dash value: **5 pt** (This creates a 5 pt dash, 5 pt gap repeating pattern.)
- First Gap value: **3 pt** (This creates a 5 pt dash, 3 pt gap repeating pattern.)
- Change the next Dash value to **2 pt**, and change the next Gap value to **4 pt**

The values below Dashed Line should now be: 5 pt, 3 pt, 2 pt, 4 pt.

▶ **Tip:** The Preserve Exact Dash And Gap Lengths button (⬚) allows you to retain the appearance of the dashes without aligning to the corners or the dash ends.

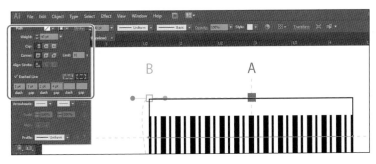

5   With the line still selected, change the Stroke color to the light yellow swatch named cup 65% in the Control panel.

6   Select the Selection tool (↖), and click to select the cup shape.

7   Change the Stroke weight to **6 pt** in the Control panel. Change the fill color to the swatch named cup and the stroke color to the brown swatch named cup stroke.

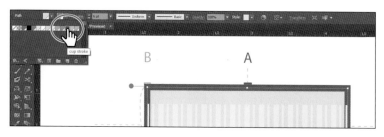

● **Note:** If you find you cannot click the Align Stroke To Outside button (it's dimmed), the cup path may not be closed. With the cup path selected, choose Object > Join and try again.

8   Click the word "Stroke" in the Control panel to reveal the Stroke panel. Click the Align Stroke To Outside button (▣).

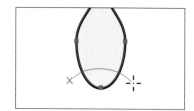

9   Choose Select > All On Active Artboard, and then choose Object > Group.

Cutting with the Knife tool

Next, you'll cut the spoon with the Knife tool (✐) to create two closed paths.

1   Choose 3 Spoon from the Artboard Navigation menu in the lower-left corner of the Document window.

2   Choose Select > All On Active Artboard. Artwork needs to be selected to cut it with the Knife tool.

3   Click and hold down the mouse on the Scissors tool (✂), and select the Knife tool (✐). Notice the Knife pointer (✐) in the Document window.

4   Press the Caps Lock key to view a more precise cursor (-¦-).

    This precise cursor can be useful when trying to cut with the Knife tool.

5   Position the pointer off the left side of the bottom end of the spoon, and drag across in the shape of an arch.

    The Knife tool allows you to cut across selected content in a freeform path. When you release the mouse, the spoon shape is cut into two closed paths.

6   Choose Edit > Undo Knife Tool.

Next, you'll make a straight cut with the Knife tool.

7 Position the pointer off the left side of the end of the spoon. Press and hold Alt+Shift (Windows) or Option+Shift (Mac OS), and drag all the way across the shape. See the figure for help.

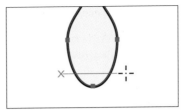

The Alt (Windows) or Option (Mac OS) keys allow you to cut in a straight line. Pressing Alt+Shift (Windows) or Option+Shift (Mac OS) allows you to cut in a straight line that is also constrained to 45°.

8 Choose Select > Deselect.

9 Select the Selection tool (◄), and drag the bottom part of the spoon path down a little bit to see that the spoon path is now cut into two closed paths.

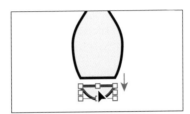

10 Choose Select > All On Active Artboard.

11 With the spoon shapes selected, choose Object > Transform > Rotate. In the Rotate dialog box, change the value to **−45** and click OK.

Now, you'll put the cup group and spoon on the artboard named Ice Cream.

12 Choose View > Fit All In Window.

13 With the Selection tool, drag the selected spoon shapes onto the ice cream path (see the figure), and choose Object > Arrange > Bring To Front.

14 Drag the cup group below the ice cream path and choose Object > Arrange > Send To Back. See the figure for position.

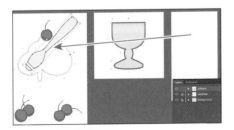 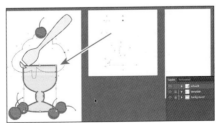

Drag the spoon, and arrange it.   Drag the cup, and arrange it.

15 Choose Select > Deselect, and then choose File > Save.

16 Press the Caps Lock key to deselect it.

Adding arrowheads

You can add arrowheads to both ends of a path using the Stroke panel. There are many different arrowhead styles to choose from in Illustrator, as well as arrowhead editing options.

Next, you'll add different arrowheads to a path.

1   Click the Layers panel icon (⬛) to show the Layers panel, if necessary. Click the eye icon (👁) to the left of the layer named template to hide its contents.

2   Make sure that 1 Ice Cream dish artboard is chosen from the Artboard Navigation menu in the lower-left corner of the Document window. Choose View > Fit Artboard In Window.

3   Select the Selection tool (▶), and click the black line segment below the orange text "THE MONTH."

● **Note:** You can also edit the Stroke options in the Stroke panel (Window > Stroke).

4   Click the underlined word "Stroke" in the Control panel to open the Stroke panel. In the Stroke panel, change the following options:

   • Stroke Weight: **50 pt**

   • Choose Arrow 20 from the menu directly to the right of the word "Arrowheads." This adds an arrowhead to the start (top) of the line.

   • Scale (beneath where you chose Arrow 20): **30%**

   • Choose Arrow 35 from the arrowheads menu to the far right of the word "Arrowheads." This adds an arrowhead to the end of the line.

   • Scale (beneath where you chose Arrow 35): **40%**

   • Make sure that the Place Arrow Tip At End Of Path button (➡) is selected. The Align options allow you to adjust the path to align to the tip or the end of the arrowhead.

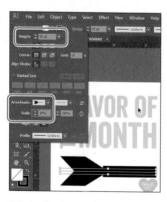

Edit the Stroke weight and first arrowhead.

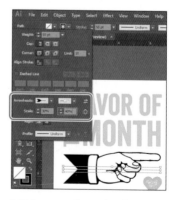

Edit the second arrowhead.

5   Change the Stroke color to the swatch named cup stroke in the Control panel.

Drawing with the Pencil tool

The Pencil tool (✐) lets you draw freeform open and closed paths as if you were drawing with a pencil on paper. Anchor points are created by Illustrator, are placed on the path as you draw, and can be adjusted when the path is complete.

Next, you will draw and edit a few lines on the ice cream path. But first, you will paint the ice cream shape.

1 With the Selection tool (▸) selected, click the ice cream shape to select it. Change the fill color to the pink swatch named ice cream, and change the stroke color to the swatch named cup stroke in the Control panel.

2 Change the Stroke weight to **6 pt** in the Control panel.

3 Click the larger spoon shape, and choose Object > Arrange > Send To Back.

   Now you can see why we cut the spoon using the Knife tool.

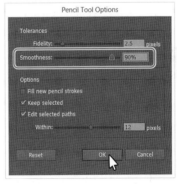

4 Choose Select > Deselect.

Next, you'll draw with the Pencil tool.

5 Double-click the Pencil tool (✐) in the Tools panel. In the Pencil Tool Options dialog box, drag the Smoothness slider to the right until the value is 90%. This reduces the number of points on the paths drawn with the Pencil tool and makes them appear smoother. Click OK.

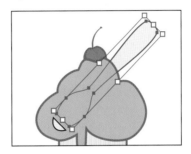

▶ **Tip:** The higher the Fidelity value, the greater the distance between anchor points and the fewer the anchor points created. Fewer anchor points can make the path smoother and less complex.

6 With the Pencil tool selected, click the Stroke color in the Control panel and select the swatch named ice cream dark. Then, change the Fill color to None (▱), if it's not already selected, in the Control panel.

7 Change the stroke weight to **8 pt** in the Control panel.

8 Select the Zoom tool (🔍) in the Tools panel, and click several times, *slowly,* on the pink ice cream shape, to zoom in.

9 Select the Pencil tool, and position the pointer inside the ice cream shape near the small spoon shape (at the red X in the figure). When you see an asterisk to the right of the Pencil tool pointer (✐*), drag an arc around the end of the spoon shape.

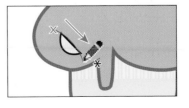

● **Note:** If you see a crosshair (-¦-) instead of the Pencil icon (✐), the Caps Lock key is active. Caps Lock turns tool icons into crosshairs for increased precision.

Tip: To draw a new path near the original without editing the original, you could double-click the Pencil tool to open the Pencil Tool Options dialog box. Deselect Edit Selected Paths, click OK, and then draw the new path.

Note: If the drip seems to disappear after you create it, with it selected, choose Object > Arrange > Bring To Front.

The asterisk that appears next to the pointer indicates that you are about to create a new path. If you don't see the asterisk, it means that you are about to redraw a shape that the pointer is near. Notice that, as you draw, the path may not look perfectly smooth. When you release the mouse button, the path is smoothed based on the Smoothness value that you set in the Pencil Tool Options dialog box.

10 Position the pointer below the drip part of the ice cream path. Begin drawing a "drip" shape beneath it. As you draw, press the Alt (Windows) or Option (Mac OS) key. The Pencil tool displays a small circle next to it (🖊) to indicate that you're creating a closed path. When the path looks like

a "drip," release the mouse button but don't release the Alt or Option key until the path closes. The beginning and ending anchor points are connected with the shortest line possible.

11 With the new closed path selected, press the letter "I" to select the Eyedropper tool (🖊). Click the ice cream path to sample the stroke and fill and to apply it to the new "drip" shape. Leave the drip selected.

Editing with the Pencil tool

Using the Pencil tool, you can also edit any path and add freeform lines and shapes to any shape. Next, you will edit the "drip" using the Pencil tool.

1 With the drip still selected, double-click the Pencil tool (🖊). In the Pencil Tool Options dialog box, click Reset. Ensure that the Fidelity is 10, and change the Smoothness to **70%**. Make sure that the Edit Selected Paths option is selected (this is important for the next step). Click OK.

Tip: You may find that it redraws the entire "drip" instead of editing it. You can zoom in to redraw a part of the path.

2 Position the Pencil tool on the drip path, and notice that the asterisk (*) disappears from the pointer. This indicates that you are about to redraw the selected path. Try redrawing the drip.

3 Choose View > Fit Artboard In Window.

4 Choose File > Save, and then choose File > Close.

FLAVOR OF
THE MONTH

Cherry

Review questions

1 Describe how to draw straight vertical, horizontal, or diagonal lines using the Pen tool (✐).

2 How do you draw a curved line using the Pen tool?

3 How do you draw a corner point on a curved line?

4 Name two ways to convert a smooth point on a curve to a corner point.

5 Which tool would you use to edit a segment on a curved line?

6 How can you change the way the Pencil tool (✏) works?

Review answers

1 To draw a straight line, click twice with the Pen tool (✐). The first click sets the starting anchor point, and the second click sets the ending anchor point of the line. To constrain the straight line vertically, horizontally, or along a 45° diagonal, press the Shift key as you click to create the second anchor point with the Pen tool.

2 To draw a curved line with the Pen tool, click to create the starting anchor point, drag to set the direction of the curve, and then click to end the curve.

3 To draw a corner point on a curved line, press the Alt (Windows) or Option (Mac OS) key and drag the direction handle on the endpoint of the curve to change the direction of the path. Continue dragging to draw the next curved segment on the path.

4 To convert a smooth point on a curve to a corner point, use the Direct Selection tool (▷) to select the anchor point, and then use the Convert Anchor Point tool (⌐) to drag a direction handle to change the direction. Another method is to choose a point or points with the Direct Selection tool and then click the Convert Selected Anchor Points To Corner button (⌐) in the Control panel.

5 To edit a segment on a curved line, select the Direct Selection tool and drag the segment to move it, or drag a direction handle on an anchor point to adjust the length and shape of the segment.

6 To change the way the Pencil tool (✏) works, double-click the Pencil tool in the Tools panel to open the Pencil Tool Options dialog box. There you can change the smoothness, fidelity, and other options.

6 COLOR AND PAINTING

Lesson overview

In this lesson, you'll learn how to do the following:

- Understand color modes and the main color controls.

- Create, edit, and paint with colors using a variety of methods.

- Name and save colors, and build a color palette.

- Work with color groups.

- Use the Color Guide panel and the Edit Colors/Recolor Artwork features.

- Copy paint and appearance attributes from one object to another.

- Create and paint with patterns.

- Work with Live Paint.

 This lesson takes approximately an hour and a half to complete.

Download the project files for this lesson from the Lesson & Update Files tab on your Account page at www.peachpit.com and store them on your computer in a convenient location, as described in the Getting Started section of this book.

Your Accounts page is also where you'll find any updates to the chapters or to the lesson files. Look on the Lesson & Update Files tab to access the most current content.

Spice up your illustrations with colors by taking advantage of color controls in Adobe Illustrator CC. In this information-packed lesson, you'll discover how to create and paint fills and strokes, use the Color Guide panel for inspiration, work with color groups, recolor artwork, create patterns, and more.

Getting started

In this lesson, you will learn about the fundamentals of color and create and edit colors for a park sign and logo, using the Color panel, Swatches panel, and more.

1   To ensure that the tools and panels function exactly as described in this lesson, delete or deactivate (by renaming) the Adobe Illustrator CC preferences file. See "Restoring default preferences," on page 3.

2   Start Adobe Illustrator CC.

● **Note:** If you have not already downloaded the project files for this lesson to your computer from your Account page, make sure to do so now. See "Getting Started" at the beginning of the book.

3   Choose File > Open, and open the L6end.ai file in the Lesson06 folder, located in the Lessons folder, to view a final version of the park sign you will paint.

4   Choose View > Fit All In Window.

Leave the L6end.ai file open for reference.

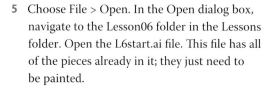

5   Choose File > Open. In the Open dialog box, navigate to the Lesson06 folder in the Lessons folder. Open the L6start.ai file. This file has all of the pieces already in it; they just need to be painted.

● **Note:** In Mac OS, when opening lesson files, you may need to click the round, green button in the upper-left corner of the Document window to maximize the window's size.

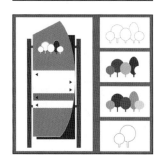

6   Choose File > Save As. In the Save As dialog box, navigate to the Lesson06 folder and name it **parksign.ai**. Leave the Save As Type option set to Adobe Illustrator (*.AI) (Windows) or the Format option set to Adobe Illustrator (ai) (Mac OS), and click Save. In the Illustrator Options dialog box, leave the options at their default settings and then click OK.

7   Choose Window > Workspace > Reset Essentials.

● **Note:** If you don't see "Reset Essentials" in the menu, choose Window > Workspace > Essentials before choosing Window > Workspace > Reset Essentials.

Understanding color

There are so many ways to experiment with and apply color to your artwork in Adobe Illustrator CC. As you work with color, it's important to keep in mind the medium in which the artwork will be published, such as a print piece or a website. The colors you create need to be described in the correct way for the medium. This usually requires that you use the correct color mode and color definitions for your colors. The first part, color modes, will be described next.

Exploring color modes

Before starting a new illustration, you should decide which color mode the artwork should use, *CMYK* or *RGB*.

- **CMYK**—Cyan, magenta, yellow, and black are the colors used in four-color process printing. These four colors are combined and overlapped in a screen pattern to create a multitude of other colors. Select this mode for printing.

- **RGB**—Red, green, and blue light are added together in various ways to create an array of colors. Select this mode if you are using images for on-screen presentations or the Internet.

When creating a new document, you select a color mode by choosing File > New and picking the appropriate document Profile, such as Print, which uses CMYK for the color mode. You can change the color mode by clicking the arrow to the left of Advanced and making a selection in the Color Mode menu.

▶ **Tip:** To learn more about color and graphics, search for "About color" in Illustrator Help (Help > Illustrator Help).

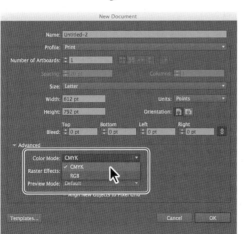

When a color mode is selected, the applicable panels open, displaying colors in the selected color mode. You can change the color mode of a document, after a file is created, by choosing File > Document Color Mode and then selecting either CMYK or RGB in the menu.

Understanding the main color controls

In this lesson, you will learn about the traditional methods of coloring (also called *painting*) objects in Illustrator. This includes painting objects with colors and patterns using a combination of panels and tools, such as the Control panel, Color panel, Swatches panel, Color Guide panel, Color Picker, and the paint buttons in the Tools panel.

You'll begin by looking at finished artwork to which color has already been applied in some areas, and then you'll explore some of more widely used options available for creating and applying color.

1 Click the L6end.ai document tab at the top of the Document window.

2 Choose 1 from the Artboard Navigation menu in the lower-left corner of the Document window, and then choose View > Fit Artboard In Window.

3 Select the Selection tool (⬆), and click the large, light brown shape in the sign.

● **Note:** Depending on your screen resolution, your Tools panel may either be a double or single column.

Objects in Illustrator can have a fill, a stroke, or both, as you've seen. At the bottom of the Tools panel, notice the Fill and Stroke boxes. The Fill box is brown for the selected object, and the Stroke box is none. Click the Stroke box, and then click the Fill box (making sure that the Fill box is the last selected). Notice that the box you click is brought to the front of the other. When a color is selected, it will apply to the fill or stroke of the selected object (whichever is in front).

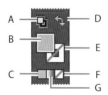

A. Default Fill And Stroke button
B. Fill box
C. Color button
D. Swap Fill And Stroke button
E. Stroke box
F. None button
G. Gradient button

▶ **Tip:** You can Shift-click the color spectrum bar at the bottom of the Color panel to rotate through different color modes, such as CMYK and RGB, or click the panel menu icon (▤) and choose a color mode.

4 Click the Color panel icon (◉) on the right side of the workspace, if it isn't open already. Click the double-arrow to the left of the word "Color" in the panel tab to show more options, if necessary.

The Color panel displays the current fill and stroke of the selected content. The CMYK sliders in the Color panel show the percentages of cyan, magenta, yellow, and black used to create the selected color. The color spectrum bar at the bottom lets you quickly and visually select a fill or stroke color from a spectrum of colors.

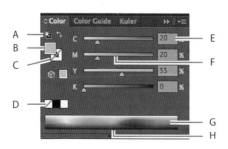

A. Default Fill And Stroke button
B. Fill box
C. Stroke box
D. None box
E. Color value
F. Color slider
G. Color spectrum bar
H. Drag to expand the color spectrum

5 Click the Swatches panel icon (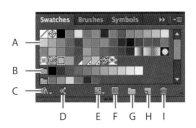) on the right side of the workspace.

You can name and save different types of colors, gradients, and patterns in the Swatches panel as swatches so that you can apply and edit them later. Swatches are listed in the Swatches panel in the order in which they were created, but you can reorder or organize the swatches into groups to suit your needs. All documents start with a set number of swatches, but any colors in the Swatches panel are available to the current document only (by default), since each document has its own defined swatches.

A. Swatch
B. Color group
C. Swatch Libraries menu
D. Open Kuler panel
E. Show Swatch Kinds menu

F. Swatch options
G. New Color group
H. New Swatch
I. Delete Swatch

6 Click the Color Guide panel icon ( ) on the right side of the workspace. Click the brown swatch in the upper-left corner of the panel to set the base color (labeled "A" in the figure below).

The Color Guide panel can provide color inspiration while you create your artwork. Either starting with the current color in the Fill box or by using an existing library of colors, it can help you pick color tints, analogous colors, and more. Those colors can then be applied directly to artwork using various methods, saved as swatches or within groups, or edited using the Edit Colors feature.

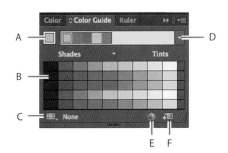

A. Set base color to the current color
B. Color variations
C. Limits the color group to colors in a swatch library

D. Harmony Rules menu and active color group
E. Edit Or Apply Colors button
F. Save color group to Swatch panel

● **Note:** The colors you see in the panel may be different, and that's okay.

7 Click the Color panel icon ( ). Using the Selection tool, click various shapes in the L6end.ai file to see how their paint attributes are reflected in the Color panel and the Tools panel.

8 Leave the L6end.ai file open for reference, or choose File > Close to close it without saving your changes.

Working with color

As you will see in this section, Illustrator provides a lot of ways to arrive at the color you need. You'll start by applying an existing color to a shape and then work your way through the most widely used ways to create and apply color.

● **Note:** Throughout this lesson, you'll be working on a document with a color mode that was set to CMYK when the document was created, which means that the majority of colors you create will, by default, be composed of cyan, magenta, yellow, and black.

Applying an existing color

As was mentioned previously, every new document in Illustrator has a series of default colors available for you to use in your artwork in the form of swatches in the Swatches panel. The first method of working with color you will explore is to paint a shape with an existing color.

1 Click the parksign.ai document tab at the top of the Document window, if you did not close the L6end.ai document.

2 Choose 1 from the Artboard Navigation menu in the lower-left corner of the Document window (if it's not chosen already), and then choose View > Fit Artboard In Window.

3 With the Selection tool (▶), click to select the large, red shape.

4 Click the Fill color in the Control panel, and the Swatches panel appears. Click to apply the swatch named sign bg. Positioning the pointer over a swatch in the list to show a tool tip with the swatch name. Press the Escape key to hide the Swatches panel.

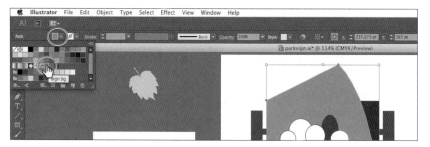

The Control panel has both Fill color and Stroke color options. By selecting artwork and clicking one or the other, you indicate which part of the object you want to paint (the stroke or the fill).

5 Choose Select > Deselect to ensure that nothing is selected.

Creating and saving a custom color as a swatch

At times, you may also need to create a specific color. Next, you'll create a color using the Color panel, and then you will save the color as a swatch in the Swatches panel.

1   With the Selection tool (), click to select the white bar above the green bar, in the middle of the artboard (on the sign).

2   If the Color panel is not visible, click the Color panel icon (). Click the Color panel menu icon (), choose CMYK from the menu (if it's not already selected), and then choose Show Options from the same menu (if necessary).

3   In the Color panel, click the Fill box (if it's not selected) to apply the color to the fill of the selected shape. Drag the bottom of the Color panel down to reveal more of the color spectrum bar. Click in the light green part of the color spectrum to apply a light green color to the fill.

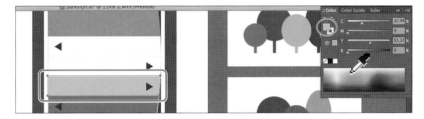

If artwork is selected when you create a color in the Color panel, the color is automatically applied. You can also create a color in the Color panel with no artwork selected and apply it later.

4   Type the following values in the CMYK text fields: C=**42**, M=**0**, Y=**62**, K=**0**. This ensures that we are all using the same light green color.

▶ **Tip:** The CMYK values are each a percentage of 100.

Now that you've created a color, you can save it as a swatch in the Swatches panel so that later you can edit or apply it elsewhere.

5   Click the Swatches panel icon (), and click the New Swatch button () at the bottom of the panel to create a swatch from the color you just created. In the New Swatch dialog box, name the color **light green** and, leaving the rest of the options as they are, click OK.

▶ **Tip:** Naming colors can be an art form. You can name them according to their value (C=45, ...), appearance (light green), or use (text header), among other attributes.

Notice that the new light green swatch is highlighted in the Swatches panel (it has a white border around it). That's because it is applied to the selected shape.

6 With the Selection tool, select the third white tree from the left on the top of the sign (see the figure).

7 Click the Fill box at the bottom of the Tools panel to make sure that you change the fill (not the stroke) of the tree.

8 In the Swatches panel on the right, select the light green swatch to apply it.

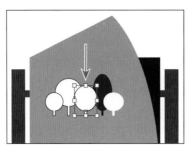  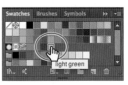

Select the tree.　　　　　　　　Select the　　Apply the swatch.
　　　　　　　　　　　　　　　　　Fill box.

When applying a swatch from the Swatches panel, it's always important to select the stroke or the fill in the Tools panel (or Color panel) so that it paints the right part.

▶ **Tip:** You may be getting used to this by now, but you have to hide the Swatches panel in order to choose Select > Deselect.

9 Change the Stroke color to the None swatch (⬜) in the Control panel to remove the stroke.

10 Choose Select > Deselect.

Creating a copy of a swatch

Next, you will create another swatch by copying and editing the swatch you made.

1 In the Swatches panel, click the New Swatch button (🔲) at the bottom.

Clicking the New Swatch button creates a swatch from the fill or stroke color (whichever is active or up front at the bottom of the Tools panel).

● **Note:** If the tree shape had still been selected, it would be filled with the new color.

2 In the New Swatch dialog box, change the name to **orange** and change the values to C=**15**, M=**45**, Y=**70**, K=**0**. Notice the Color Mode menu. You can change the color mode of a specific color to RGB, CMYK, Grayscale, or another mode, when you create it. Click OK.

3 With the Selection tool (▶), click the white bar above the light green filled bar to select it. Click the Fill color in the Control panel, and click to select the color named orange.

Creating a spot color

In this section, you will see how to load a color library, such as the PANTONE color system, and how to add a PANTONE MATCHING SYSTEM (PMS) color to the Swatches panel.

1   In the Swatches panel, click the Swatch Libraries Menu button () at the bottom of the panel. Choose Color Books > PANTONE+ Solid Coated.

    The PANTONE+ Solid Coated library appears in its own panel.

2   Type **755** in the Find field. As you type, the list is filtered, showing a smaller and smaller range of swatches. Type another **5** so that 7555 appears in the search field. Click the swatch beneath the search field to add it to the Swatches panel. Click the X to the right of the search field to stop filtering them. Close the PANTONE+ Solid Coated panel.

Open the color library.

Filter the list of colors.

Select the swatch.

● **Note:** When you exit Illustrator and then relaunch it, the PANTONE library panel does not reopen. To automatically open the panel whenever Illustrator opens, choose Persistent from the PANTONE+ Solid Coated panel menu.

3   Choose 2 Artboard 2 from the Artboard Navigation menu in the lower-left corner of the Document window.

4   With the Selection tool (🠕), click the first white-filled tree shape on the left. From the Fill color in the Control panel, choose the PANTONE 7555 C color to fill the shape.

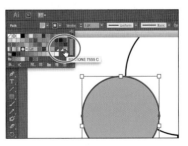

5   Change the Stroke color to None (▱).

6   Choose Select > Deselect, and then choose File > Save.

Why does my PANTONE swatch look different from the other swatches in the Swatches panel?

In the Swatches panel, you can identify spot-color swatches by the spot-color icon (⊙) when the panel is in List view or by the dot in the lower corner (▧) when the panel is in Thumbnail view. Process colors do not have a spot-color icon or a dot. To learn more about color libraries and spot colors, search for "About color" in Illustrator Help (Help > Illustrator Help).

Creating and saving a tint of a color

A *tint* is a mixture of color with white to make the color lighter. You can create a tint from a global process color, like CMYK, or from a spot color.

Next, you will create a tint of the Pantone swatch.

1   With the Selection tool (▶), click the white tree shape just to the right of the tree shape filled with the Pantone color.

2   In the Swatches panel, apply the new Pantone color to the *fill* of the shape.

● **Note:** Don't forget! You need to make sure that the Fill box is selected in the Tools panel (or Color panel) to apply the color to the fill.

3   Click the Color panel icon (▨) to expand the Color panel. Make sure that the Fill box is selected in the Color panel, and then drag the tint slider to the left to change the tint value to **70%**.

● **Note:** You may need to choose Show Options from the Color panel menu to see the slider.

4   Click the Swatches panel icon (▦) on the right side of the workspace. Click the New Swatch button (▤) at the bottom of the panel to save the tint. Notice the tint swatch in the Swatches panel. Position the pointer over the swatch icon to see its name, PANTONE 7555 C 70%.

Create the tint.

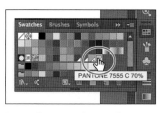

Notice the tint in the panel.

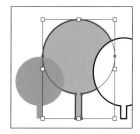

Notice the result.

5 Change the Stroke color to None () for the selected tree shape.

6 For the remaining three tree shapes, apply the PANTONE 7555 C swatch, the tint swatch (PANTONE 7555 C 70%), and then the PANTONE 7555 C swatch to their fills.

7 Change the Stroke color to None () for each of the tree shapes.

8 Choose Select > Deselect, and then choose File > Save.

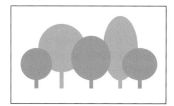

Adjusting colors

When working with colors, Illustrator offers an Edit Colors menu option (Edit > Edit Colors) that allows you to convert colors between color modes, blend colors, invert colors, and much more, for selected artwork. Next, you will change the logo with the PANTONE 7555 C color applied to use CMYK colors instead of Pantone.

1 While still on Artboard 2, choose Select > All On Active Artboard to select all of the shapes with the Pantone color and tint applied.

2 Choose Edit > Edit Colors > Convert To CMYK.

The colors in the selected shapes are now composed of CMYK. Using this method for converting to CMYK does not affect the Pantone color swatches in the Swatches panel. It simply converts the selected *artwork* colors to CMYK.

● **Note:** Currently, Convert to RGB in the Edit Color menu is dimmed (you cannot select it). That's because the Document Color Mode is CMYK. To convert select content color to RGB using this method, choose File > Document Color Mode > CMYK.

Copying appearance attributes

At times, you may want to simply copy appearance attributes, like character, paragraph, fill, and stroke, from one object to another. This can speed up your creative process.

1 Choose 1 from the Artboard Navigation menu in the lower-left corner of the Document window to return to the artboard with the sign on it.

2 Using the Selection tool (▶), select the first white tree (on the left) at the top of the sign (the one with the stroke applied).

3 Select the Eyedropper tool (✒) in the Tools panel. Click the green bar just above the bottom brown bar (see the figure).

The tree has the attributes from the painted bar applied, including a cream-colored stroke.

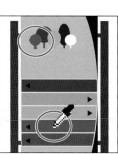

▶ **Tip:** You can double-click the Eyedropper tool in the Tools panel, before sampling, to change the attributes that the Eyedropper picks up and applies.

4 Click the Stroke color in the Control panel, and change the color to None ().

5 Choose Select > Deselect, and then choose File > Save.

Creating a color group

In Illustrator, you can save colors in color groups, which consist of related color swatches in the Swatches panel. Organizing colors by their use, such as grouping all colors for a logo, can be helpful for organization and more, as you'll soon see. Only spot, process, and global colors can be in a group.

Next, you will create a color group of some of the swatches you've created for the logo, to keep them organized.

● **Note:** If objects are selected when you click the New Color Group button, an expanded New Color Group dialog box appears. In this dialog box, you can create a color group from the colors in the artwork and convert the colors to global colors.

1   In the Swatches panel, click swatch named aqua to select it. Holding down the Shift key, click the forest green swatch to the right to select five color swatches. Ctrl-click (Windows) or Command-click (Mac OS) the orange swatch to remove it from the selection.

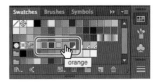

2   Click the New Color Group button (▢) at the bottom of the Swatches panel. Change the Name to **tree logo** in the New Color Group dialog box, and click OK to save the group.

3   With the Selection tool (▶), click a blank area of the Swatches panel to deselect the color group you just created.

Each swatch in a color group can still be edited independently by double-clicking a swatch in the group and editing the values in the Swatch Options dialog box.

For the next step, you may want to drag the bottom of the Swatches panel down so that you can see all of the swatches in the panel.

4   Click the white swatch in the top row of the Swatches panel, and drag it to the right of the forest green swatch in the tree logo color group.

When dragging a color into a color group, make sure that you see a line appear on the right edge of the forest green swatch (see the figure). Otherwise, you may drag the white swatch to the wrong place. You can always choose Edit > Undo Move Swatches and try again. Aside from dragging colors in or out of a color group, you can rename a color group, reorder the colors in the group, and more.

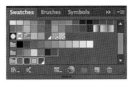

Note the new color group.

Deselect the swatches.

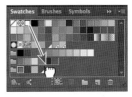

Drag the white swatch.

Working with color in the Color Guide panel

The Color Guide panel can provide you with color inspiration as you create your artwork. You can use it to pick color tints, analogous colors, and much more and then either apply them directly to artwork, edit them using several methods, or save them as a group in the Swatches panel.

Next, you will use the Color Guide panel to select different colors for a version of the tree logo and then you'll save those colors as a color group in the Swatches panel.

1 Choose 3 Artboard 3 from the Artboard Navigation menu in the lower-left corner of the Document window.

2 With the Selection tool (￫), click the first tree on the left (with the aqua color fill). Make sure that the Fill box is selected in the Tools panel.

3 Click the Color Guide panel icon (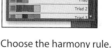) on the right side of the workspace to open the panel. Click the Set Base Color To The Current Color button (▣).

This allows the Color Guide panel to suggest colors based on the color showing in the Set Base Color To The Current Color button.

Next, you'll experiment with colors using Harmony Rules.

4 Choose Analogous from the Harmony Rules menu (circled in the figure) in the Color Guide panel.

A base group of colors is created to the right of the base color (aqua), and a series of tints and shades of those colors appears in the body of the panel.

● **Note:** The colors you see in the Color Guide panel may be different from what you see in the figure. That's okay.

▶ **Tip:** You can also choose a different color variation (different from the default Tints/Shades), such as Show Warm/Cool, by clicking the Color panel menu icon (▤) and choosing one.

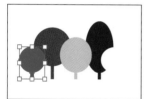
Select the tree.

Set the base color.

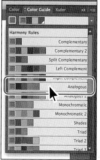
Choose the harmony rule.

There are lots of harmony rules to choose from, each instantly generating a color scheme based on any color you want. The base color you set (aqua) is the basis for generating the colors in the color scheme.

5 Choose File > Save.

6 Click the Save Color Group To Swatch Panel button (image) to save the base colors in the Analogous harmony rule in the Swatches panel as a group.

7 Click the Swatches panel icon (image). Scroll down to see the new group added.

Save new color group.

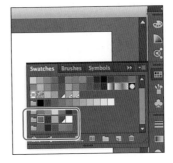
Note the saved color group.

Next, you'll experiment with the colors in the color group that you just created to create an alternate group of colors.

8 Choose Select > Deselect.

9 Click the Color Guide panel icon (image), to open the Color Guide panel.

● **Note:** If you choose a different color variation than the one suggested, your color will differ from those in the rest of this section.

10 In the list of swatches in the Color Guide panel, select the fifth color from the left, in the third row (see the figure).

If the tree were still selected, it would have been filled with the blue. You can apply or save any of the colors in the Color Guide panel as an individual swatch.

11 Click the Set Base Color To The Current Color button (image) to ensure that all colors that the panel creates are based on that same blue. Choose Complementary 2 from the Harmony Rules menu.

12 Click the Save Color Group To Swatch Panel button (image) to save the colors as a group in the Swatches panel.

Editing a color group in the Edit Colors dialog box

When you create color groups, in the Swatches panel or in the Color Guide panel, you can edit the swatches in the group either individually, from the Swatches panel, or together. In this section, you will learn how to edit the colors of a color group in the Swatches panel using the Edit Color dialog box. Later, you will apply those colors to a version of the logo.

1   Choose Select > Deselect (if it's available), and then click the Swatches panel icon () to show the panel.

Deselecting right now is important! If artwork is selected when you edit the color group, the edits can apply to the selected artwork.

2   Click the color group icon ( ) to the left of the colors in the color group you just saved to select the group. Click the Edit Color Group button ( ) at the bottom of the Swatches panel to open the Edit Colors dialog box.

The Edit Color Group button appears in multiple locations, like the Swatches and Color Guide panels. The Edit Colors dialog box allows you to edit a group of colors in various ways or even to create new color groups. On the right side of the Edit Colors dialog box, under the "Color Groups" section, all of the existing color groups in the Swatches panel are listed.

▶ **Tip:** With no artwork selected, you could also double-click the color group icon to open the Edit Colors dialog box.

3   Select the name Color Group 2 above the Color Groups, on the right side of the dialog box (circled in the figure below), and rename the group **logo2**. This is one way you can rename a color group.

Next, you will make a few changes to the colors in the logo2 group. On the left side of the Edit Colors dialog box, you can edit the colors of each color group, either individually or together, and edit them visually or precisely using specific color values. In the color wheel, you'll see markers (circles) that represent each color in the selected group.

▶ **Tip:** You'll notice that all of the colors in the group move and change together. This is because they are linked together, by default.

4   In the color wheel, drag the largest blue circle, called a *marker*, in the lower-left section of the color wheel, down and to the right just a little bit. The largest marker is the base color of the color group that you set in the Color Guide panel initially.

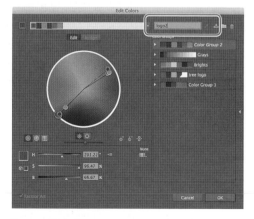

Rename the color group.

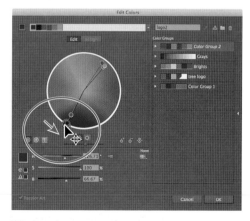

Edit the color group.

Moving the color markers away from the center of the color wheel increases saturation, and moving them toward the center decreases saturation. Moving a color marker around the color wheel (clockwise or counter-clockwise) edits the hue.

● **Note:** You can match the H, S, B (hue, saturation, brightness) values below the color wheel in the Edit Colors dialog box to mimic what you see in the figure, if you want to match exactly the color we achieved.

5 Drag the Adjust Brightness slider below the color wheel to the right, to brighten all the colors at once.

Next, you will edit the colors in the group independently and then save the colors as a new named group.

6 Click the Unlink Harmony Colors button (⬚) in the Edit Colors dialog box to edit the colors independently (circled in the figure below, right).

The lines between the color markers (circles) and the center of the color wheel become dotted, indicating that you can edit the colors independently.

Next, you will edit just one of the colors, since they are now unlinked, and you will edit that color by using specific color values rather than by dragging the color in the color wheel.

7 Click the Color Mode icon (⬚) to the right of the H, S, B values below the color wheel, and choose CMYK from the menu, if the CMYK sliders are not already visible. Click to select lightest orange marker in the color wheel, as shown in the figure on the right, below. Change the CMYK values to C=**10**, M=**50**, Y=**100**, and K=**0**. Notice that the marker has moved in the color wheel, and it's the only one that moved. Leave the dialog box open.

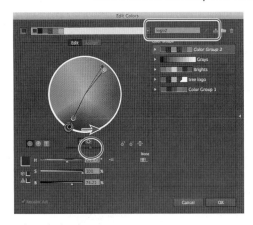
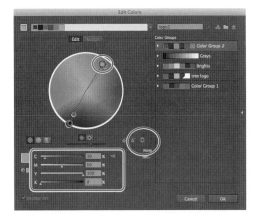

Adjust the brightness.   Unlink the colors, and edit the CMYK values.

● **Note:** It's okay if the color markers in your Edit Colors dialog box are different from those shown in the figure above.

8 Click the Save Changes To Color Group button (⬚) in the upper-right corner of the Edit Colors dialog box, to save the changes to the color group.

If you decide to make changes to colors in another color group, you can select the color group on the right side of the Edit Colors dialog box and edit the colors on the left side. You can then save the changes to the group, or you can save those colors as a new color group, by clicking the New Color Group button () in the upper-right corner of the dialog box.

9 Click OK to close the Edit Colors dialog box. The subtle changes to the colors in the group should show in the Swatches panel.

10 Choose File > Save.

Note: If a dialog box appears after clicking OK, click Yes to save the changes to the color group in the Swatches panel.

Editing colors in artwork

You can also edit the colors in selected artwork, using the Recolor Artwork command. It's really useful when global swatches weren't used in the artwork, and, as a result, updating a series of colors in selected artwork may take a lot of time.

Next, you will edit the colors for one of the logos that was created with colors that were not saved in the Swatches panel.

1 Choose 4 Artboard 4 from the Artboard Navigation menu in the lower-left corner of the Document window.

2 Choose Select > All On Active Artboard to select all of the artwork.

3 Click the Recolor Artwork button (⬤) in the Control panel to open the Recolor Artwork dialog box.

▶ **Tip:** You can also access the Recolor Artwork dialog box by selecting the artwork and then choosing Edit > Edit Colors > Recolor Artwork.

The Recolor Artwork dialog box options allow you to edit, reassign, or reduce the colors in your selected artwork and to create and edit color groups. You'll probably notice that it looks an awful lot like the Edit Colors dialog box. The big difference is that the Edit Colors dialog box only allows you to edit colors, but in the Recolor Artwork dialog box you can also change the color applied to the selected artwork.

4 In the Recolor Artwork dialog box, click the Hide Color Group Storage icon (◀) on the right side of the dialog box.

Like in the Edit Colors dialog box, all of the color groups in the Swatches panel appear on the right side of the Recolor Artwork dialog box (in the Color Groups storage area). In the Recolor Artwork dialog box, you can apply colors from these color groups to the selected artwork.

5 Click the Edit tab to edit the colors in the artwork using the color wheel.

6   Make sure that the Link Harmony Colors icon (⊡) is showing so that you can edit all of the colors independently. If it looks like this (⊡), click it to unlink.

When you created a color group, you worked with the color wheel and the CMYK sliders to edit color. This time, you will adjust color using a different method.

▶ **Tip:** If you want to return to the original logo colors, click the Get Colors From Selected Art button (▨).

7   Click the Display Color Bars button (▥) to show the colors in the selected artwork as bars. Click the cream color bar to select it. At the bottom of the dialog box, change the CMYK values to C=**5**, M=**10**, Y=**40**, K=**0**. If the Recolor Artwork dialog box isn't in the way, you should see the artwork changing.

8   Click the green color bar to select it instead of the cream color bar. With the pointer over the green color bar, right-click (Windows) or Control-click (Mac OS) and choose Select Shade from the menu that appears. Click in the shade menu, and drag to change the color of the color bar.

Editing the colors as bars is just another way to view and edit the colors, and there are so many options for editing. To learn more about these options, search for "Color groups (harmonies)" in Illustrator Help (Help > Illustrator Help).

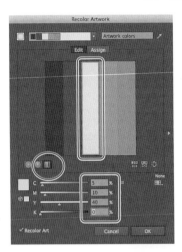 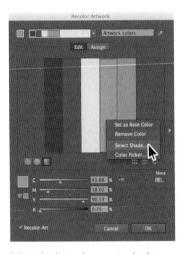 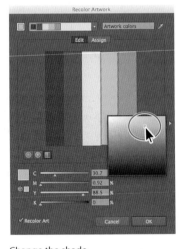

Click the cream color bar, and edit it.   Select shade on the green color bar.   Change the shade.

▶ **Tip:** You can save the edited colors as a color group by clicking the Show Color Group Storage icon (▨) on the right side of the dialog box and then clicking the New Color Group button (▥).

The edit options in the Recolor Artwork dialog box are almost identical to the options in the Edit Colors dialog box. Instead of editing color and creating color groups to apply later, you are dynamically editing colors in the selected artwork.

9   Click OK in the Recolor Artwork dialog box.

10 Choose Select > Deselect, and then choose File > Save.

Working with Adobe Kuler

Adobe Kuler is a web-based application used to experiment with, create, and share color themes that you use in a project. Illustrator CC has a Kuler panel that enables you to view and use the color themes that you have created In the Kuler application.

Note: For the Kuler panel to work, Internet connectivity is essential when you launch Illustrator CC. If you do not have Internet connectivity launching Illustrator, the Kuler panel cannot be used.

The Kuler panel (Window> Kuler) displays the themes you have created and synced with your account on the Kuler website (kuler.adobe.com). The Adobe ID used In Illustrator CC is automatically used to sign in to the Kuler website, and the Kuler panel is refreshed with your Kuler themes.

Note: If the credentials you are using with Illustrator CC do not have an associated Kuler ID, then a Kuler ID Is automatically created using the Illustrator CC credentials. You can then access the Kuler website using your Adobe ID credentials.

1   Choose Window > Kuler, to open the Kuler panel.

2   The Kuler panel automatically refreshes to display the latest themes available in your Kuler account. If the Kuler panel does not display the latest themes, click Refresh.

Note: Your Kuler panel will most likely be empty.

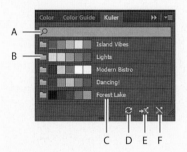

A. Theme search by name

B. Theme folder icon

C. Theme name

D. Refresh

E. Launch Kuler website

F. Icon that indicates the themes cannot be edited

For more information about working with the Kuler panel, search for "Kuler panel" in Illustrator Help (Help > Illustrator Help).

—From Illustrator Help

Assigning colors to your artwork

As you've seen, with artwork selected, clicking the Recolor Artwork button (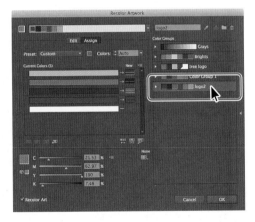) opens the Recolor Artwork dialog box. In the Recolor Artwork dialog box, you can edit colors in existing artwork, as you've seen, but you can also "assign" colors from an existing color group to your artwork. Next, you will assign a color group to create a version of the logo.

1 Choose 3 from the Artboard Navigation menu in the lower-left corner of the Document window.

2 Choose Select > All On Active Artboard to select the logo trees.

3 Click the Recolor Artwork button ( ) in the Control panel.

4 Click the Show Color Group Storage icon ( ) (the small arrow) on the right side of the dialog box to show the color groups, if they aren't already showing. Make sure that, in the top left of the dialog box, the Assign button is selected.

On the left side of the Recolor Artwork dialog box, notice that the five colors of the selected logo are listed in the Current Colors column, in what is called "hue-forward" sorting. That means they are arranged, from top to bottom, in the ordering of the color wheel: red, orange, yellow, green, blue, indigo, and violet.

● **Note:** If the colors of the logo do not change, make sure that Recolor Art is selected at the bottom of the Recolor Artwork dialog box.

5 Under Color Groups in the Recolor Artwork panel, select the logo2 color group you created earlier.

On the left side of the Recolor Artwork dialog box, notice that the colors of the color group named logo2 are *assigned* to the colors in the logo. The Current Colors column shows what the color was in the logo, and an arrow to the right of each of those colors points to the New column, which contains what the color has become (or has been *reassigned to*). Notice that the white color has not been modified and that there is no arrow pointing to a color in the New column. That's because white, black, and grays are typically *preserved*, or unchanged.

6 Click the Hide Color Group Storage icon ( ) to hide the color groups. Drag the dialog box by the title bar at the top so that you can see the artwork.

6   With the Selection tool selected, drag the leaf to the left a little. Notice that the blue tile moves with the artwork.

7   Click the Symbols panel (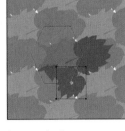) icon to open the panel. Drag the symbol named medium leaf just to the right of the original leaf.

8   Drag the small leaf symbol from the Symbols panel just below the two other symbols. You can arrange them in the next step.

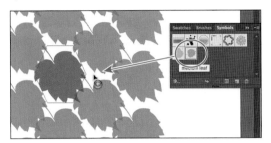

Drag the symbols into the pattern.

Arrange the leaves.

After adding the new content to the pattern, you can see that the pattern tile does not contain the new content.

9   Select Size Tile To Art in the Pattern Options panel.

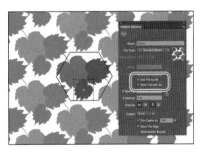

The Size Tile To Art selection fits the tile area (the blue hex shape) to the bounds of the artwork, changing the spacing between the repeated objects. With Size Tile To Art deselected, you could manually change the width and the height of the pattern definition area in the Width and Height fields to include more content or to edit the spacing between. You can also edit the tile area manually with the Pattern Tile Tool button (⊞) in the upper-left corner of the Pattern Options panel.

● **Note:** In this step, you can see the leaves more clearly. At this point, try to arrange the leaves like you see in the figure.

10 Change the H Spacing to **−18 pt**, and change the V Spacing to **−18 pt**.

11 For Overlap, click the Bottom In Front button (▨), to see the change in the pattern.

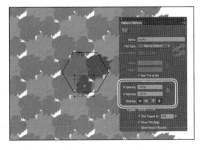

The artwork in a pattern may begin to overlap, due to the size of the tile or the spacing values. By default, when objects overlap horizontally, the left object is on top; when objects overlap vertically, the top object is on top.

▶ **Tip:** The spacing values can be either positive or negative values, to move the tiles apart or to bring them closer together.

12 Change the H Spacing and V Spacing values back to **0 in**.

The Pattern Options panel has a host of other pattern editing options, including the ability to see more or less of the pattern, called Copies. To learn more about the Pattern Options panel, search for "Create and edit patterns" in Illustrator Help.

13 Select Show Swatch Bounds at the bottom of the Pattern Options panel to see the dotted area that will be saved in the swatch. Deselect Show Swatch Bounds.

Tip: If you want to create pattern variations, you can click Save A Copy in the bar along the top of the Document window. This saves the current pattern in the Swatches panel as a copy and allows you to continue creating.

14 Click Done in the bar along the top of the Document window. In the dialog box that appears, click OK.

15 Choose File > Save.

Applying your pattern

You can assign a pattern using a number of different methods. In this lesson, you will use the Swatches panel to apply the pattern. You can also apply the pattern using the Fill color in the Control panel.

1 Choose View > Fit Artboard In Window.

2 With the Selection tool (⬧), click the shape filled with the Sticks pattern swatch off the left edge of the artboard.

3 Select the leaves swatch from the Fill color in the Control panel.

4 Choose Select > Deselect, and then choose File > Save.

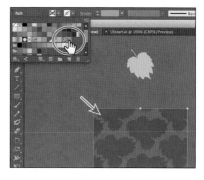

● **Note:** Your pattern may look different, and that's okay.

Editing your pattern

Next, you will edit the leaves pattern in Pattern Editing mode.

1 In the Swatches panel, double-click the leaves pattern swatch to edit it.

Tip: You can also select an object filled with a pattern swatch and, with the Fill box selected in the Tools panel, choose Object > Pattern > Edit Pattern.

2 In Pattern Editing mode, with the Selection tool selected (⬧), choose Select > All to select all three green leaves.

3 In the Control panel, change the Fill color to the swatch named **forest green** (in a color group). Right now, there are different green colors applied.

4 Choose Select > Deselect.

Review questions

1 Describe what a *global color* is.

2 How can you save a color?

3 How can you choose color harmonies for color inspiration?

4 Name two things that the Recolor Artwork dialog box allows you to do.

5 How do you add pattern swatches to the Swatches panel?

6 Explain what Live Paint allows you to do.

Review answers

1 A *global color* is a color swatch that, when you edit it, automatically updates all artwork that has it applied. All spot colors are global; however, process colors can be either global or local.

2 You can save a color for painting other objects in your artwork by adding it to the Swatches panel. Select the color, and do one of the following:

   • Drag it from the Fill box, and drop it over the Swatches panel.
   • Click the New Swatch button (⬛) at the bottom of the Swatches panel.
   • Choose New Swatch from the Swatches panel menu.
   • Choose Create New Swatch from the Color panel menu.

3 You can choose color harmonies from the Color Guide panel. Color harmonies are used to generate a color scheme based on any color you want.

4 You use the Recolor Artwork dialog box to change the colors used in selected artwork, create and edit color groups, or reassign or reduce the colors in your artwork, among other functions.

5 You can add pattern swatches to the Swatches panel either by creating content for the pattern or by deselecting all content and choosing Object > Pattern > Make. In Pattern Editing mode, you can edit the pattern and preview it. You can also drag artwork into the swatch list in the Swatches panel.

6 Live Paint lets you paint vector graphics intuitively, by automatically detecting and correcting gaps that might otherwise affect the application of fills and strokes. Paths divide the drawing surface up into areas, any of which can be colored, regardless of whether the area is bounded by a single path or by segments of multiple paths.

7 WORKING WITH TYPE

Lesson overview

In this lesson, you'll learn how to do the following:

- Create area and point type.
- Convert between area and point type.
- Import text.
- Create columns of text.
- Change text attributes.
- Modify text with the Touch Type tool.
- Create and edit paragraph and character styles.
- Copy and apply text attributes by sampling type.
- Reshape text with a warp.
- Create type on a path and on shapes.
- Wrap type around an object.
- Create text outlines.

This lesson takes approximately an hour to complete.

Download the project files for this lesson from the Lesson & Update Files tab on your Account page at www.peachpit.com and store them on your computer in a convenient location, as described in the Getting Started section of this book.

Your Accounts page is also where you'll find any updates to the chapters or to the lesson files. Look on the Lesson & Update Files tab to access the most current content.

Text as a design element plays a major role in your illustrations. Like other objects, type can be painted, scaled, rotated, and more. In this lesson, discover how to create basic text and interesting text effects.

Getting started

You'll be working in one art file during this lesson, but before you begin, restore the default preferences for Adobe Illustrator CC. Then, open the finished art file for this lesson to see the illustration.

1   To ensure that the tools and panels function exactly as described in this lesson, delete or deactivate (by renaming) the Adobe Illustrator CC preferences file. See "Restoring default preferences," on page 3.

2   Start Adobe Illustrator CC.

● **Note:** If you have not already downloaded the project files for this lesson to your computer from your Account page, make sure to do so now. See "Getting Started" at the beginning of the book.

3   Choose File > Open. Locate the file named L7end.ai in the Lesson07 folder in the Lessons folder that you copied onto your hard disk. Open the L7end.ai file.

In this lesson, you will create the text for this poster. Leave it open for reference later in the lesson, if you like.

● **Note:** In Mac OS, when opening lesson files, you may need to click the round, green button in the upper-left corner of the Document window to maximize the window's size.

4   Choose File > Open. In the Open dialog box, navigate to the Lesson07 folder in the Lessons folder. Open the L7start.ai file.

This file already has non-text components in it. You will add all of the text elements to complete the poster and card.

5   Choose File > Save As. In the Save As dialog box, navigate to the Lesson07 folder and name the file **zoo.ai**. Leave the Save As Type option set to Adobe Illustrator (*.AI) (Windows) or the Format option set to Adobe Illustrator (ai) (Mac OS), and then click Save. In the Illustrator Options dialog box, leave the Illustrator options at their default settings and then click OK.

6   Choose View > Smart Guides, to deselect the Smart Guides.

7   Choose Window > Workspace > Reset Essentials.

● **Note:** If you don't see "Reset Essentials" in the Workspace menu, choose Window > Workspace > Essentials before choosing Window > Workspace > Reset Essentials.

Working with type

Type features are some of the most powerful tools in Illustrator. You can add a single line of type to your artwork, create columns and rows of text like you do in Adobe InDesign, flow text into a shape or along a path, and work with letterforms as graphic objects. You can create text in three different ways: as point type, area type, and type on a path. You will learn about each as you proceed through this lesson.

Creating point type

Point type is a horizontal or vertical line of text that begins where you click and expands as you enter characters. Each line of text is independent—the line expands or shrinks as you edit it but doesn't wrap to the next line unless you add a paragraph return or soft return. Entering text this way is useful for adding a headline or a few words to your artwork. Next, you will enter some text at the bottom of the poster.

1 Ensure that 1 Flyer is chosen in the Artboard Navigation menu in the lower-left corner of the Document window, and choose View > Fit Artboard In Window.

2 Select the Zoom tool (🔍) in the Tools panel, and click the upper-left corner of the artboard twice, *slowly*.

3 Choose Window > Layers to show the panel. Select the Text layer, if it's not already selected, to ensure that the content you create is on that layer. Click the Layers panel tab to collapse it.

4 Select the Type tool (T), and click in the white area to the left of the vertical guide in the upper-left corner of the artboard. The cursor appears on the artboard. Type **ZOO TALES** (in upper case).

By clicking with the Type tool, you create a point type object.

● **Note:** Point type that is scaled is printable, but the font size may not be a whole number (such as 12 pt).

5 Select the Selection tool (▶) in the Tools panel, and notice the bounding box around the text. Drag the right, middle bounding point (NOT the circle), to the right. Notice that the text stretches as you drag any bounding point.

Position the pointer.

Type the text.

Drag the point.

6 Choose Edit > Undo Scale, and then choose View > Fit Artboard In Window.

Creating area type

Area type uses the boundaries of an object to control the flow of characters, either horizontally or vertically. When the text reaches a boundary, it automatically wraps to fit inside the defined area. Entering text in this way is useful when you want to create one or more paragraphs, such as for a sign or a brochure.

To create area type, you click with the Type tool where you want the text and drag to create an area type object (also called a *text area*). When the cursor appears, you can type. You can also convert an existing shape or object to a type object by clicking the edge of an object (or inside the object) with the Type tool.

Next, you will create an area type object and enter more text.

1 Choose View > Smart Guides to select the Smart Guides.

2 Choose View > zoo sign, to zoom in to the zoo sign at the bottom of the artboard. The zoo sign view is at the bottom of the View menu, and you may need to scroll.

3 Select the Type tool (**T**). Position the cursor to the left of the striped orange and black tail, in the white area (see the red X in the figure). Click and drag down and to the right to create a text area with an approximate width of 1.5 in and a height of 1 in.

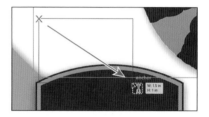

4 With the cursor in the new text area, type **Safari Zoo** (without a period).

5 Select the Selection tool (**↖**), and notice the bounding box around the text. Drag the right-center bounding point to the left, until the two words wrap within the object.

6 Drag the text object down and to the left of the black sign shape with the green stroke. Notice that you need to drag directly from the text, not from a blank area in the type area.

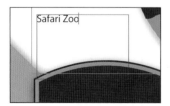

Type the text.

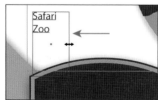

Resize the text object.

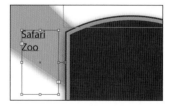

Note the result.

7 Choose Select > Deselect, and then choose File > Save.

Notice the out port (▶) of the left type object and the in port (▶) of the right type object (both circled in the previous figure). The port arrows indicate how the text is flowing from one to the other. If you delete the second type object, the text is pulled back into the original object as overflow text. Although not visible, the overflow text is not deleted. Later on, you will flow the text into a new text object you create.

▶ **Tip:** Another way to thread text between objects is to select an area type object, select the object (or objects) you want to link to, and then choose Type > Threaded Text > Create.

7   Choose Select > Deselect, and then choose File > Save.

Creating columns of text

You can easily create columns and rows of text by using the Area Type options. This can be useful for a single text area with multiple columns (instead of separate threaded text areas) or for organizing text, like a table or simple chart, for instance. Next, you'll add a few columns to an existing text area.

1   While still on the 2 Card artboard, with the Selection tool (▶), click to select the text area that starts with the orange text "Lion Circle..."

2   Choose Type > Area Type Options. In the Area Type Options dialog box, in the Columns section, change the Number to **2** and select Preview. The text won't change in appearance, but you should see the column guides. Click OK.

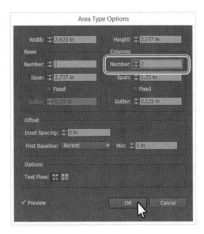

● **Note:** If the cursor is still in the type object, you don't have to select the text area with the Selection tool to access the Area Type options.

● **Note:** To learn more about the large number of options in the Area Type Options dialog box, search for "Creating Text" in Illustrator Help (Help > Illustrator Help).

Next, you'll drag the bottom of the type area up to see the columns at work.

3   Drag the bottom, middle bounding point up until the text flows into the second column, like you see in the figure. Try to balance the text in the columns, as well (make them even).

4   Choose Select > Deselect.

5   Choose File > Save.

Formatting type

When it comes to text, you can format it using character and paragraph formatting, apply fill and stroke attributes to it, and change its transparency. You can apply these changes to one character, a range of characters, or all characters in a type object that you select.

As you'll soon see, selecting the type object, rather than selecting the text inside, lets you apply global formatting options to all of the text in the object, including options from the Character and Paragraph panels, fill and stroke attributes, and transparency settings.

In this section, you'll discover how to change text attributes, such as size and font, and how to save that formatting as text styles.

Changing font family and font style

In this section, you'll learn two different methods for selecting a font. First, you'll change the font of selected text using the Font menu in the Control panel.

● **Note:** You may see the word "Character" instead of the Font menu listed in the Control panel. Click the word "Character" to reveal the Character panel.

1 Choose 1 Flyer from the Artboard Navigation menu in the lower-left corner of the Document window.

2 Select the Zoom tool (🔍) in the Tools panel, and click twice, slowly, in the center of the main threaded text object.

▶ **Tip:** If you double-click text with the Selection or Direct Selection tool, the Type tool becomes selected.

3 Select the Type tool (**T**) in the Tools panel, and position the pointer over the text. When the pointer changes to (Ⲓ), click to insert the cursor in the text. Choose Select > All, or press Ctrl+A (Windows) or Command+A (Mac OS), to select all the text in both threaded text objects.

If you miss the text, you will create point type. Choose Edit > Undo Type, if that's the case, and try again.

● **Note:** You most likely will need to use the scrollbar to the right of the font list to scroll through the list.

4 Click the arrow to the right of the Font menu, and scroll to find Myriad Pro. It may already be highlighted in the list.

5 Click the arrow to the left of Myriad Pro in the menu, and choose Semibold.

This sets the Font Family to Myriad Pro and the Font Style to Semibold for all of the threaded text.

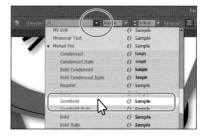

● **Note:** You can also choose the Font Family (such as Myriad Pro) and then choose the Font Style in the Font Style menu in the Control panel or in the Character panel.

Document setup options

By choosing File > Document Setup, you can access the Document Setup dialog box. In this dialog box, there are many text options, including the Highlight Substituted Fonts and Highlight Substituted Glyphs options, which are in the Bleed and View Options section.

In the Type Options section at the bottom of the dialog box, you can set the document language, change double and single quotes, edit the values for superscript, subscript, small caps, and more.

6 Scroll down the artboard so that you can see the text that starts with "Thursdays at..."

7 Click three times anywhere in the text to select the entire paragraph. Choose Type > Font to see a list of available fonts. Scroll down, and choose Adobe Garamond Pro > Bold Italic. If your font list is long, you may need to scroll quite far to find this font.

Note: Be careful when selecting text. If you attempt to drag across the text to select it, you may wind up creating a new text object.

Next, you will use Font search to locate a font. This next method is the most dynamic method for selecting a font.

8 Insert the cursor in the text "Safari Zoo" to the far left of the "Thursdays at..." text, and choose Select > All.

9 With the text selected, click whatever font is listed in the Font menu in the Control panel.

▶ **Tip:** Once a font name is selected, you can also click the X on the right side of the Font Family field to remove the current font shown.

10 Begin typing the letters "**ga**."

Notice that a menu appears beneath where you are typing. Illustrator filters through the list and displays the font names which contain "ga," regardless of where "ga" is in the font name and regardless of whether it's capitalized.

11 Continue typing an "r" to make it "gar," and the list is filtered further.

12 In the menu that appears beneath where you are typing, click to select "Adobe Garamond Pro" and Adobe Garamond Pro Regular is applied to the selected text.

When the menu of fonts appears, you could also use the arrow keys (up and down) to navigate the list of fonts. When the font you want is chosen, you can press Enter or Return to apply it.

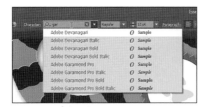 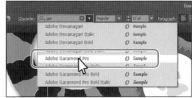

Continue typing with an "r."   Choose Adobe Garamond Pro.

Font styles are specific to each font family. Although you may have the Adobe Garamond Pro font family on your system, you may not have the bold or italic styles of that family.

Changing font size

1 With the "Safari Zoo" text and Type tool (T) still selected, choose 36 pt from the preset sizes in the Font Size menu in the Control panel.

2 Type **37** in the Font Size field in the Control panel, and press Enter or Return.

The text may not fit anymore, and the overset icon (⊞) appears in the out port of the text object. Because it's an area type object, it doesn't resize when the text resizes.

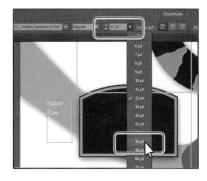

> ▶ **Tip:** You can dynamically change the font size of selected text using keyboard shortcuts. To increase the font size in increments of 2 points, press Ctrl+Shift+> (Windows) or Command+Shift+> (Mac OS). To reduce the font size, press Ctrl+Shift+< (Windows) or Command+Shift+< (Mac OS).

3 Select the Selection tool (▶), and drag the lower-right corner of the text object down and to the right until the text fits. Make sure that the word "Zoo" is still on its own line in the text object. You'll adjust the text later to make it look better.

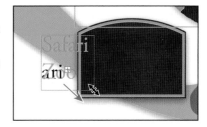

> ▶ **Tip:** You can click the Eyeglass icon (🔍) to the left of the field and choose to search the first word only. You can also open the Character panel (Window > Type > Character) and search for fonts by typing the name.

> ● **Note:** You may see the word "Character" instead of the Font Size field in the Control panel. Click the word "Character" to reveal the Character panel.

4   Choose View > Fit Artboard In Window.

5   With the Selection tool (), click the "ZOO TALES" text object at the top of the artboard.

6   Type **74** in the Font Size field in the Control panel, and press Enter or Return.

7   Drag the text object down, if need be, so that it stays on the artboard. Leave the text object selected.

    Notice that the text object resizes since it's point type.

Changing font color

You can change the appearance of text by applying fills, strokes, and more. In this example, you will change the stroke and then the fill of selected text.

1   With the "ZOO TALES" text object still selected, click the Stroke color in the Control panel. When the Swatches panel appears, select White. The text stroke changes to white.

2   Change the Stroke weight of the text to **2 pt** in the Control panel.

3   Select the Type tool (**T**) in the Tools panel, and click on the text in the threaded text frames in the middle of the artboard. Press Ctrl+A (Windows) or Command+A (Mac OS) to select all of the text.

4   Click the Fill color in the Control panel. When the Swatches panel appears, select white. Change the Font Size by typing **15 pt** in the Control panel.

● **Note:** The text that once fit in the two threaded text objects no longer fits. That's okay, since you'll get it all to fit shortly.

5 Choose Select > Deselect.

6 Select the Selection tool (**▶**). Shift-click the two text objects, at the bottom of the artboard, that contain the words "Safari Zoo" and "Thursdays at…"

Note: You may find that, if a text object contains text with different formatting, like a heading and body text, this method will not work.

7 Change the Fill color in the Control panel to white.

You can either select the text or the text object to change most of the formatting, including fill and stroke.

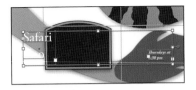

8 Choose Select > Deselect, and then choose Chose File > Save.

Changing additional text attributes

You can change many additional text attributes in the Character panel, which you can access by clicking the underlined word "Character" in the Control panel or by choosing Window > Type > Character. Below are the formatting options available in the Character panel when all options are showing.

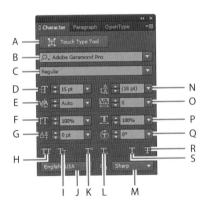

A. Touch Type tool	K. Superscript
B. Font family	L. Subscript
C. Font style	M. Text anti-aliasing
D. Font size	N. Leading
E. Kerning	O. Tracking
F. Vertical scale	P. Horizontal scale
G. Baseline shift	Q. Character rotation
H. All caps	R. Strikethrough
I. Small caps	S. Underline
J. Language	

In this section, you will apply some of the many possible attributes to experiment with the different ways you can format text.

1 Select the Type tool (**T**), and click in either of the threaded text objects that contain the placed text. Choose Select > All.

It's difficult to see the text since it's white and the background is white. You'll fix that next by turning on a layer.

2 Click the Layers panel icon (■) to expand the panel. Click the visibility column to the left of the layer named Background. Click the Layers panel tab to collapse it.

3 Click the word "Character" in the Control panel, and click the down arrow to the left of the Leading () field until the value is 17 pt.

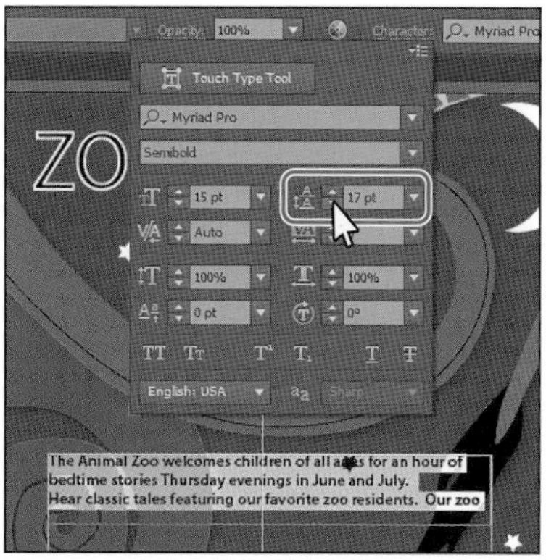

Leading is the vertical space between lines. Notice the change in the vertical distance between the lines. Adjusting the leading can be useful for fitting text into a text area. Like other Character panel options, you can also type in a value for the Leading.

4 With the Type tool selected, insert the cursor in the text "Safari Zoo." With the cursor in the text, triple-click to select the entire paragraph.

5 Choose Window > Type > Character. With the text selected, click the Tracking icon () in the Character panel, to select the Tracking field, and type **–50**. Press Enter or Return.

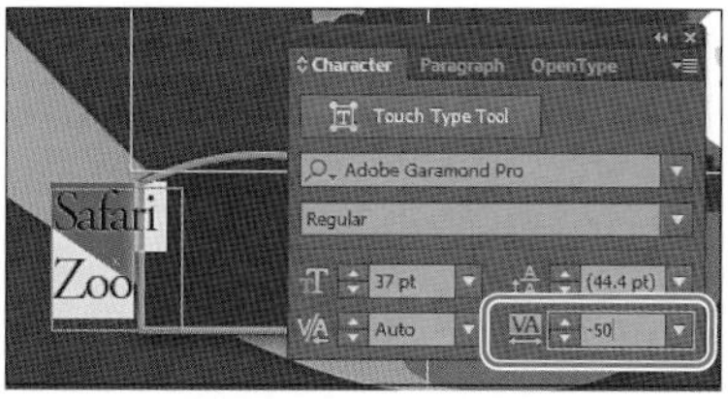

Tracking changes the spacing between characters. A positive value pushes the letters apart horizontally; a negative value pulls the letters closer together.

● **Note:** If you choose to open the Character panel (Window > Type > Character), you may need to click the double arrow next to the word "Character" in the panel tab to reveal more options.

6 Choose Type > Change Case > UPPERCASE.

7 With the Selection tool (), drag the lower-right corner of the "SAFARI ZOO" text object to the right and down until the text fits again on two lines.

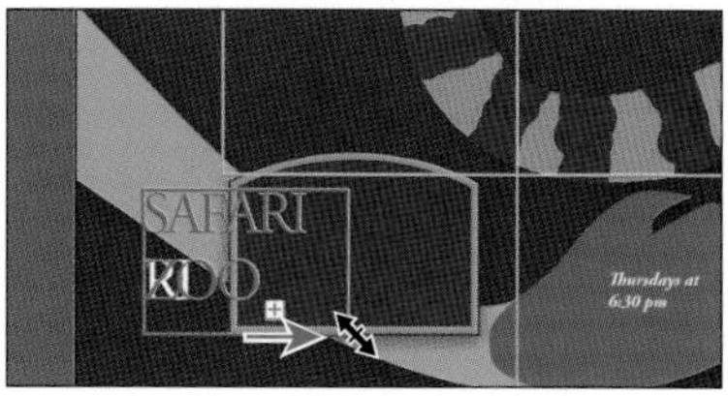

8 With the Type tool, insert the cursor in the text that begins with "Thursdays at…" With the cursor in the text, triple-click to select the entire paragraph.

9 Change the Font Size to **33 pt** in the Character panel. You'll need to either click the up arrow or type the value in.

10 With the Selection tool, drag the lower-right corner of the "Thursdays at…" text object to the right and down until the text fits again on two lines.

11 Click the double-arrow on the left side of the Character panel tab to show more options. With the text still selected, click the Vertical Scale icon (![icon]) in the Character panel to select the value and type **120**. Press Enter or Return to close the panel.

Leave the Character panel open.

12 Choose View > Fit Artboard In Window, and then choose Select > Deselect.

Modifying text with the Touch Type tool

Using the Touch Type tool, you can modify the properties of a character, like size, scale, and rotation, using a mouse cursor or touch controls. This is a very visual (and more fun) way of applying the character formatting properties: baseline shift, horizontal and vertical scale, rotation, and kerning.

Next, you are going to use the Touch Type tool to alter the appearance of the "ZOO TALES" headline at the top of the artboard.

1 Select the Zoom tool (![icon]), and click the headline "ZOO TALES," several times, to zoom in closely. Make sure you can still see all of the "ZOO TALES" text.

2 With the Selection tool (![icon]), click to select the "ZOO TALES" text object. Select whatever font is listed in the Font menu in the Control panel, and type **Gar**. In the menu that appears beneath where you are typing, click to select Adobe Garamond Pro Bold.

> **Tip:** You can also click and hold down the mouse button on the Type tool (T) in the Tools panel, and select the Touch Type tool (![icon]) from the menu.

3 Click the Touch Type Tool button at the top of the Character panel.

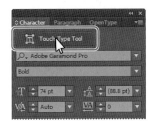

A message appears at the top of the Document window telling you to tap a character to select it.

4 Click the letter "Z" to select it. A box with a dot above it appears around the letter. The different points around the box allow you to adjust the character in different ways, as you'll see.

5 Choose View > Smart Guides.

> **Tip:** By dragging the upper-left corner point of the box, you can adjust just the vertical scale. By dragging the lower-right corner of the box, you can adjust the horizontal scale.

6 Click and drag the upper-right corner of the box away from the center, to make the letter larger. Stop dragging when you see roughly 190% for width (W:) and height (H:) in the measurement label.

Notice that the movement is constrained—width and height change together proportionally. You just adjusted the horizontal scale and the vertical scale for the letter "Z" in the Character panel.

7   Look in the Character panel to see that the Horizontal Scale and Vertical Scale
    values are roughly 190%.

Position the pointer.   Drag to resize the letter "Z."   Notice the scaling.

8   With the letter "Z" still selected, position the pointer in the center of the letter.
    The pointer will change appearance (▶). Click and drag the letter down until the
    Baseline value shows approximately −24 pt in the gray measurement label.

    You just edited the baseline shift of the letter in the Character panel.

9   Click the "O" to the right of the "Z," and drag the rotate handle (the circle
    above the letter) counter-clockwise until you see approximately 20° in the
    measurement label.

10 Click and drag the upper-right corner of the box around the selected "O," away
    from the center, to make the letter larger. Stop dragging when you see roughly
    125% for width (W:) and height (H:) in the measurement label.

Drag the letter "Z."   Rotate the letter "o."   Drag to resize the letter "o."

11 Drag the letter "O" from the center, to the
    left, until it looks something like the figure.

    ▶ **Tip:** You can also nudge the selected letter with the
    arrow keys.

▶ **Tip:** Dragging a
character left adjusts
the kerning between
that character and the
character to the left.
Dragging a character
right adjusts the
kerning between that
character and the
character to the right.

12 Click to select the second letter "O" in "ZOO," and change the following using the Touch Type tool:

- Rotate the letter clockwise 35° (clockwise rotation shows a negative value).
- Click and drag (what was) the upper-right corner of the box, away from the center, until you see roughly 105% for width (W:) and height (H:) in the measurement label.
- Drag the letter from the center into the position you see in the figure.

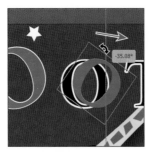

Rotate the letter "O."

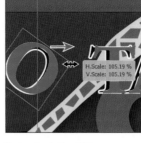

Resize the letter "O."

Drag the letter into position.

13 Click to select the letter "T" in "TALES," and change the following using the Touch Type tool:

- Click and drag the upper-right corner of the box, away from the center, until you see roughly 150% for width (W:) and height (H:) in the measurement label.
- Drag the letter from the center down and to the left (a bit closer to the second "O" in "ZOO"), into the position you see in the figure.
- Click and drag the upper-left point up until you see a Vertical Scale of 185%.

Resize the letter "T."

Drag the letter "T" into position.

Change the Vertical Scale.

14 Click the letter "A" in "TALES." Drag the letter straight to the left to make it closer to the "T." See the figure for placement. Try not to drag up or down. The measurement label will show Baseline Shift: 0 pt.

Changing paragraph attributes

As with character attributes, you can set paragraph attributes, such as alignment or indenting, before you enter new type or to change the appearance of existing type. If you select several type paths and type containers, you can set attributes for them all at the same time. Most of this type of formatting is done in the Paragraph panel, which you can access by clicking the underlined word "Paragraph" in the Control panel or by choosing Window > Type > Paragraph. Below are the formatting options available in the Paragraph panel.

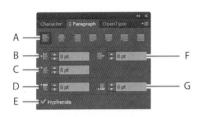

A. Alignments
B. Left indent
C. First-line left indent
D. Space before paragraph

E. Hyphenate
F. Right indent
G. Space after paragraph

Next, you'll add more space after all the paragraphs in the main text.

1   Choose View > Fit Artboard In Window.

2   Position the pointer over the Touch Type tool (⊞) in the Tools panel, click and hold down the mouse button, and select the Type tool (T). Insert the cursor in the text in middle of the artboard that begins with "The Animal Zoo welcomes..."

3   Click the word "Paragraph" in the Control panel to open the Paragraph panel.

4   Type **11 pt** in the Space After Paragraph text field (in the lower-right corner), and press Enter or Return.

Setting a spacing value after paragraphs, rather than pressing the Return key, is useful for maintaining consistency and ease of editing later.

5   With the Selection tool (▶), click the text "SAFARI ZOO" and then Shift-click the text "Thursdays at 6:30 pm" to select the two text objects only. Choose Window > Type > Paragraph, to open the Paragraph panel. In the panel, click the Align Center button (▤).

● **Note:** You can also click the Paragraph panel tab in the Character panel group, if the Character panel is still open.

6   Close the Paragraph panel group.

7   Choose Select > Deselect, and then choose File > Save.

Working with glyphs

Glyphs are characters within a certain typeface that may be harder to find, like a bullet point or a registration symbol. In Illustrator, the Glyphs panel is used to insert type characters, like trademark symbols (™). The panel shows all of the characters (glyphs) available for a given font.

1   Select the Zoom tool (🔍) in the Tools panel, and drag a marquee around the first threaded text object in the middle of the artboard.

2   Select the Type tool (T) in the Tools panel, and click to place the cursor right after the text "The Animal Zoo" in the first line.

3   Choose Type > Glyphs to open the Glyphs panel.

4   In the Glyphs panel, scroll down until you see a copyright symbol (©). Double-click the symbol to insert it at the text insertion point. Close the Glyphs panel.

▶ Tip: The Glyphs panel lets you select another font in the bottom of the panel. You can also increase the size of the glyph icons by clicking the larger mountain (⬔) in the lower-right corner or make the icons smaller by clicking the smaller mountain (⬔).

5   With the Type tool, select the copyright symbol (©) you just inserted.

6   Click the word "Character" in the Control panel (or choose Window > Type > Character), and click the Superscript button (T¹) near the bottom of the panel.

Instead of applying the generic Superscript option, you can also change the font size and edit the Baseline Shift (A↕) in the Character panel for more control.

7   Click with the Type tool between the word "Zoo" and the copyright symbol until the cursor is inserted. The Character panel closes.

▶ Tip: To remove kerning changes, insert the cursor in the text and choose Auto from the Kerning menu.

8   Click the word "Character" again, and choose −25 from the Kerning menu in the Character panel.

Kerning is similar to tracking, but it adds or subtracts space between a pair of characters. It's useful for situations such as this one, when you're working with a glyph.

9   Choose Select > Deselect, and then choose File > Save.

Resizing and reshaping type objects

You can create unique type object shapes by reshaping them using a variety of methods, including the Direct Selection tool. In this next section, you'll reshape and resize type objects to better fit text in them.

1   Choose View > Fit All In Window.

At times, you may need to reflow the text between text objects. Next, you will learn how to resize, unlink, relink, and reshape type objects.

2   With the Selection tool (▸), click the text in the main type object on the larger artboard that is threaded, to select it. Drag the right, middle point to the left to the vertical guide.

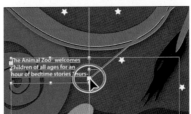

3   Double-click the out port (▶) in the lower-right corner of the text object (where the thread [blue line] is coming out).

Because the two text objects were threaded, double-clicking the out port of the first text object (or the in port of the second type object) breaks the connection between them. Any text threaded between the three type objects flows back into the first one. The other text object is still there, but it has no stroke or fill.

● **Note:** It may be difficult to double-click on the out port since you are zoomed out. You may wish to zoom in closer to the type area.

4   Using the Selection tool, drag the bottom, middle handle of the bounding box down until the text "...favorite stuffed animal!" is the last text in the object. The text object changes in size vertically.

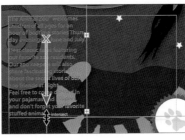

5   With the Selection tool, click the out port (⊞) in the lower-right corner of the type object. The pointer changes to the loaded text icon (▤).

6 Position the loaded text icon (⊞) to the right of the existing type object and down from its top edge (see the figure). Click, and a new type object is created that should roughly fit into the aqua guide box. Leave the new type object selected.

When type objects are threaded, you can move them anywhere and still maintain the connection between them. When type objects are resized, especially those in the beginning of the thread, text can reflow. Now you will link the new type object to the type object on the Card artboard.

● **Note:** It may be difficult to click the out port since there is other artwork there. You can always move the type object, click the out port, and continue on to the next steps. Later, moving it back into position.

7 With the Selection tool, click the out port (⊞) in the lower-right corner of the new type object. The pointer changes to the loaded text icon (⊞).

8 Choose View > Outline to see the artwork edges.

9 On the 2 Card artboard, position the loaded text icon on the edge (boundary) of the existing type object (see the figure), and click when the pointer changes to this (▸⊕).

10 Choose View > Preview.

11 Using the Selection tool, on the 1 Flyer artboard, drag the bottom, middle handle of the right-hand type object up until the text "...for supporting this program." is the last text in the object. The text object changes in size vertically.

12 With the Type tool (T), position the pointer over the threaded text on the 2 Card artboard. When the cursor changes to (Ɪ), click three times to select the paragraph.

13 Change the Font Size to **11 pt** in the Control panel. Click the word "Character" in the Control panel and, in the Character panel, change the Leading to **15 pt**.

14 Select the Direct Selection tool (▸). Click the upper-right corner of the type object to select the anchor point. Drag that point to the left to adjust the shape of the path to fit the orange shape.

You may need to adjust the shape or the size/leading to fit the last paragraph in the type object, if you see the overset icon (⊞).

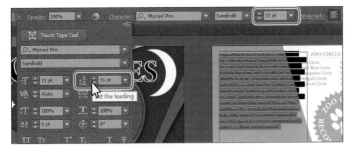

Adjust the Font Size and Leading.

Edit the type object.

15 Choose File > Save.

Creating and applying text styles

Styles allow you to format text consistently and are helpful when text attributes need to be globally updated. Once a style is created, you only need to edit the saved style. Then, all text formatted with that style is updated.

Illustrator provides two types of text styles:

- **Paragraph**—Retains character and paragraph attributes and applies them to an entire paragraph.
- **Character**—Retains the character attributes and applies them to selected text.

Creating and applying a paragraph style

First, you will create a paragraph style for the body copy.

1 Choose 1 Flyer from the Artboard Navigation menu in the lower-left corner of the Document window (if it's not already chosen). Choose View > Fit Artboard In Window.

2 With the Type tool (**T**) selected, insert the cursor anywhere in the first paragraph in the first threaded type object that starts with "The Animal Zoo©...," except for next to the © (copyright symbol).

You do not need to select text to create a paragraph style, but you do have to place the text insertion point in the text that has the attributes you want to save.

3 Choose Window > Type > Paragraph Styles, and click the Create New Style button (⬚) at the bottom of the Paragraph Styles panel.

This creates a new paragraph style in the panel, called Paragraph Style 1. This style captures the character and paragraph formatting from the paragraph.

4 Double-click the style name Paragraph Style 1 in the list of styles. Change the name of the style to **Body**, and press Enter or Return to edit the name inline.

By double-clicking the style to edit the name, you are also applying the new style to the paragraph (where the cursor is). This means that if you edit the Body paragraph style, this paragraph will update, as well.

● **Note:** Make sure not to select the threaded text on the card, on the artboard 2 Card.

5 With the Type tool selected, click and drag from before the first word in the paragraph that starts with the text "Hear classic tales…" to after the last word "… for supporting this program." in the second "column" to select it.

6 Click the Body style in the Paragraph Styles panel.

Notice that a plus sign (+) appears to the right of the Body style name. The plus sign indicates that the style has an override. An *override* is any formatting that doesn't match the attributes defined by the style, for example, if you changed the font size for the selected paragraph.

● **Note:** If you place a Microsoft Word document and choose to keep the formatting, the styles used in the Word document may be brought into the Illustrator document and may appear in the Paragraph Styles panel.

7 Press the Alt (Windows) or Option (Mac OS) key, and select the Body style again in the Paragraph Styles panel to overwrite existing attributes on the selected text.

The text attributes of the Body style are applied to the selected text, including the Space After value, so the text may no longer all fit in the two columns.

8 Choose Select > Deselect.

9 Select the Selection tool (🔾), and click to select the type object on the right (the right column). Click and drag the bottom bounding point down until the text "supporting this program" is the last to appear in the column (if necessary).

10 With the Type tool selected, click three times in the first paragraph in the first type object that starts with "The Animal Zoo©…" to select it.

11 Alt-click (Windows) or Option-click (Mac OS) the Body style in the Paragraph Styles panel.

12 Choose Select > Deselect.

The copyright symbol has lost its formatting. The formatting applied to the copyright was local formatting. Alt-clicking (Windows) or Option-clicking (Mac OS) the style name removed it.

Editing a paragraph style

After creating a paragraph style, you can easily edit the style formatting. Then, anywhere the style has been applied, the formatting will be automatically updated.

1 Double-click to the right of Body in the Paragraph Styles panel list to open the Paragraph Style Options dialog box.

2 Select the Indents And Spacing category on the left side of the dialog box.

3 Change the Space After to **8 pt**.

Since Preview is selected, by default, you can move the dialog box out of the way to see the text change.

4 Click OK.

5 Choose File > Save.

There are many options for working with paragraph styles, most of which are found in the Paragraph Styles panel menu, including duplicating, deleting, and editing paragraph styles.

Tip: You can also choose Paragraph Style Options from the Paragraph Styles panel menu (▤).

● **Note:** You may need to click and drag the bottom bounding point up until the text "supporting this program" is the last to appear in the column (if necessary).

Creating and applying a character style

Character styles, unlike paragraph styles, can only be applied to selected text and can only contain character formatting. Next, you will create a character style from text styling within the columns of text.

1 Choose View > Zoom In, twice, to zoom in to the threaded text in the center.

2 Using the Type tool (**T**), in the first paragraph, select "The Animal Zoo©."

3 Click the Fill color, and select the swatch named gold in the Control panel.

4 Click the word "Character" in the Control panel, and choose Italic from the Font Style menu, and then click the Underline button (**T̲**) to underline the text.

● **Note:** You may see the word "Character" instead of the Font Style menu in the Control panel. Click the word "Character" to reveal the Character panel.

Change the text color.

Edit other attributes.

5 In the Paragraph Styles panel group, click the Character Styles panel tab.

6 In the Character Styles panel, Alt-click (Windows) or Option-click (Mac OS) the Create New Style button (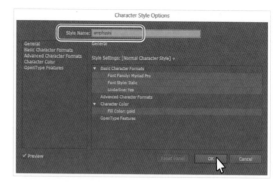) at the bottom of the Character Styles panel.

Alt-clicking (Windows) or Option-clicking (Mac OS) the Create New Style button in the Character or Paragraph Styles panel allows you to name the style as it is added to the panel.

7 Name the style **emphasis**, and click OK.

The style records the attributes applied to your selected text.

8 With the text still selected, Alt-click (Windows) or Option-click (Mac OS) the style named emphasis in the Character Styles panel to assign the style to that text so that it will update if the style changes.

● **Note:** You must select the entire phrase rather than just placing the cursor in the text.

9 In the next column (text object), select the text "This program is free" and apply the emphasis style while pressing the Alt (Windows) or Option (Mac OS) key.

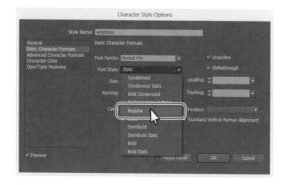

10 Choose Select > Deselect.

Editing a character style

After creating a character style, you can easily edit the style formatting, and, anywhere the style is applied, the formatting will be automatically updated.

1 Double-click to the right of the emphasis style name in the Character Styles panel (*not* the style name itself). In the Character Style Options dialog box, make sure that Preview is selected. Click the Basic Character Formats category on the left side of the dialog box, and choose Regular from the Font Style menu. Click OK.

If you don't see the text align options in the Control panel, click the word "Paragraph" to reveal the Paragraph panel.

Next, you'll reposition the text on the path so that all of the text appears.

10 Select the Selection tool, and position the pointer over the line on the left edge of the text (just to the left of the "B"). When you see this cursor (▸₊), click and drag to the left—all the way to the left end of the path.

Tip box:

> **Tip:** With the path or the text on the path selected, you can choose Type > Type On A Path > Type On A Path Options to set more options.

11 Choose Select > Deselect, and then choose File > Save.

Creating type on a closed path

Next, you will add text around a circle.

1 Select the Zoom tool (🔍) in the Tools panel, and click the yellow paw print three times, slowly, to zoom in.

2 With the Selection tool (▸), Shift-click the threaded type object and the yellow paw print to select both and choose Object > Hide > Selection.

3 Select the Type tool (T), and position the pointer over the edge of the white circle. The Type cursor (ⓘ) changes to a Type cursor with a circle (ⓘ). This indicates that, if you click (*don't click*), text will be placed *inside* of the circle, creating a type object in the shape of a circle.

4 While pressing the Alt (Windows) or Option (Mac OS) key, position the pointer over the left side of the circle. The insertion point with an intersecting wavy path (⤵) appears. Click and type **ZOO CIRCLE**. The text flows on the circular path. Click three times to select the text.

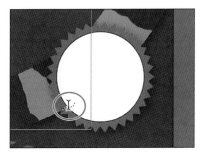

> ● **Note:** Instead of pressing the Alt (Windows) or Option (Mac OS) key to allow the Type tool to type on a path, you can select the Type On A Path tool (➚) by holding down the Type tool in the Tools panel.

5 With the text still selected, in the Control panel, change the font size to **16 pt**, the Font Style to Bold (the Font Family should already be Adobe Garamond Pro) and the Fill color to the swatch named gold.

Next, you will adjust the position of the text.

● **Note:** Brackets appear at the beginning of the type, at the end of the path, and at the midpoint between the start and end brackets. All of these brackets can be adjusted to reposition the text in the path.

6   Select the Selection tool in the Tools panel. Position the pointer over the line on the left end of the text (to the left of the word "ZOO"). That line is called a *bracket*. When you see this cursor (⯆), with an arrow pointing to the right, drag up around the circle in a clockwise fashion. See the figure for position.

Editing type on a path options

When you create type on a path, you can set options to change the appearance of the text, including: effects, alignment, and spacing. Next, you'll edit the type on a path options for the text on the circle.

● **Note:** To learn about the Type On A Path options, search for "Creating type on a path" in Illustrator Help (Help > Illustrator Help).

1   With the path type object selected with the Selection tool, choose Type > Type On A Path > Type On A Path Options. In the Type On A Path Options dialog box, select Preview and change the following options:

• Choose **Skew** from the Effect menu and then choose **Rainbow**.
• Align To Path: **Ascender**
• Spacing: **–18 pt**

Click OK.

2   With the Selection tool (▶), position the pointer over the line on the left end of the text (to the left of the word "ZOO"). When you see this cursor (⯆), drag down around the circle in a counter-clockwise fashion. See the figure for position.

Now, you will create text that flows along the bottom of the circle shape. To do so, you will copy the text on a path you just created and make some simple edits.

3   With the type on a path still selected, choose Edit > Copy.

4   Choose Object > Lock > Selection, to lock the copied type on a path.

5   Choose Edit > Paste In Front, to paste a copy in the same position.

6   Choose Type > Type On A Path > Type On
    A Path Options. In the Type On A Path
    Options dialog box, select Preview and
    change the following options:

    • Flip: **Selected** (to flip the direction of the
      text along the path)
    • Align To Path: **Descender**
    • Spacing: **20 pt**

    Click OK.

7   Select the Type tool (**T**), and triple-click the text "ZOO CIRCLE."
    Type **BECOME A MEMBER**.

8   Select the Selection tool. Position the pointer
    over the line on the left end of the text (to the left
    of the word "BECOME..."). When you see this
    cursor (⤵), with an arrow pointing to the left, drag
    down and to the left.

9   Choose Object > Show All, and then choose
    Object > Unlock All.

10 Choose Select > Deselect.

Wrapping text around an object

In Illustrator, you can easily wrap text around objects, like type objects, imported
images, and vector artwork, to avoid text running over those objects or to create
interesting design effects. Next, you will wrap text around the text on a path object.

1   With the Selection tool, click directly on the "ZOO CIRCLE" text to select it.
    Choose Object > Arrange > Bring To Front.

2   Choose Object > Text Wrap > Make. Click OK if a dialog box appears. The text
    in the column wraps around the text on a path shape.

    If you move the object with the text wrap applied, the text responds and
    wraps differently.

3   Choose Object > Text Wrap > Text
    Wrap Options. In the Text Wrap
    Options dialog box, change Offset to
    13 pt and select Preview to see the
    change. Click OK.

● **Note:** To wrap text
around an object, the
object that the text is
to wrap around must
be in the same layer as
the text and must be
located above the text
in the layer hierarchy.

● **Note:** Your text may wrap differently, and that's okay.

4   With the Selection tool (🠕), drag the bottom, middle point of the threaded text box down to make sure that the text "...for supporting this program" is the last showing.

5   Choose View > Fit Artboard In Window.

6   Choose Select > Deselect.

Creating text outlines

Converting text to outlines means converting text into *vector outlines* that you can edit and manipulate as you would any other graphic object. Text outlines are useful for changing the look of large display type, but they are rarely useful for body text or other type at small sizes. The file recipient doesn't need to have your fonts installed to open and view the file correctly.

When you create outlines from text, you should consider that text as no longer editable. Also, bitmap fonts and outline-protected fonts cannot be converted to outlines, and outlining text that is less than 10 points in size is not recommended. When type is converted to outlines, the type loses its *hints*—instructions built into outline fonts to adjust their shape to display or print optimally at many sizes. You must also convert all type in a selection to outlines; you cannot convert a single letter within a type object.

Next, you will convert the main heading to outlines and position content.

● **Note:** To keep your original text, you can save a layer with the original text (and hide the layer).

1   With the Selection tool (🠕), click the heading text "Zoo Tales" at the top of the artboard to select it. Choose Type > Create Outlines. Drag it into position like you see in the figure.

The text is no longer linked to a particular font. Instead, it is now artwork, much like any other vector art in your illustration.

2   With the Selection tool, drag the text "Thursdays at 6:30 pm" at the bottom of the artboard into position, like you see in the figure.

3   Choose View > Guides > Hide Guides, and then choose Select > Deselect.

4   Choose File > Save, and then choose File > Close.

Review questions

1 Name two methods for creating a text area in Adobe Illustrator.

2 What does the Touch Type tool let you do?

3 What is *overflow text*?

4 What is *text threading*?

5 What is the difference between a *character style* and a *paragraph style*?

6 What is the advantage of converting text to outlines?

Review answers

1 The following methods can be used for creating text areas:

- With the Type tool (**T**), click the artboard and start typing when the cursor appears. A text area is created to accommodate the text.

- With the Type tool, drag to create a text area. Type when a cursor appears.

- With the Type tool, click a path or closed shape to convert it to text on a path or click in a text area. Alt-clicking (Windows) or Option-clicking (Mac OS) when crossing over the stroke of a closed path creates text around the shape.

2 The Touch Type tool allows you to visually edit certain character formatting options for individual characters in text. You can edit the character rotation, kerning, baseline shift, and horizontal and vertical scale of text.

3 *Overflow text* is when text does not fit within an area type object. A red plus sign (⊞) in an out port indicates that the object contains additional text.

4 *Text threading* allows you to continue text from one object to the next by linking type objects. Linked type objects can be of any shape; however, the text must be entered in an area or along a path (not at a point).

5 A *character style* can be applied to selected text only. A *paragraph style* is applied to an entire paragraph. Paragraph styles are best for indents, margins, and line spacing.

6 Converting text to outlines eliminates the need to send the fonts along with the file when sharing with others.

8 WORKING WITH LAYERS

Lesson overview

In this lesson, you'll learn how to do the following:

- Work with the Layers panel.

- Create, rearrange, and lock layers and sublayers.

- Move objects between layers.

- Copy and paste objects and their layers from one file to another.

- Merge layers into a single layer.

- Make a layer clipping mask.

- Locate objects in the Layers panel.

- Apply an appearance attribute to objects and layers.

- Isolate content in a layer.

 This lesson takes approximately 45 minutes to complete.

Download the project files for this lesson from the Lesson & Update Files tab on your Account page at www.peachpit.com and store them on your computer in a convenient location, as described in the Getting Started section of this book.

Your Accounts page is also where you'll find any updates to the chapters or to the lesson files. Look on the Lesson & Update Files tab to access the most current content.

Pasting layers

To complete the television, you'll copy and paste the remaining pieces of artwork from another file. You can paste a layered file into another file and keep the layers intact.

1   Choose Window > Workspace > Reset Essentials.

2   Choose File > Open, and open the show.ai file, located in the Lesson08 folder in the Lessons folder on your hard disk.

3   Click the Layers panel icon () to show the panel. To see how the objects in each layer are organized, Alt-click (Windows) or Option-click (Mac OS) the eye icon ( ) for each layer in the Layers panel to show one layer and hide the others. You can also click the triangles ( ) to the left of the layer names to expand and collapse the layers for further inspection. When you're finished, make sure that all the layers are showing and that they are collapsed.

4   Choose Select > All, and then choose Edit > Copy to select and copy the game show content to the clipboard.

5   Choose File > Close to close the show.ai file without saving any changes. If a warning dialog box appears, click No (Windows) or Don't Save (Mac OS).

6   In the tv.ai file, click the Layers panel menu icon ( ) and choose Paste Remembers Layers. A check mark next to the option indicates that it's selected.

When Paste Remembers Layers is selected, artwork is pasted into the layer(s) from which it was copied, regardless of which layer is active in the Layers panel. If the option is not selected, all objects are pasted into the active layer and the layers from the original file are not pasted in.

● **Note:** If the target document has a layer of the same name, Illustrator combines the pasted content into a layer of the same name.

7   Choose Edit > Paste, to paste the game show content onto the television.

The Paste Remembers Layers option causes the show.ai layers to be pasted as four separate layers at the top of the Layers panel (Shadow/highlight, Text, Game board, and Background).

8 With the Selection tool (▶), drag the new content on top of the gray, rounded rectangle to center it as best you can. See the figure for placement help.

Now, you'll move the newly pasted layers into the Screen layer.

9 In the Layers panel, select the Shadow/ highlight layer (if it's not already selected) and Shift-click the Background layer name. Drag any of the four selected layers down on top of the Screen layer. The artwork should not change in appearance.

Drag the selected layers.   Note the result.

The four pasted layers become sublayers of the Screen layer. Notice that they keep their individual layer colors.

10 Choose Select > Deselect, and then choose File > Save.

Creating a clipping mask

The Layers panel lets you create clipping masks to control whether artwork on a layer (or in a group) is hidden or revealed. A *clipping mask* is an object or group of objects which masks (with its shape) artwork below it, in the same layer or sublayer, so that only artwork within the shape is visible.

Now, you'll create a clipping mask with the white, rounded rectangle shape at the top of the Screen layer.

1 Drag the bottom of the Layers panel down to reveal all of the layers.

In the Layers panel, a masking object must be above the objects it masks. You can create a clipping mask for an entire layer, a sublayer, or a group of objects. Because you want to mask all of the content in the Screen layer, the clipping object needs to be at the top of the Screen layer, which is what you did in the previous section.

2 Click the <Path> sublayer at the bottom of
   the Screen layer. Drag the selected <Path>
   sublayer up onto the Screen layer name.
   When the layer is highlighted, release the
   mouse button to position the <Path> on the
   top of the layer.

● **Note:** Deselecting
the artwork on
the artwork on
the artboard is not
necessary to complete
the next steps, but
it can be helpful for
viewing the artwork.

   The white, rounded rectangle will now be on
   top of the other artwork on the Screen layer.

3 Select the Screen layer to highlight it in the Layers panel. Click the Make/
   Release Clipping Mask button (▣) at the bottom of the Layers panel.

▶ **Tip:** To release the
clipping mask, you can
select the Screen layer
again and click the
same Make/Release
Clipping Mask button.

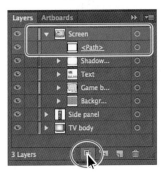

   The name of the <Path> sublayer is underlined to indicate that it is the masking
   shape. On the artboard, the <Path> sublayer has hidden the parts of the screen
   content that extended outside of the shape.

Merging layers

To streamline your artwork, you can merge layers, sublayers, or groups to combine
the contents into one layer, sublayer, or group. Note that items will be merged into
the layer or group that you selected last. Next, you will merge a few layers into one.

1 Click the Text sublayer in the Layers panel to
   highlight it, and then Shift-click to highlight
   the Background sublayer.

   Notice that the current layer indicator (◣)
   shows the last highlighted layer as the active
   layer. The last layer you select determines the
   name and color of the merged layer.

● **Note:** Layers can
only merge with other
layers that are on the
same hierarchical level
in the Layers panel.
Likewise, sublayers can
only merge with other
sublayers that are in
the same layer and on
the same hierarchical
level. Objects can't be
merged with other
objects.

2   Click the Layers panel menu icon (), and choose Merge Selected to merge the content from the three sublayers into the Background sublayer.

The objects on the merged layers retain their original stacking order and are added above the objects in the destination layer.

3   Double-click the thumbnail to the left of the Background layer name, or double-click directly to the right of the Background layer name. In the Layer Options dialog box, choose Green from the Color menu to match the Screen layer color. Click OK.

Changing the layer color to match the main layer isn't necessary. The Layer Options dialog box has a lot of the options you've already worked with, including naming layers, Preview or Outline mode, locking layers, and showing and hiding layers. You can also deselect the Print option in the Layer Options dialog box, and any content on that layer will not print.

4   Alt-click (Windows) or Option-click (Mac OS) the eye icon (👁) to the left of the Screen layer to hide the other layers. Click the blank visibility column to the left of the Shadow/highlight sublayer to show its content on the artboard. Make sure that the Background layer is hidden.

5   Choose Select > All On Active Artboard.

● **Note:** The Align options may not appear in the Control panel but are indicated by the word "Align." The number of options displayed in the Control panel depends on your screen resolution.

6   Make sure that Align To Selection (▣▾) is chosen in the Control panel, and then click the Horizontal Align Center button (▤) and the Vertical Align Center button (▥) in the Control panel, to align the content to each other.

7   In the Layers panel, click the Layers panel menu icon (), and choose Show All Layers. Then, choose Select > Deselect.

8   Choose File > Save.

Locating layers

When working in artwork, there may be times when you select content on the artboard and then want to locate that same content in the Layers panel. This can help you to determine how content is organized.

1   With the Selection tool (▶), click to select one of the small knobs.

In the Layers panel, you will see the selection indicator to the far right of the Side panel layer and knobs sublayer name.

2   Click the Locate Object button (◉) at the bottom of the Layers panel to reveal the object within the knobs sublayer.

Clicking the Locate Object button will open the layer so that the layer content can be seen, and the Layers panel will scroll, if necessary, to reveal the selected content. With an Illustrator file that has a lot of layered content, this can be helpful.

3   Choose Select > Deselect.

4   Click the triangle to the left of the Screen and Side panel layer names to hide the contents of each layer.

Applying appearance attributes to layers

You can apply appearance attributes, such as styles, effects, and transparency, to layers, groups, and objects, using the Layers panel. When an appearance attribute is applied to a layer, any object on that layer takes on that attribute. If an appearance attribute is applied only to a specific object on a layer, it affects only that object, not the entire layer.

● **Note:** To learn more about working with appearance attributes, see Lesson 13, "Applying Appearance Attributes and Graphic Styles."

You will apply an effect to an object on one layer. Then, you'll copy that effect to another layer to change all objects on that layer.

1   Click the triangle to the left of the TV body layer name to show the contents of the layer.

Note: Clicking the target icon also selects the object(s) on the artboard. You could simply select the content on the artboard to apply an effect.

2 Click the target icon () to the right of the bottom <Path> object in the target column.

Clicking the target icon indicates that you want to apply an effect, style, or transparency change to that layer, sublayer, group, or object. In other words, the layer, sublayer, group, or object is *targeted*. The content is also selected in the Document window. When the target button appears as a double ring icon (either ⊙ or ⊙), the item is targeted; a single ring icon indicates that the item is not targeted.

Note: There are two Stylize commands in the Effect menu. Choose the top Stylize menu command, which is in the Illustrator Effects.

3 Choose Effect > Stylize > Drop Shadow. In the Drop Shadow dialog box, change the following options:

- Mode: **Multiply** (the default setting)
- Opacity: **50%**
- X Offset: **0 in**
- Y Offset: **0.1 in**
- Blur: **0.1 in** (if necessary)

Click OK. A drop shadow appears on the edge of the television shape.

Notice that, on the <Path> sublayer, the target icon (⊙) is now shaded, indicating that the object has appearance attributes applied to it.

4 Click the Appearance panel icon (⊙) on the right side of the workspace to reveal the Appearance panel. If the Appearance panel isn't visible, choose Window > Appearance. Notice that Drop Shadow has been added to the list of appearance attributes for the selected object.

5 Choose Select > Deselect.

You will now use the Layers panel to copy an appearance attribute into a layer and then edit it.

6   Click the Layers panel icon () on the right side of the workspace to show the Layers panel. Click the arrow to the left of the Side panel layer to reveal its contents. If necessary, first scroll down or drag the bottom of the Layers panel down to display the entire list.

7   Press the Alt (Windows) or Option (Mac OS) key, and drag the shaded target icon of the bottom <Path> sublayer in the TV body layer to the target icon of the knobs sublayer, without releasing the mouse button. When the target icon of the knobs sublayer turns light gray, release the mouse button and then release the modifier key.

● **Note:** You can drag and copy the shaded target icon to any layer, sublayer, group, or object to apply the properties found in the Appearance panel.

The drop shadow is now applied to the knobs sublayer and all content in that sublayer, as indicated by the shaded target icon.

Now, you'll edit the drop shadow effect for the knobs to make the shadow more prominent.

8   In the Layers panel, click the target icon () to the right of the knobs sublayer name.

This automatically selects the objects on the sublayer and deselects the object on the TV body layer.

9   Click the Appearance panel icon () on the right side of the workspace to reveal the Appearance panel. In the Appearance panel, click the words "Drop Shadow," scrolling down to find them in the list, if necessary.

10 In the Drop Shadow dialog box, change the Opacity to **80%**, and then click OK.

This will make a subtle gradient change to the knobs.

11 Choose Select > Deselect.

12 Choose File > Save.

Isolating layers

When a layer is in Isolation mode, objects on that layer are isolated so that you can easily edit them without affecting other layers. Next, you will enter Isolation mode for a layer and make a simple edit.

1   Click the Layers panel icon () on the right side of the workspace to show the Layers panel. Click the triangles to the left of the layers in the Layers panel to close them all.

2   Click to select the Side panel layer.

3   Choose Enter Isolation Mode from the Layers panel menu (▼≡).

In Isolation mode, the contents of the Side panel layer appear on top of all the objects on the artboard. The rest of the content on the artboard is dimmed and locked, much like when you enter Isolation mode for a group. The Layers panel now shows a layer called Isolation Mode and a sublayer that contains the Side panel content.

4   Select the Selection tool (▶), if it's not already selected, and Shift-click the two small knobs at the top of the side panel to select them.

5   Press the down arrow key twice to move the knobs down.

6   Press the Escape key to exit Isolation mode.

Notice that the content is no longer locked and that the Layers panel reveals all the layers and sublayers again.

7   Choose Select > Deselect.

Now that the artwork is complete, you may want to combine all the layers into a single layer and then delete the empty layers. This is called *flattening* artwork. Delivering finished artwork in a single-layer file can prevent accidents, such as hiding layers or omitting parts of the artwork during printing. To flatten specific layers without deleting hidden layers, you can select the layers you want to flatten and then choose Merge Selected from the Layers panel menu.

For a complete list of shortcuts that you can use with the Layers panel, see "Keyboard shortcuts" in Illustrator Help.

8   Choose File > Save, and then choose File > Close.

Review questions

1 Name at least two benefits of using layers when creating artwork.

2 How do you hide layers? How do you show individual layers?

3 Describe how to reorder layers in a file.

4 What is the purpose of changing the color for a layer?

5 What happens if you paste a layered file into another file? Why is the Paste Remembers Layers option useful?

6 How do you create a layer clipping mask?

7 How do you apply an effect to a layer? How can you edit that effect?

Review answers

1 The benefits of using layers when creating artwork include: organizing content, selecting content more easily, protecting artwork that you don't want to change, hiding artwork that you aren't working with so that it's not distracting, and controlling what prints.

2 To hide a layer, click to deselect the eye icon (👁) to the left of the layer name in the Layers panel. Select the blank, leftmost column (the Visibility column) to show a layer.

3 You reorder layers by selecting a layer name in the Layers panel and dragging the layer to its new location. The order of layers in the Layers panel controls the document's layer order—topmost in the panel is front-most in the artwork.

4 The color for a layer controls how selected anchor points and direction lines are displayed on a layer and helps you identify the different layers in your document.

5 The paste commands paste layered files or objects copied from different layers into the active layer, by default. The Paste Remembers Layers option keeps the original layers intact when the objects are pasted.

6 Create a clipping mask on a layer by selecting the layer and clicking the Make/Release Clipping Mask button (▣) in the Layers panel. The topmost object in the layer becomes the clipping mask.

7 Click the target icon for the layer to which you want to apply an effect. Then, choose an effect from the Effect menu or by clicking the Add New Effect button (fx.) in the Appearance panel. To edit the effect, make sure that the layer is selected and then click the name of the effect in the Appearance panel. The effect's dialog box opens, and you can change the values.

9 WORKING WITH PERSPECTIVE DRAWING

Lesson overview

In this lesson, you'll learn how to do the following:

- Understand perspective drawing.
- Use grid presets.
- Adjust the perspective grid.
- Draw and transform content in perspective.
- Edit grid planes and content.
- Bring content into perspective.
- Create text and bring it into perspective.
- Bring symbols into perspective.
- Edit symbols in perspective.

This lesson takes approximately an hour and a half to complete.

Download the project files for this lesson from the Lesson & Update Files tab on your Account page at www.peachpit.com and store them on your computer in a convenient location, as described in the Getting Started section of this book.

Your Accounts page is also where you'll find any updates to the chapters or to the lesson files. Look on the Lesson & Update Files tab to access the most current content.

In Adobe Illustrator CC, you can easily draw or render artwork in perspective, using the perspective grid. The perspective grid allows you to approximately represent a scene, on a flat surface, as it is naturally perceived by the human eye.

Getting started

In this lesson, you'll explore working with the perspective grid, by adding content to and editing content on the grid. Before you begin, you'll restore the default preferences for Adobe Illustrator. Then, you'll open the finished art file for this lesson to see what you'll create.

1 To ensure that the tools and panels function exactly as described in this lesson, delete or deactivate (by renaming) the Adobe Illustrator CC preferences file. See "Restoring default preferences," on page 3.

2 Start Adobe Illustrator CC.

● **Note:** If you have not already downloaded the project files for this lesson to your computer from your Account page, make sure to do so now. See "Getting Started" at the beginning of the book.

3 Choose File > Open, and open the L9end.ai file in the Lesson09 folder, located in the Lessons folder on your hard disk.

You are going to create some product boxes for a makeup ad.

4 Choose View > Fit Artboard In Window and leave the file open for reference, or choose File > Close.

● **Note:** In Mac OS, when opening lesson files, you may need to click the round, green button in the upper-left corner of the Document window to maximize the window's size.

5 Choose File > Open. Navigate to the Lesson09 folder, located in the Lessons folder on your hard disk. Open the L9start.ai file.

6 Choose File > Save As. In the Save As dialog box, navigate to the Lesson09 folder and name the file **L9ad.ai**. Leave the Save As Type option set to Adobe Illustrator (*.AI) (Windows) or the Format option set to Adobe Illustrator (ai) (Mac OS), and then click Save. In the Illustrator Options dialog box, leave the Illustrator options at their default settings and then click OK.

7 Choose Reset Essentials from the workspace switcher in the Application bar.

● **Note:** If you don't see "Reset Essentials" in the menu, choose Window > Workspace > Essentials before choosing Window > Workspace > Reset Essentials.

8 Choose View > Fit Artboard In Window.

Understanding the perspective grid

In Illustrator, using the perspective grid and the Perspective Selection tool, you can easily draw or render artwork in perspective. You can define the perspective grid in one-point, two-point, or three-point perspective, define a scale, move the grid planes, and draw objects directly in perspective. You can even attach flat art onto the grid planes by dragging with the Perspective Selection tool.

1   Click the Layers panel icon (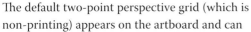) to expand the Layers panel. In the Layers panel, select the Perspective layer. Click the Layers panel icon to collapse the panel again.

2   Select the Perspective Grid tool (⊞) in the Tools panel.

The default two-point perspective grid (which is non-printing) appears on the artboard and can be used to draw and snap content in perspective. The two-point grid (for short), is composed of several *planes* or surfaces, by default—left (blue), right (orange), and a ground plane.

The figure below shows the default perspective grid and its parts. It may be helpful to refer back to this figure as you progress through the lesson.

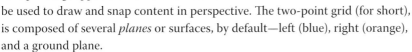

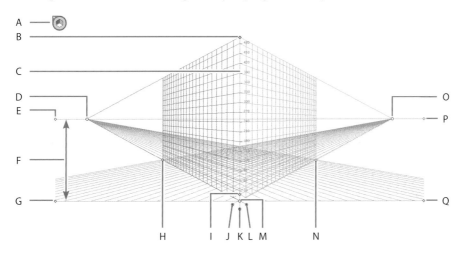

A. Plane Switching Widget	**I.** Grid cell size
B. Vertical grid extent	**J.** Right grid plane control
C. Perspective Grid ruler (not showing, by default)	**K.** Horizontal grid plane control
	L. Left grid plane control
D. Left vanishing point	**M.** Origin
E. Horizon line	**N.** Extent of grid
F. Horizon height	**O.** Right vanishing point
G. Left ground level point	**P.** Horizon level
H. Extent of grid	**Q.** Right ground level point

Working with the perspective grid

In order to begin working with content in perspective, it is helpful to see and set up the perspective grid the way you want.

Using a preset grid

Note: A one-point perspective can be very useful for roads, railway tracks, or buildings viewed so that the front is directly facing the viewer. Two-point perspective is useful for drawing a cube, such as a building, or for two roads going off into the distance, and it typically has two vanishing points. Three-point perspective is usually used for buildings seen from above or below.

To begin the lesson, you'll work with the perspective grid, starting with an Illustrator preset. The perspective grid, by default, is set up as a two-point perspective. You can easily change the grid to a one-point, two-point, or three-point grid, using presets, which is what you'll do next.

1 Choose View > Perspective Grid > Three Point Perspective > [3P-Normal View]. Notice that the grid changes to a three-point perspective.

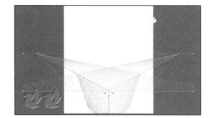

In addition to showing vanishing points for each wall, there is now a point showing those walls receding into the ground or high in space.

2 Choose View > Perspective Grid > Two Point Perspective > [2P-Normal View]. Notice that the grid changes back to the default two-point perspective.

Adjusting the perspective grid

To create artwork in the perspective you want, you can adjust the grid using the Perspective Grid tool or using the Define Grid command. You can make changes to the grid if you have content on it, although it will be easier to establish what your grid looks like before you add content. In this section, you'll make a few adjustments to the grid. First, you'll move the grid where you're going to draw some boxes. You can also draw content in the default grid position and move that content later.

1 Make sure that the Smart Guides are on (View > Smart Guides).

2 With the Perspective Grid tool (⊞), position the pointer over the left ground level point. When the pointer changes (▶⊹), drag it to the left and up, to move the whole perspective grid. Match the position in the figure as closely as you can.

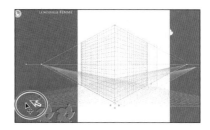

The left and right ground level points allow you to drag the perspective grid to different parts of the artboard or to a different artboard altogether.

Next, you'll change the height of the grid.

3 With the Perspective Grid tool, position the pointer over the Vertical Grid Extent point, indicated by the X in the figure. When the pointer changes (▶⊞), drag it down to roughly match the figure to shorten the vertical extent.

Dragging the vertical extent dow~ ͵ a way to minimize the grid ͵͞ drawing objects that ͵ you will see lat~

4 Positi~

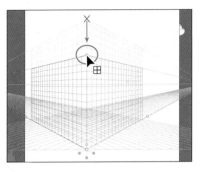

● **Note:** Throughout this section, a red X in the figures shows where to drag from. Also, the gray lines seen in some of these figures indicate the initial position of the perspective grid, before it was adjusted.

▶ **Tip:** The location of the ground level in relation to the horizon line will determine how far above or below eye level the object will be viewed.

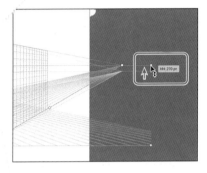

͵ac OS), *twice*, to zoom out.

͝n Point.

....ₛ points so that they move together.

...͵ospective Grid tool, position the pointer over the right vanishing point. When the pointer includes a horizontal arrow (▶..), drag to the right until the measurement label shows an X value of approximately 15 in.

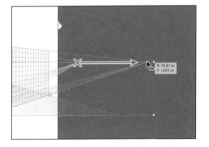

This changes both planes on the grid, and the product box you create will have a more visible right face.

Setting the grid up for your drawing is an important step in creating the artwork with the perspective you desire. Next, you will access some of the perspective grid options you have already adjusted, and more, using the Define Perspective Grid dialog box.

8 Choose View > Fit Artboard In Window.

9 Choose View > Perspective Grid > Define Grid.

10 In the Define Perspective Grid dialog box, change the following options:

- Units: **Inches**
- Gridline Every: **0.3 in**

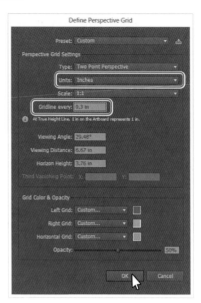

▶ **Tip:** After setting the Define Perspective Grid settings, you can save them as a preset to access later. In the Define Perspective Grid dialog box, change the settings and then click the Save Preset button (⊡).

Changing the Gridline Every option adjusts the grid cell size and can help you be more precise when drawing and editing on the grid, since content snaps to the lines of the grid by default. Notice that you can also change the Scale of the grid, which you might want to do if real-world measurements are involved. You can also edit settings, like Horizon Height and Viewing Angle, on the artboard, using the Perspective Grid tool. Leave the Grid Color & Opacity settings at their defaults.

When you have finished making changes, click OK.

The grid should now look pretty close to this (but doesn't have to exactly match):

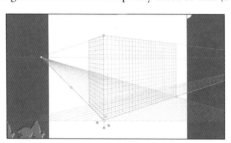

● **Note:** To learn more about the options in the Define Perspective Grid dialog box, search for "Perspective drawing" in Illustrator Help (Help > Illustrator Help).

11 Choose View > Perspective Grid > Lock Grid.

This command restricts the grid movement and other grid-editing features of the Perspective Grid tool. You can only change the visibility and the grid plane position, which you will work with later in this lesson.

● **Note:** When you select a tool other than the Perspective Grid tool, you cannot edit the perspective grid. Also, if the perspective grid is locked, you can edit it by choosing View > Perspective Grid > Define Grid.

12 Choose File > Save.

Drawing objects in perspective

To draw objects in perspective, you can use the line group tools or the rectangle group tools (except for the Flare tool) while the grid is visible. Before you begin drawing using any of these tools, you need to select a grid plane to attach the content to, using the Plane Switching Widget or keyboard shortcuts.

When the perspective grid is showing, a Plane Switching Widget appears in the upper-left corner of the Document window, by default. Whichever grid plane is selected in the widget is the active grid plane of the perspective grid

A. Left Grid(1)
B. Horizontal Grid(2)
C. Right Grid(3)
D. No Active Grid(4)

to which you'll add content. In the figure, you can see each of the planes that you can select, as well as their keyboard shortcut.

1 Select the Rectangle tool (▣) in the Tools panel.

2 Select Left Grid(1), in the Plane Switching Widget (if it's not already selected).

3 Position the pointer at the origin of the perspective grid (where the two planes meet, at the bottom). Notice that the cursor has an arrow pointing to the left (◂┤), indicating that you are about to draw on the left grid plane. Drag up and to the left, until the gray measurement label shows an approximate width of 2.4 in and a height of approximately 3 in. As you drag, the pointer should be snapping to the grid lines.

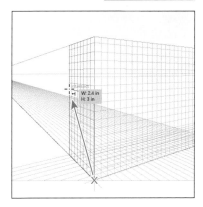

▶ **Tip:** You can turn off grid-snapping by choosing View > Perspective Grid > Snap To Grid. Snapping is enabled by default.

When drawing in perspective, you will find that you can still use the usual keyboard shortcuts for drawing objects, such as Shift-drag to constrain.

4 With the rectangle selected, change the Fill color in the Control panel to the orange/red swatch named Box Left. Press the Escape key to hide the Swatches panel.

5 Change the Stroke color to None (▱), in the Control panel.

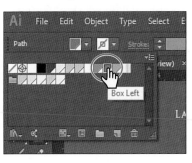

There are many ways to add content to the perspective grid. Next, you'll create another rectangle a different way.

● **Note:** Zooming in brings into view more gridlines that are closer to the vanishing point. That's why, depending on the zoom level, your grid may not match the figures exactly, and that's okay.

6 Press Ctrl++ (Windows) or Command++ (Mac OS), *twice*, to zoom in to the grid.

7 With the Rectangle tool still selected, click Right Grid(3) in the Plane Switching Widget to draw in perspective on the right grid plane.

8 Position the pointer over the upper-right corner of the last rectangle you drew. When the word "anchor" appears, click. In the Rectangle dialog box, the width and height of the last rectangle you drew are showing. Click OK.

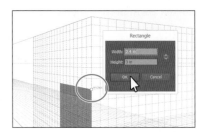

Notice that the pointer now has an arrow pointing to the right (➡), indicating that you are about to draw on the right grid plane.

9 Click the Graphic Styles panel (▦) to show the panel. With the new rectangle still selected, click the graphic style named Box Right to apply it.

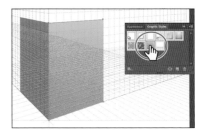

A *graphic style* is something you can use to save formatting from content you create and then apply it elsewhere. It's a great way to apply a gradient to another object so that it looks the same as the first one.

● **Note:** To learn more about working with graphic styles, see Lesson 13, "Applying Appearance Attributes and Graphic Styles."

10 With the Rectangle tool still selected, click Horizontal Grid(2) in the Plane Switching Widget to draw in perspective on the ground plane.

11 Position the pointer over the upper-left corner point of the first rectangle you drew (on the left plane). When the word "anchor" appears, along with a large, hollow anchor point, click and drag to the upper-right corner point of the second rectangle you created. When a large, hollow anchor point appears on the second anchor point, release the mouse button.

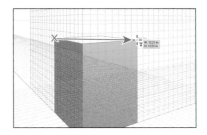

12 With the rectangle selected, change the Fill color in the Control panel to the orange/red swatch named Box Top.

13 Choose View > Perspective Grid > Hide Grid, to hide the perspective grid and to see your artwork.

Selecting and transforming objects in perspective

You can select objects in perspective using selection tools, like the Selection tool and using the Perspective Selection tool (▶). The Perspective Selection tool uses the active plane settings to select the objects. If you use the Selection tool to drag an object that was drawn in perspective, it maintains its original perspective but it doesn't change to match the perspective grid.

Next, you will move and resize several of the rectangles you drew.

1 Choose View > Fit Artboard In Window.

2 Choose View > Perspective Grid > Show Grid.

3 Position the pointer over the Perspective Grid tool (▦), click and hold down the mouse button, and then select the Perspective Selection tool (▶). Click the rectangle on the right grid plane with the gradient fill to select it. Notice that the right grid plane (Right Grid(3)) is now selected in the Plane Switching Widget and the perspective grid appears.

4 With the Perspective Selection tool still selected, drag the upper-right point of the rectangle up and to the left. When the measurement label shows a width of about 2.1 in and a height of 3.3 in, release the mouse button. Make sure that the rectangle is snapping to the grid lines.

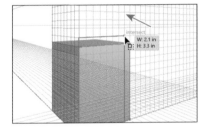

▶ **Tip:** Zooming in to the grid may make it easier when resizing content.

Notice that the rectangle that you resized is behind the rectangle that is the top of the box. Content on the perspective grid has the same stacking order as content you draw off of the perspective grid.

5 Choose Object > Arrange > Bring To Front.

6 With the Perspective Selection tool, click to select the first rectangle you created (on the left plane). Click the word "Transform" in the Control panel, and then click the bottom, middle point of the reference point locator (▦) in the Control panel. With the Constrain Width And Height Proportions option deselected (▦), change the Height to **3.3 in**.

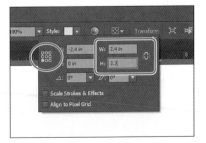

● **Note:** Depending on the resolution of your screen, you may see the Transform options in the Control panel.

7 Select the Zoom tool (🔍) in the Tools panel, and click several times on the top of the box to zoom in.

● **Note:** Select the top of the box (the rectangle) on its left side, since the right side of the box is arranged on top of it.

8 With the Perspective Selection tool, click to select the red rectangle that is the top of the box. Drag the rectangle up from its center above the other two rectangles.

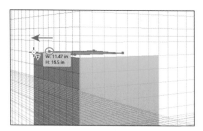

Dragging artwork on the horizontal grid up or down, with the Perspective Selection tool, makes it smaller and larger. Dragging it up moves the artwork "farther away" in perspective, and dragging it down moves it "closer" in perspective.

▶ **Tip:** You can also move objects from one plane to another using a keyboard command. With the objects selected, begin dragging them with the Perspective Selection tool, without releasing the mouse button yet. Press the number 1, 2, or 3 key (depending on which grid you intend to attach the objects to) to switch to the grid plane of your choice.

9 Press Ctrl++ (Windows) or Command++ (Mac OS), *twice*, to zoom in to the grid.

10 Drag the leftmost point of the top rectangle so that it snaps to the upper-left corner of the rectangle on the left plane. Drag the rightmost point of the top rectangle so that it snaps to the upper-right corner of the rectangle on the right plane.

Snap the left anchor point.   Snap the right anchor point.

11 Choose File > Save, and then choose Select > Deselect.

Duplicating content in perspective

You can easily duplicate content on the grid using copy and paste or other methods. Next, you will duplicate an object in perspective, as well as move an object perpendicular to an existing object.

1   Choose View > Fit Artboard In Window.

2   Choose View > Perspective Grid > Unlock Grid, so you can edit the grid again.

3   Select the Perspective Grid tool (⊞) in the Tools panel, and position the pointer over the right grid extent widget, indicated by the red X in the figure below. When the pointer changes (►⊞), drag to the left until it reaches the right edge of the rectangle.

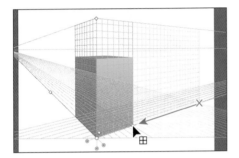

Changing the extent of the grid plane allows you to see more or less of the gridlines.

Next, you will begin to create another product box to the left of the box you've already created. To do this, you will copy content.

4   Select the Perspective Selection tool (►◉) in the Tools panel. Click to select the gradient-filled rectangle on the right grid plane. Begin dragging the rectangle to the left. As you drag, press Alt+Shift (Windows) or Option+Shift (Mac OS). Stop dragging when the measurement labels shows a dX value of approximately −1.4 in. Release the mouse button, and then release the keys.

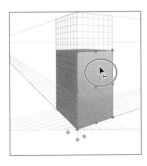
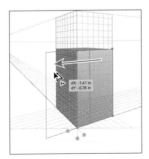

▶ **Tip:** You can also use the Transform Again command (Object > Transform > Transform Again) or the keyboard shortcut Ctrl+D (Windows) or Command+D (Mac OS) to move objects in perspective.

The Shift key constrains the movement to 45° on the grid, and the Alt (Windows) or Option (Mac OS) key copies the object.

5 Drag the upper-right point of the new rectangle up and to the left to make the rectangle narrower and taller. Stop dragging when the measurement label shows an approximate width of 0.62 in and a height of 5.8 in.

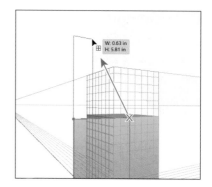

> ▶ **Tip:** For more precision, you can also zoom in on the artwork or change the size of the selected rectangle by changing the W and H values in the Control panel or in the Transform panel (Window > Transform).

Moving objects in a perpendicular direction

With the new rectangle in place, you are going to move the rectangle in a direction perpendicular to the current location. This technique is useful when creating parallel objects, such as the legs of a chair.

● **Note:** The keyboard shortcut 5, for perpendicular movement, (and the keyboard shortcuts 1, 2, 3, and 4 for plane switching) while drawing or moving objects, works only from the main keyboard and not from the extended numeric keypad.

1 With the rectangle still selected, hold down the number 5 key and drag the rectangle to the right a bit. When the measurement label shows a dX value of approximately 0.25 in, release the mouse and then release the 5 key.

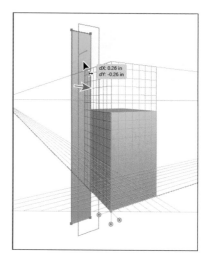

This action moves the object parallel to its current location. You could also press the Alt key (Windows) or Option key (Mac OS), while dragging, to copy the object that you are dragging.

2 Press the Escape key to hide the perspective grid.

3 Choose Select > Deselect, and then choose File > Save.

Moving planes and objects together

As you saw in the beginning of this lesson, it's usually best to adjust the grid before there is artwork on it. But Illustrator allows you to move objects perpendicularly, similar to what you just did, by moving the grid planes instead. This can be better for more precise perpendicular movement.

Next, you will move a grid plane and artwork together.

1 Press Ctrl+Shift+I (Windows) or Command+Shift+I (Mac OS) to show the perspective grid again.

2 Select the Zoom tool (🔍), and click the lower-left corner of the original box twice, *slowly*, to zoom in to the grid.

3 Select the Perspective Selection tool (▶🔲). Position the pointer over the right grid plane control (circled in the figure). When the pointer changes (▶.), drag to the right until D: 0.5 in appears in the measurement label, and then release the mouse button. This moves the right grid plane but not the objects on it.

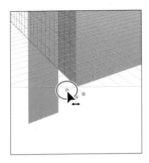
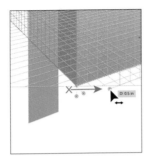

Position the pointer.　　　　Drag the right grid plane.

Notice how the plane moved but the artwork stayed in place. Next, you will put the right grid plane back where it was.

4 Double-click the same right grid plane control you just dragged (circled in the figure). In the Right Vanishing Plane dialog box, change the Location to **0 in**, make sure that Do Not Move is selected, and click OK.

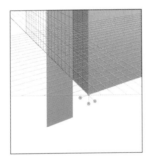

Edit the grid plane control.　　　Notice the result.

> **Tip:** If you move a plane using the grid plane control, you can also choose Edit > Undo Perspective Grid Edit to put the plane back to its original location.

In the Right Vanishing Plane dialog box, the Do Not Move option allows you to move the grid plane and not the objects on it. Copy All Objects allows you to move the grid plane and to bring a copy of the objects on the grid plane with it.

The location in the Right Vanishing Plane dialog box starts at the station point, which is 0. The station point is indicated by the very small green diamond on the perspective grid, above the horizontal grid control.

5   With the Perspective Selection tool still selected, double-click the left grid plane
    control (an arrow is pointing to it in the figure). In the Left Vanishing Plane
    dialog box, change the Location to **−1.4 in**, select Copy All Objects, and click
    OK. This moves the left plane to the left (positive values move the plane to the
    right) and copies the rectangle, moving the copy as well.

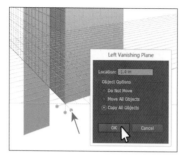 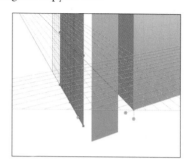

▶ **Tip:** If you select an
object or objects on the
grid plane first and then
drag the grid plane
control while holding
down the Shift key,
only the selected
objects move with the
grid plane.

There are a lot of keyboard commands associated with moving grid planes. You
can hold down the Alt key (Windows) or Option (Mac OS) and drag a grid
plane control to move the grid plane and copy the content. Dragging a grid
plane control while pressing the Shift key moves the objects with the grid plane
without copying them.

Next, you'll resize the new rectangle so that it can become the left side of the tall
box. For the following step, reference the figure as you progress.

6   Drag the lower-right point of the new rectangle, snapping it to the lower-left
    corner of the tall rectangle.

7   Choose View > Fit Artboard In Window.

8   Drag the upper-right corner point of the new rectangle up, snapping it to the
    upper-left corner of the tall rectangle.

9   Drag the left, middle point of the rectangle to the right until a width of
    approximately .65 in shows in the measurement label.

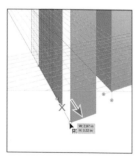  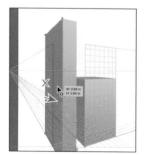

Drag the lower-right point.   Drag the upper-right point.   Change the width.

10 Choose Select > Deselect, and then choose File > Save.

Bringing content into perspective

If you have already created content that is not in perspective, Illustrator provides an option to bring objects into perspective on an active plane in the perspective grid. You will now add a flower logo to two of the boxes.

1 Choose View > Fit Artboard In Window, if necessary.

2 With the Perspective Selection tool () in the Tools panel, select Right Grid(3) in the Plane Switching Widget to make sure that the flower will be added to the right grid plane.

▶ **Tip:** You can also select the active plane by pressing keyboard shortcuts: 1=Left Grid, 2=Horizontal Grid, 3=Right Grid, and 4=No Active Grid.

3 With the Perspective Selection tool, drag one of the red flowers off of the lower-left corner of the artboard onto the right side of the larger box.

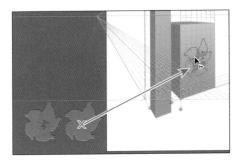

The artwork is added to the grid that is selected in the Plane Switching Widget and is behind the rectangles in the stacking order.

● **Note:** Instead of dragging an object onto the plane using the Perspective Selection tool, you can also select the object with the Perspective Selection tool, choose the plane using the Plane Switching Widget, and then choose Object > Perspective > Attach To Active Plane. This adds the content to the active plane, but it doesn't change its appearance.

4 Choose Object > Arrange > Bring To Front.

5 Choose View >Zoom In, a few times, to zoom in to the boxes.

Next, you will scale the flower artwork, making it smaller.

6 With the Perspective Selection tool, press Shift+Alt (Windows) or Shift+Option (Mac OS) and drag the upper-right corner of the flower shape toward the center until an approximate width of 1.5 in shows in the measurement label. You won't have to drag very far.

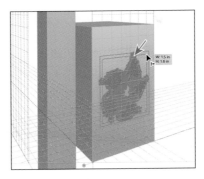

7 Choose Select > Deselect, and then choose File > Save.

Drawing with no active grid

There will be times when you need to draw or add content that is not meant to be in perspective. In a case like that, you can select No Active Grid in the Plane Switching Widget to draw without regard to the grid. You will now add a rectangle to the background of the ad.

1 Choose View > Fit Artboard In Window.

2 Click the Layers panel icon (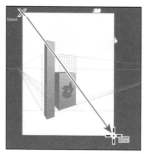), to expand the Layers panel. In the Layers panel, select the Background layer. Click the lock icon (🔒) to the left of the Background name in the panel to unlock the content of the Background layer. Leave the panel showing.

3 Select the Rectangle tool (▢) in the Tools panel. Click No Active Grid(4) in the Plane Switching Widget. This allows you to add content without perspective.

4 Starting from the upper-left corner of the artboard, drag down to the lower-right corner of the artboard to create a rectangle the size of the artboard, as shown in the figure below.

5 Click the Graphic Styles panel icon (▦) to show the panel. With the new rectangle still selected, position the pointer over the graphic style thumbnail with the yellow tooltip that shows "Background" and click to apply the style.

Select No Active Grid.

Create the rectangle.

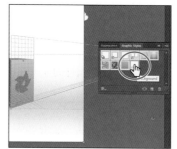
Apply the graphic style.

6 Choose Object > Arrange > Send To Back.

7 In the Layers panel, click the edit column to the left of the Background name in the panel to lock the content of the Background layer.

8 Select the Perspective layer so that any content you add will be added to the Perspective layer. Click the Layers panel tab to hide the panel.

9 Choose Select > Deselect (if necessary).

Adding and editing text in perspective

You cannot add text directly to a perspective plane when the grid is visible. However, you can bring text into perspective after creating it off of the perspective grid. Next, you will add some text and then edit it in perspective.

1   Select the Type tool (**T**) in the Tools panel. Click in a blank area on the artboard and type **La Nouvelle**, press Enter or Return, and then type **Femme**.

2   Select the text with the Type tool, change the Font to **Trajan Pro 3**, ensure that the Font Style is Regular, and change the Font Size to **20 pt** in the Control panel.

3   Click the Align Center button (■) in the Control panel, to align the text to center.

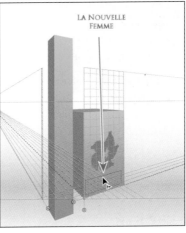

● **Note:** If you don't see the Font Formatting options in the Control panel, click the word "Character" in the Control panel to reveal the Character panel.

4   Select the Perspective Selection tool (▶●) in the Tools panel. Press the number 3 key on the keyboard to select the Right Grid(3) in the Plane Switching Widget. Drag the text below the red flower on the right side of the larger box.

5   With the text object still selected, double-click the text with the Perspective Selection tool to enter Isolation mode. The Type tool (**T**) is selected automatically.

6   Double-click the word "Femme," and change the Font Size to **24 pt** in the Control panel. Click the word "Character" in the Control panel, and change the Leading value to **22 pt**. Press the Escape key to hide the Character panel.

7   Select all of the text, and change the Fill color to **White** in the Control panel.

8   Press the Escape key until Isolation mode is exited.

▶ **Tip:** You can also enter Isolation mode to edit text by clicking the Edit Text button (■) in the Control panel. To exit Isolation mode, you can also click twice on the gray arrow that appears below the document tab at the top of the Document window.

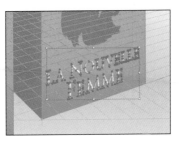

● **Note:** We zoomed in to more easily edit the text.

Moving a plane to match an object

When you want to draw or bring objects in perspective at the same depth or height as an existing object, such as the tall box, you can bring the corresponding grid to the desired height or depth. Next, you will move the right grid plane to the same depth as the right side of the tall box and add more text to it.

1   Select the Selection tool (▶), and click to select the white text "La Nouvelle Femme" that is off the upper-left corner of the artboard.

2   Choose Object > Transform > Rotate. In the Rotate dialog box, change the Angle value to **90°** and select Preview. Click OK.

You will find that, most of the time, it's best to rotate content *before* bringing it into perspective.

● **Note:** The gridlines on the right grid plane will most likely not cover the right side of the tall box. That's okay. Imagine that those gridlines go on forever in the same plane.

3   Select the Perspective Selection tool (▶▣) in the Tools panel. Click to select the right face of the tall box. Choose Object > Perspective > Move Plane To Match Object. Now, anything you add to the right grid plane will be at the same depth as the right side of the tall box.

4   With the Perspective Selection tool (▶▣), click to drag the rotated text object into the lower-left corner of the right side of the tall box. See the figure for placement help.

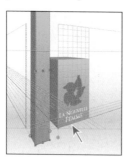  

The plane before you move it.   The plane after moving it.   The text in place.

5   Choose Object > Arrange > Bring To Front, to bring the text on top of the box.

To finish the tall box, you will add a red flower to it.

6   With the Perspective Selection tool (▶▣) selected, make sure that the Right Grid(3) in the Plane Switching Widget is selected.

7   With the Perspective Selection tool, drag the last remaining red flower off the lower-left corner of the artboard onto the right side of the tall box, just above the text.

Review questions

1 There are three preset grids. Describe briefly what each could be used for.

2 How can you show or hide the perspective grid?

3 Before drawing content on a grid plane, what must be done to ensure that the object is on the correct grid plane?

4 What does double-clicking a grid plane control allow you to do?

5 How do you move an object perpendicular to the grid?

Review answers

1 The three preset grids are: one-point perspective, two-point perspective, and three-point perspective. A one-point perspective can be very useful for roads, railway tracks, or buildings viewed so that the front is directly facing the viewer. Two-point perspective is useful for drawing a cube, such as a building, or for two roads going off into the distance, and it typically has two vanishing points. Three-point perspective is usually used for buildings seen from above or below. In addition to vanishing points for each wall, there is a vanishing point in three-point perspective showing those walls receding into the ground or high in space.

2 You can show the perspective grid by selecting the Perspective Grid tool (⊞) in the Tools panel, by choosing View > Perspective Grid > Show Grid, or by pressing Ctrl+Shift+I (Windows) or Command+Shift+I (Mac OS). To hide the grid, choose View > Perspective Grid > Hide Grid, press Ctrl+Shift+I (Windows) or Command+Shift+I (Mac OS), or press the Escape key with the Perspective Selection or Perspective Grid tools selected.

3 The correct grid plane must be selected by choosing it in the Plane Switching Widget; by using the following keyboard commands: Left Grid(1), Horizontal Grid(2), Right Grid(3), or No Active Grid(4); or by selecting content on the grid you want to choose with the Perspective Selection tool (▶⊞).

4 Double-clicking a grid plane control allows you to move the plane. You can specify whether to move the content associated with the plane and whether to copy the content as the plane moves.

5 To move an object perpendicular to the grid, with the Perspective Selection tool, hold down the number 5 key and drag the object perpendicular to the plane.

10 BLENDING COLORS AND SHAPES

Lesson overview

In this lesson, you'll learn how to do the following:

- Create and save a gradient fill.

- Apply and edit a gradient on a stroke.

- Apply and edit a radial gradient.

- Add colors to a gradient.

- Adjust the direction of a gradient blend.

- Adjust the opacity of color in a gradient blend.

- Blend the shapes of objects in intermediate steps.

- Create smooth color blends between objects.

- Modify a blend and its path, shape, and color.

 This lesson takes approximately an hour to complete.

Download the project files for this lesson from the Lesson & Update Files tab on your Account page at www.peachpit.com and store them on your computer in a convenient location, as described in the Getting Started section of this book.

Your Accounts page is also where you'll find any updates to the chapters or to the lesson files. Look on the Lesson & Update Files tab to access the most current content.

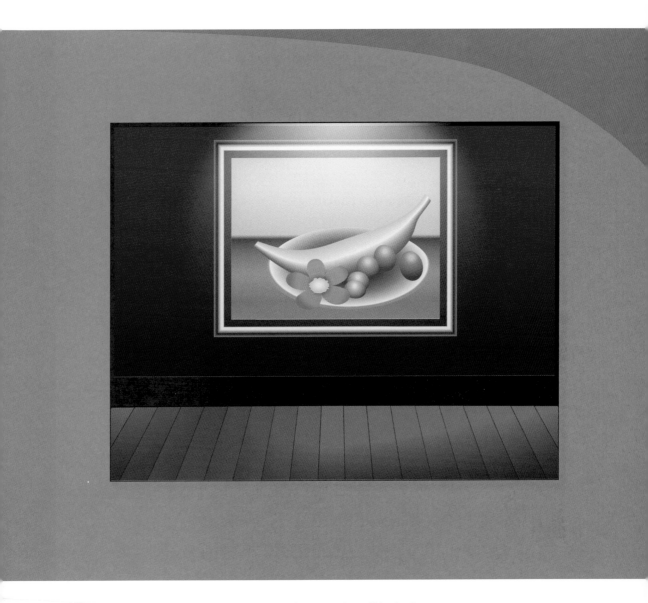

Gradient fills are graduated blends of two or more
colors. Using the Gradient tool and/or the Gradient
panel, you can create or modify a gradient fill or a
gradient stroke. With the Blend tool, you can blend
the shapes and colors of objects together into a new,
blended object or a series of intermediate shapes.

Getting started

You'll explore various ways to create your own color gradients and to blend colors and shapes together using the Gradient tool, the Gradient panel, and the Blend tool.

Before you begin, you'll restore the default preferences for Adobe Illustrator CC. Then, you'll open the finished art file for this lesson to see what you'll create.

1   To ensure that the tools and panels function exactly as described in this lesson, delete or deactivate (by renaming) the Adobe Illustrator CC preferences file. See "Restoring default preferences," on page 3.

2   Start Adobe Illustrator CC.

● **Note:** If you have not already downloaded the project files for this lesson to your computer from your Account page, make sure to do so now. See "Getting Started" at the beginning of the book.

3   Choose File > Open, and open the L10end.ai file in the Lesson10 folder, located in the Lessons folder on your hard disk.

4   Choose View > Zoom Out to make the finished artwork smaller, if you want to leave it on your screen as you work. (Use the Hand tool [🖐] to move the artwork where you want it in the window.) If you don't want to leave the document open, choose File > Close.

To begin working, you'll open an existing art file.

● **Note:** In Mac OS, when opening lesson files, you may need to click the round, green button in the upper-left corner of the Document window to maximize the window's size.

5   Choose File > Open, and open the L10start.ai file in the Lesson10 folder, located in the Lessons folder on your hard disk.

6   Choose File > Save As, name the file **gallery.ai**, and select the Lesson10 folder in the Save In menu. Leave the Save As Type option set to Adobe Illustrator (*.AI) (Windows) or the Format option set to Adobe Illustrator (ai) (Mac OS), and then click Save. In the Illustrator Options dialog box, leave the Illustrator options at their default settings and then click OK.

7   Choose Reset Essentials from the workspace switcher in the Application bar.

● **Note:** If you don't see "Reset Essentials" in the workspace switcher menu, choose Window > Workspace > Essentials before choosing Window > Workspace > Reset Essentials.

Working with gradients

A *gradient fill* is a graduated blend of two or more colors, and it always includes a starting and an ending color. You can create different types of gradient fills in Illustrator, including *linear*, in which the beginning color blends into the ending color along a line, and *radial*, in which the beginning color radiates outward, from the center point to the ending color. You can use the gradients provided with Adobe Illustrator CC or create your own gradients and save them as swatches for later use.

You can use the Gradient panel (Window > Gradient) or the Gradient tool (▦) to apply, create, and modify gradients. In the Gradient panel, the Gradient Fill or Stroke box displays the current gradient colors and gradient type applied to the fill or stroke of an object.

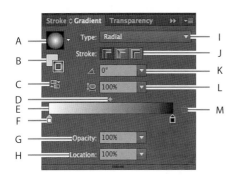

A. Gradient Fill box
B. Fill box/ Stroke box
C. Reverse Gradient
D. Gradient midpoint
E. Gradient slider
F. Color stop
G. Opacity
H. Location
I. Gradient type
J. Stroke gradient type
K. Angle
L. Aspect ratio
M. Delete Stop

In the Gradient panel, the left gradient stop (labeled F—also called a *color stop*) under the gradient slider marks the starting color; the right gradient stop marks the ending color. A *gradient color stop* is the point at which a gradient changes from one color to the next. You can add more color stops by clicking below the gradient slider. Double-clicking a color stop opens a panel where you can choose a color from swatches, color sliders, or the eyedropper.

Creating and applying a linear gradient to a fill

With the simplest, two-color linear gradient, the starting color (leftmost color stop) blends into the ending color (rightmost color stop) along a line. To begin the lesson, you'll create a gradient fill for the background shape.

1   Choose View > Fit Artboard In Window.

2   Using the Selection tool (▸), click to select the large yellow rectangle with a black border in the background.

   The background is painted with a yellow fill color and a black stroke, as shown in the Fill and Stroke boxes toward the bottom of the Tools panel. The Gradient box below the Fill and Stroke boxes shows the last created gradient. The default gradient fill is a black-and-white gradient.

3   Click the Fill box (near the bottom of the Tools panel) to activate it, and then click the Gradient box (■) below the Fill box.

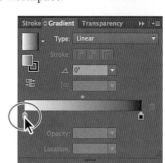

The default black-and-white gradient appears in the Fill box and is applied to the fill of the selected background shape. The Gradient panel also opens on the right side of the workspace.

4   In the Gradient panel that opens, double-click the white, leftmost gradient stop to select the starting color of the gradient.

A new panel appears when you double-click a color stop (in the step below). In this panel, you can change the color of the stop, using swatches or the Color panel, which is what you'll do next.

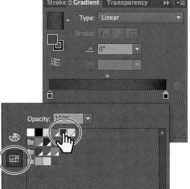

● **Note:** The colors that you will use in gradients in this lesson have been saved in color groups, grouped according to the object you are applying them to, to make them easier to find.

5   After double-clicking the white color stop, click the Swatches button (▦) in the panel that appears. Click to select the reddish swatch named wall 1. Notice the gradient change on the artboard. Press the Escape key, or click in a blank area of the Gradient panel to close the Swatches panel.

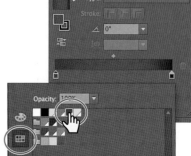

6   Double-click the black color stop on the right side of the gradient slider to edit the color (circled in the figure).

▶ **Tip:** To move between text fields, press the Tab key. Press Enter or Return to apply the last value typed.

7   In the panel that appears, click the Color button (🎨) to open the Color panel. Click the menu icon (▼≡) and choose CMYK from the menu, if CMYK values aren't showing. Change the values to C=**50**, M=**80**, Y=**70**, and K=**80**. After entering the last value, click in a blank area of the Gradient panel to return to the Gradient panel.

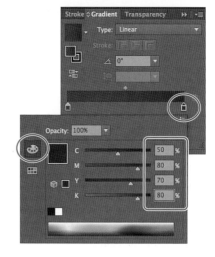

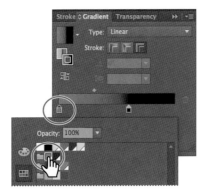

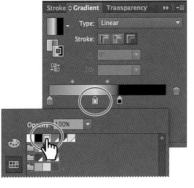

Edit the white color.   Add light yellow to the gradient.

7 Pressing the Alt (Windows) or Option (Mac OS) key, drag the light yellow color stop to the right, close to the black color stop, release the mouse button, and then release the modifier key. This is an easy way to duplicate a color in a gradient.

8 Pressing the Alt (Windows) or Option (Mac OS) key, drag the leftmost (brown) color stop to the right. Release the mouse button, and then release the modifier key, when it is positioned as you see in the figure below.

9 Click below the color ramp, between the two leftmost color stops, to add a final color stop. Double-click that new color stop and, with the swatches showing, click the swatch named frame 2 in the top color group.

▶ **Tip:** You can delete a color in the color ramp by selecting a color stop and clicking the Delete Stop button (🗑) or by dragging the color stop downward and out of the Gradient panel. Remember that the gradient must contain at least two colors!

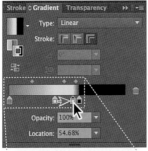

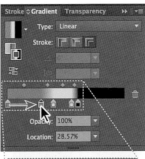

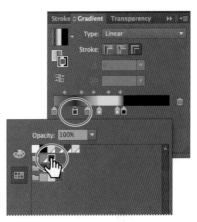

Duplicate the yellow stop.   Duplicate the leftmost color stop.   Add and edit the final color stop.

10 Choose Select > Deselect.

11 Choose View > Fit Artboard In Window, and then choose File > Save.

Creating and applying a radial gradient

As previously noted, with a *radial gradient*, the starting color (leftmost color stop) of the gradient defines the center point of the fill, which radiates outward to the ending color (rightmost color stop).

Next, you will create and apply a radial gradient fill to a plate.

1 Click the Layers panel icon () on the right side of the workspace. Make sure that the triangle to the left of the Gallery layer is toggled open. Click to select the visibility column to the left of the plate sublayer (you may need to scroll in the Layers panel).

2 Use the Selection tool (▶) to select the white ellipse in the frame of the painting.

3 Select the Zoom tool (🔍) in the Tools panel, and click the ellipse several times to zoom in.

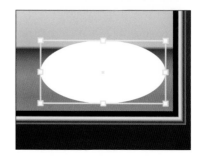

4 In the Control panel, change the Fill color to the White, Black gradient. Press the Escape key to hide the Swatches panel.

5 Click the Gradient panel icon (▣) to show the Gradient panel. In the Gradient panel, make sure that the Fill box is selected. Choose Radial from the Type menu to convert the linear gradient in the shape to a radial gradient. Keep the ellipse selected and the Gradient panel showing.

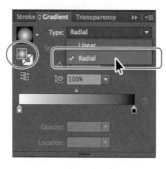

Editing the radial gradient colors

Once you have filled an object with a gradient, you can use the Gradient tool or the Gradient panel to edit the gradient, including changing the direction, color, and origin.

Next, you will use the Gradient tool to adjust the color of each color stop and to add two more colors, for a total of four colors in the radial gradient.

1 Select the Gradient tool (🔲) in the Tools panel.

2 Position the pointer over the gradient annotator (bar) in the artwork to reveal the gradient slider. Double-click the white color stop on the left end to edit the color. In the panel that appears, click the Swatches button (🔳), if it's not already selected.

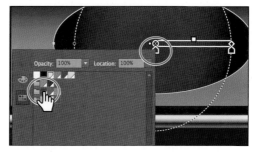

● **Note:** When you double-click the color stop, you can see the Location in the panel that appears. As you build this radial gradient, you can copy the values you see in the figures to closely match the positions of the color stops.

Select the color called plate 1 in the second color group. Press the Escape key to hide the panel.

Notice that the gradient annotator starts from the center of the ellipse and points to the right. The dashed circle around it indicates that it is a radial gradient. You can set additional options for radial gradients, as you'll soon see.

In the gradient slider, double-click the black color stop on the right. In the panel that appears, select the light yellow swatch at the top of the swatches panel. Press the Escape key to close the panel.

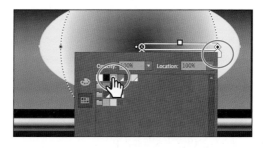

3 Position the pointer beneath the gradient slider. When the pointer with a plus sign (▶+) appears, click to add another color to the gradient (circled in the figure). Double-click the new color stop. In the panel that appears, select the plate 2 swatch in the second color group. Press the Escape key to close the panel.

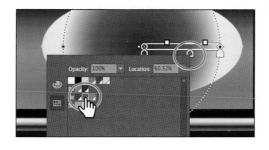

4 Position the pointer beneath the gradient slider, and click to add a fourth (and final) color stop just to the left of the rightmost (light yellow) color stop. See the figure for placement. Double-click the new color stop beneath the gradient slider. In the panel that appears, select the plate 3 swatch in the second color group. Make sure that the Location is 97%. Press the Escape key to close the panel.

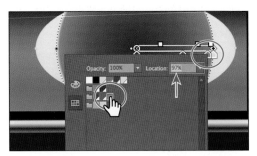

Once the colors are set in the gradient, you can always delete, add more, or even change the order of colors. Next, you will change the order of the last two colors.

5 Double-click the leftmost color stop, and change the Location value to **42%** in the panel that appears. Press Enter or Return to change the value and hide the panel.

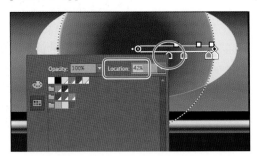

6 Drag the rightmost (light yellow) color stop to the left (just to the left of the closest brown color stop). Drag the rightmost brown color stop to the right, all the way to the end of the gradient slider. See the figure for how they should be arranged. Notice that they are still close to each other.

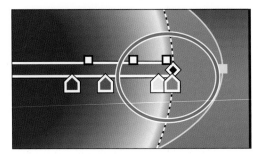

7 Choose File > Save.

Adjusting the radial gradient

Next, you will change the aspect ratio of the gradient, adjust the position, and change the radius and the origin of the radial gradient.

1   With the Gradient tool (▣), position the pointer over the small white box on the right end of the gradient annotator. Click and drag to the right, stopping just past the right edge of the ellipse shape, and release the mouse button. This lengthens the gradient.

● **Note:** You may not see the dotted circle as you drag the end of the gradient annotator. That's okay. It appears if you position the pointer over the gradient annotator bar first, before dragging the right end point.

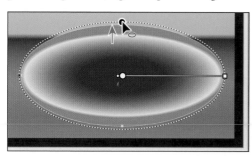

2   In the Gradient panel, ensure that the Fill box is selected and then change the Aspect Ratio (▣) to **40%** by selecting it from the menu.

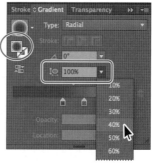

● **Note:** The aspect ratio is a value between 0.5% and 32,767%. As the aspect ratio gets smaller, the ellipse flattens and widens.

    The aspect ratio changes a radial gradient into an elliptical gradient and makes the gradient better match the shape of the plate.

3   With the Gradient tool selected, position the pointer over the gradient on the plate. Position the pointer over the top black circle that appears on the dotted path. When the pointer changes to (▶○), drag up to just past the top of the ellipse shape to change the aspect ratio.

When you release the mouse button, notice that the Aspect Ratio value in the Gradient panel is larger than the 40% set previously (it's now closer to 50%).

Next, you will drag the gradient slider to reposition the gradient in the ellipse.

4 With the Gradient tool, click and drag the gradient slider up a little bit to move the gradient in the ellipse. Make sure that the bottom edge of the dotted ellipse is above the edge of the yellow path.

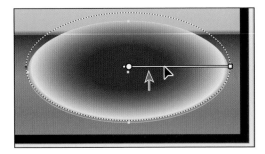

Drag the gradient slider up.

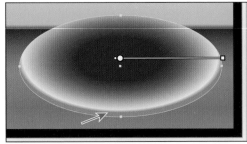

Note the "depth" you've added to the plate.

5 With the Gradient tool, click the small white dot to the left of the leftmost color stop and drag to the left.

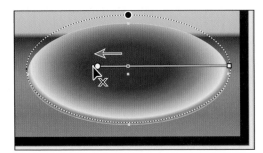

Change the origin of the gradient.

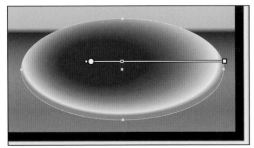

Note the result.

This dot repositions the center of the gradient (the leftmost color stop), without moving the entire gradient bar, and changes the radius of the gradient.

6 Choose Edit > Undo Gradient, to put the gradient back to the center.

7 Choose Select > Deselect, and then choose File > Save.

Applying gradients to multiple objects

You can apply a gradient to multiple objects by selecting all the objects, applying a gradient color, and then dragging across the objects with the Gradient tool.

Now, you'll paint a flower with a radial gradient fill and then edit the colors in it.

1 Choose View > Fit Artboard In Window.

2 Click the Layers panel icon (⬛) to open the Layers panel. Click to select the visibility column to the left of the flower sublayer. Click the panel tab to hide it.

3   Select the Zoom tool (🔍) in the Tools panel, and drag a marquee across the blue flower shapes to zoom in.

4   Select the Selection tool (▶), and click to select one of the blue flower shapes.

5   Choose Select > Same > Fill Color to select all five blue flower shapes.

6   In the Control panel, choose the gradient named flower from the Fill color. Press the Escape key to hide the Swatches panel, if necessary.

When you apply a gradient to the fill or stroke of multiple selected objects, they are applied independently.

Now, you'll adjust the gradient on the shapes so that the gradient blends across all of them as one object, and then you'll adjust the gradient itself.

7   Make sure that the Fill box (at the bottom of the Tools panel) is selected.

8   Double-click the Gradient tool (▨) in the Tools panel to select the tool and to show the Gradient panel. Drag from the center of the yellow shape (in the middle of the flower) to the outer edge of one of any one of the petal shapes, as shown in the figure, to apply the gradient uniformly. Leave the flower shapes selected.

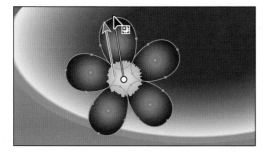
Drag across the flower shapes with the Gradient tool.

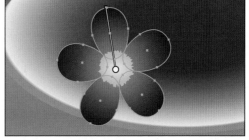
Note the result.

Exploring other methods for editing gradient colors

Up to this point, you've added, edited, and adjusted the position of colors on the color ramp. Next, you will reverse a gradient and adjust the midpoint between colors on the color ramp.

1   In the Gradient panel, with the Fill box selected, click the Reverse Gradient button (▨).

You can also reverse the colors in a gradient by using the Gradient tool (▨) to drag across the gradient on the artboard in the opposite direction. This will make it so that the dark color is in the center of the gradient.

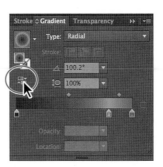

2 In the color ramp, in the Gradient panel, drag the leftmost dark color stop to the right until you see approximately 20% in the Location box at the bottom of the Gradient panel (it doesn't have to be exact).

3 Drag the diamond icon (located between the leftmost color stop and the middle color stop to the left), closer to the leftmost color stop. Drag until the Location box shows a value of approximately 30% (it doesn't have to be exact).

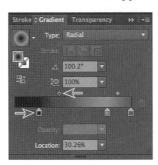 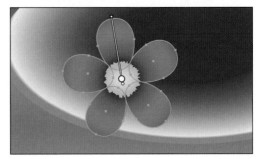

Another way to apply a color to a gradient is to sample the color from the artwork, using the Eyedropper tool, or to drag a color swatch onto a color stop.

4 With the flower shapes still selected, click to select the leftmost color stop (the dark color) in the Gradient panel.

5 Choose View > Fit Artboard In Window.

6 Select the Eyedropper tool ( ) in the Tools panel. In the artwork, Shift-click the black rectangle at the bottom of the wall.

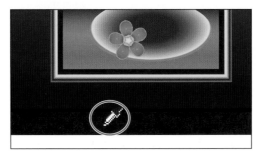

Shift-clicking with the Eyedropper tool applies the sampled color to the selected color stop in the gradient, rather than replacing the entire gradient with the color in the selected artwork.

The flower petals are complete. Now, you will group them with the flower center shape and apply a warp to give the whole flower some dimension.

7 Select the Zoom tool ( ) in the Tools panel, and drag a marquee across the blue flower shapes to zoom in.

8 With the Selection tool ( ), Shift-click the yellow center shape in the flower.

9 Choose Object > Group.

10 Choose Effect > Warp > Arc. In the Warp Options dialog box, with Horizontal selected, change the Bend to **–20%** and then click OK.

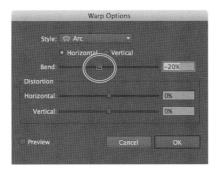 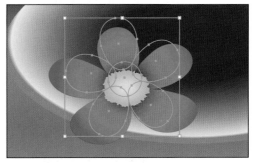

11 Choose Select > Deselect, and then choose File > Save.

Adding transparency to gradients

By specifying varying opacity values for the different color stops in your gradient, you can create gradients that fade in or out and that show or hide underlying images. Next, you will create a light for the painting and apply a gradient that fades to transparent.

1 Choose View > Fit Artboard In Window.

2 Click the Layers panel icon () to open the Layers panel. Click to select the visibility column to the left of the <Path> object.

3 Using the Selection tool (), click to select the white ellipse that is now on the artboard.

4 Click the Gradient panel icon () to open the panel. Ensure that the Fill box is selected, click the Gradient menu arrow (), and then select White, Black.

> **Tip:** The Fading Sky and Super Soft Black Vignette default gradients are also great starting points for fading to transparency.

5 Choose Radial from the Type menu in the Gradient panel. Double-click the rightmost color stop (the black color). In the panel that appears, click the Swatches button () and select the color swatch named White. Press the Escape key once to hide the swatches.

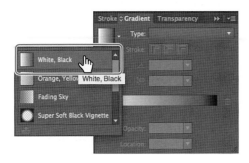 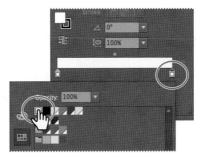

6 With the rightmost color stop selected in the Gradient panel, change the Opacity to **0%**. See the result in the middle part of the figure below.

7 Drag the gradient midpoint (the diamond shape) to the left until you see a value of approximately 30% in the Location field. Click the Gradient panel tab to collapse the Gradient panel group.

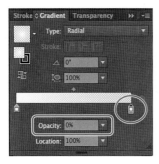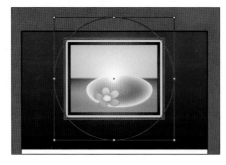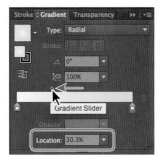

8 Press Ctrl+– (Windows) or Command+– (Mac OS) once to zoom out to see the entire selected circle.

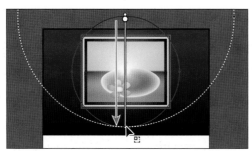

9 Select the Gradient tool (▭) in the Tools panel. Holding down the Shift key, drag from the top to the bottom of the ellipse shape. Release the mouse button, and then release the key.

▶ **Tip:** Be careful not to drag the black circle, which would change the Aspect Ratio.

10 In the Control panel, change the Stroke Color to [**None**].

11 Choose Effect > Blur > Gaussian Blur. In the Gaussian Blur dialog box, change the Radius to **60** (or what looks good to you) and then click OK.

12 Choose Select > Deselect, and then choose File > Save.

Working with blended objects

You can blend two distinct objects to create and distribute shapes evenly between two objects. The two shapes you blend can be the same or different. You can also blend between two open paths to create a smooth transition of color between objects, or you can combine blends of colors and objects to create color transitions in the shape of a particular object.

When you create a blend, the blended objects are treated as one object, called a *blend object*. If you move one of the original objects or edit the anchor points of the original object, the blend changes accordingly. You can also expand the blend to divide it into distinct objects.

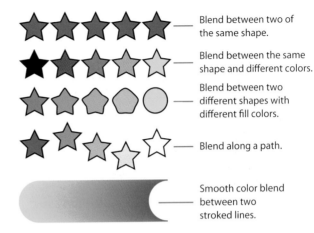

Blend between two of the same shape.

Blend between the same shape and different colors.

Blend between two different shapes with different fill colors.

Blend along a path.

Smooth color blend between two stroked lines.

Creating a blend with specified steps

Next, you'll use the Blend tool to blend three shapes that make up a wood floor of the gallery.

1   Choose View > Fit Artboard In Window.

2   Click the Layers panel icon ( ) to open the Layers panel. Click to select the visibility column to the left of both the floor and the fruit sublayers.

3   Click the visibility column to hide the <Path>, flower, plate, painting, and wall sublayers. Click the Layers panel tab to collapse the panel group.

Before you blend shapes, you can set the options for how they blend, which is what you'll do next.

4   Double-click the Blend tool ( ) in the Tools panel to open the Blend Options dialog box. Change the following options:

   • Spacing: **Specified Steps**

   • Number of steps: **4**

   Click OK.

▶ **Tip:** You can also make a blend by selecting objects and choosing Object > Blend > Make.

5   Scroll down in the Document window so that you can see the three brown floor shapes.

6 Using the Blend tool, position the pointer over the gradient-filled rectangle on the far left. Click when the pointer displays an asterisk (⬛*). Then, hover over the middle rectangle until the pointer displays a plus sign (⬛+), indicating that you can add an object to the blend. Click the middle rectangle to add it to the blend. There is now a blend between these two objects.

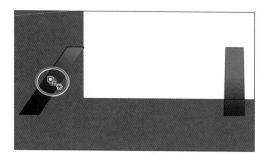 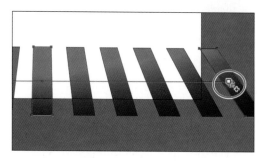

7 Click the rightmost rectangle with the Blend tool pointer (displaying the plus sign) to add it to the blend and to complete the blend object.

● **Note:** If you wanted to end the current path and blend other objects, you would first click the Blend tool in the Tools panel and then click the other objects, one at a time, to blend them.

8 With the blended rectangles still selected, choose Object > Blend > Blend Options. In the Blend Options dialog box, change the Specified Steps to **9** and then click OK.

 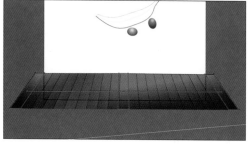

▶ **Tip:** To edit the blend options for an object, you can also select the blend object and then double-click the Blend tool.

9 Choose Select > Deselect.

Modifying a blend

Now, you'll create another blend and edit the shape of the path, called the *spine*, that the objects blend along.

1   Select the Zoom tool (🔍) in the Tools panel, and drag a marquee across the green grapes to zoom in. You may need to scroll up in the Document window.

2   With the Blend tool (🔳) selected, click the first green grape on the left and then click the green grape on the right to create a blend.

3   Double-click the Blend tool (🔳) in the Tools panel to open the Blend Options dialog box. Change the specified steps to **3**. Click OK.

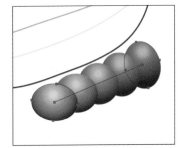

4   Choose View > Outline.

In Outline mode, you can see the outlines of the two original grapes and a straight path between them. These three objects are what a blend object is composed of, by default. It can be easier to edit the path between the original objects in Outline mode.

5   Make sure that the Smart Guides are selected (View > Smart Guides).

6   Select the Direct Selection tool (▷) in the Tools panel. Click the anchor point on the right end of the path to select that anchor point. In the Control panel, click the Convert Selected Anchor Points To Smooth button (🔲) to smooth the curve. With the Direct Selection tool, drag the bottom direction handle up and to the left. See the figure for help.

● **Note:** You are editing the spine. However you edit the spine, the blend objects will follow.

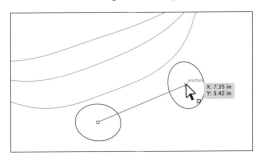
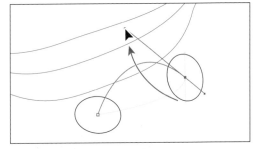

7   Choose View > Preview to see the change, and then choose Select > Deselect.

Next, you'll edit the position of the grape on the left and see the effect on the blend.

8   With the Selection tool (▶), click the blended grapes to select them.

9   Double-click anywhere on the blend object to enter Isolation mode.

This temporarily ungroups the blended objects and lets you edit each original grape (but not the grapes created by blending), as well as the spine.

▶ **Tip:** A quick way to reshape the spine of a blend is to blend the shapes along another path. You can draw another path, select the blend, as well, and then choose Object > Blend > Replace Spine.

Tip: You can reverse a blend by choosing Object > Blend > Reverse Front To Back.

10 Click to select the grape on the left. With the Selection tool, press Shift+Alt (Windows) or Shift+Option (Mac OS) and drag a corner bounding point toward the center to make the grape smaller. Release the mouse button, and then release the keys.

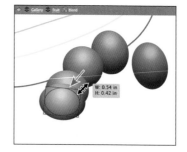

11 Press the Escape key to exit Isolation mode.

The blended objects are considered a single blend object. If you need to edit all the grapes (including the grapes that the blend created), you can expand the blend. Expanding the blend converts it to individual objects. You can no longer edit the blend as a single object because it has become a group of individual grape shapes. Next, you will expand the blend.

Tip: To release, or remove, a blend from the original objects, select the blend and choose Object > Blend > Release.

12 Choose Object > Blend > Expand. With the grapes still selected, notice the word "Group" on the left side of the Control panel.

The blend is now a group of individual shapes that you can edit independently.

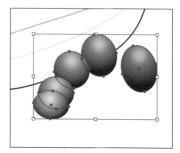

13 Choose Select > Deselect.

14 Choose File > Save.

Creating and editing smooth color blends

You can choose several options for blending the shapes and colors of objects to create a new object. When you choose the Smooth Color blend option in the Blend Options dialog box, Illustrator combines the shapes and colors of the objects into many intermediate steps, creating a smooth, graduated blend between the original objects.

Now, you'll combine three shapes into a smooth color blend to make a banana.

1 Choose View > Fit Artboard In Window. Press Ctrl++ (Windows) or Command++ (Mac OS) twice to zoom in.

You will now blend the three paths that are behind the blended grapes. All of the paths have a stroke color and no fill. Objects that have strokes blend differently than those that have no stroke.

2 With the Blend tool ( ), position the pointer over the top line until it displays an asterisk ( ), and then click. Click the middle (yellow) line with the Blend tool pointer that displays a plus sign ( ) to add it to the blend. Position the pointer over the third line (away from the grapes), and click when a plus sign appears next to the pointer ( ). Leave the blend object selected.

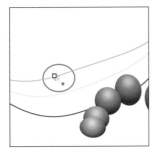 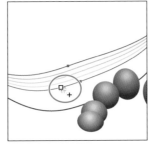 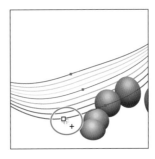

Next, you'll change the blend settings for the banana so that it blends as smooth color, rather than in specified steps.

3   Double-click the Blend tool (⬚) in the Tools panel. In the Blend Options dialog box, choose Smooth Color from the Spacing menu to set up the blend options, which will remain set until you change them. Click OK.

4   Choose Select > Deselect.

When you make a smooth color blend between objects, Illustrator automatically calculates the number of intermediate steps necessary to create the transition between the objects. Once you've applied a smooth color blend to objects, you can edit it. Next, you will edit the paths that make up the blend.

▶ **Tip:** Creating smooth color blends between paths can be difficult in certain situations. For instance, if the lines intersect or the lines are too curved, unexpected results can occur.

5   Using the Selection tool (▶), double-click the color blend (the banana) to enter Isolation mode. Click to select the middle path, and change the Stroke color in the Control panel to any color you want. Notice how the colors are blended. Choose Edit > Undo Apply Swatch to return to the original stroke color.

6   Double-click away from the blend paths to exit Isolation mode.

7   Choose View > Fit Artboard In Window.

8   Open the Layers panel, and click to select the visibility column for all of the sublayers, including the Mask sublayer, to make all objects visible on the artboard.

9   In the Layers panel, click to select the Gallery layer.

10 Click the Make/Release Clipping Mask button (⬚) at the bottom of the Layers panel.

This uses the first shape (the Mask shape) as a clipping mask to hide artwork that is outside the bounds of the shape.

11 Choose File > Save, and close all open files.

Review questions

1 What is a *gradient*?

2 Name two ways to apply a gradient to a selected object.

3 How do you adjust the blend between colors in a gradient?

4 Name two ways you can add colors to a gradient.

5 How can you adjust the direction of a gradient?

6 What is the difference between a *gradient* and a *blend*?

7 Describe two ways to blend the shapes and colors of objects.

8 What is the difference between selecting a smooth color blend and specifying the number of steps in a blend?

9 How do you adjust the shapes or colors in a blend? How do you adjust the path of a blend?

Review answers

1 A *gradient* is a graduated blend of two or more colors or of tints of the same color. Gradients can be applied to the stroke or fill of an object.

2 To apply a gradient to a selected object, select an object, and do one of the following:

- Select the Stroke or Fill box, and then click the Gradient box (⬛) in the Tools panel to fill an object with the default white-to-black gradient or with the last selected gradient.

- Change the Fill color or Stroke color in the Control panel to apply a gradient to selected content.

- Select the Stroke or Fill box in the Tools panel, and then click a gradient swatch in the Swatches panel.

- Use the Eyedropper tool (🖊) to sample a gradient from an object in your artwork, and then apply it to the selected object.

- Select the Stroke or Fill box in the Gradient panel, and then choose a gradient by clicking the Gradient menu arrow (⬛).

3   To adjust the blend between colors in a gradient, with the Gradient tool (■) selected and with the pointer over the gradient annotator or in the Gradient panel, you can drag the diamond icons or the color stops of the gradient slider.

4   To add colors to a gradient, in the Gradient panel, click beneath the gradient slider to add a gradient stop to the gradient. Then, double-click the color stop to edit the color, using the panel that appears to mix a new color or to apply an existing color swatch. You can select the Gradient tool in the Tools panel, position the pointer over the gradient-filled object, and then click beneath the gradient slider that appears in the artwork to add a color stop.

5   Drag with the Gradient tool to adjust the direction of a gradient. Dragging a long distance changes colors gradually; dragging a short distance makes the color change more abrupt. You can also rotate the gradient using the Gradient tool and change the radius, aspect ratio, starting point, and more.

6   The difference between a *gradient* and a *blend* is the way that colors combine together—colors blend together within a gradient and between objects in a blend.

7   You can blend the shapes and colors of objects by doing one of the following:

   •   Click each object with the Blend tool (⬚) to create a blend of intermediate steps between the objects, according to preset blend options.

   •   Select the objects and choose Object > Blend > Blend Options to set the number of intermediate steps, and then choose Object > Blend > Make to create the blend.

   Objects that have painted strokes blend differently than those with no strokes.

8   When you choose Smooth Color blend, Illustrator automatically calculates the number of intermediate steps necessary to create a seamlessly smooth blend between the selected objects. Specifying the number of steps lets you determine how many intermediate steps are visible in the blend. You can also specify the distance between intermediate steps in the blend.

9   You can use the Direct Selection tool (▷) to select and adjust the shape of an original object, thus changing the shape of the blend. You can change the colors of the original objects to adjust the intermediate colors in the blend. You can also use the Convert Anchor Point tool (∧) to change the shape of the path, or *spine*, of the blend by dragging anchor points or direction handles on the spine.

11 WORKING WITH BRUSHES

Lesson overview

In this lesson, you'll learn how to do the following:

- Use four brush types: Calligraphic, Art, Bristle, and Pattern.
- Apply brushes to paths.
- Paint and edit paths with the Paintbrush tool.
- Create an Art brush from a raster image.
- Change brush color and adjust brush settings.
- Create new brushes from Adobe Illustrator artwork.
- Work with the Blob Brush tool and the Eraser tool.

This lesson takes approximately an hour to complete.

Download the project files for this lesson from the Lesson & Update Files tab on your Account page at www.peachpit.com and store them on your computer in a convenient location, as described in the Getting Started section of this book.

Your Accounts page is also where you'll find any updates to the chapters or to the lesson files. Look on the Lesson & Update Files tab to access the most current content.

The variety of brush types in Adobe Illustrator CC lets you create a myriad of effects simply by painting or drawing using the Paintbrush tool or the drawing tools. You can work with the Blob Brush tool, choose from the Art, Calligraphic, Pattern, Bristle, or Scatter brushes, or create new brushes based on your artwork.

Getting started

You will learn how to work with the different brush types in the Brushes panel and how to change brush options and create your own brushes. Before you begin, you'll restore the default preferences for Adobe Illustrator CC. Then, you'll open the finished art file for the lesson to see the finished artwork.

1 To ensure that the tools and panels function exactly as described in this lesson, delete or deactivate (by renaming) the Adobe Illustrator CC preferences file. See "Restoring default preferences," on page 3.

2 Start Adobe Illustrator CC.

● **Note:** If you have not already downloaded the project files for this lesson to your computer from your Account page, make sure to do so now. See "Getting Started" at the beginning of the book.

3 Choose File > Open, and open the L11end.ai file in the Lesson11 folder, located in the Lessons folder on your hard disk.

4 If you want, choose View > Zoom Out to make the finished artwork smaller and then adjust the window size and leave the artwork on your screen as you work. (Use the Hand tool [✋] to move the artwork to where you want it in the Document window.) If you don't want to leave the artwork open, choose File > Close.

To begin working, you'll open an existing art file.

● **Note:** In Mac OS, when opening lesson files, you may need to click the round, green button in the upper-left corner of the Document window to maximize the window's size.

5 Choose File > Open, to open the L11start.ai file in the Lesson11 folder in the Lessons folder on your hard disk.

6 Choose View > Fit Artboard In Window.

7 Choose File > Save As. In the Save As dialog box, name the file **cruiseposter.ai** and select the Lesson11 folder. Leave the Save As Type option set to Adobe Illustrator (*.AI) (Windows) or the Format option set to Adobe Illustrator (ai) (Mac OS), and then click Save. In the Illustrator Options dialog box, leave the Illustrator options at their default settings and then click OK.

8 Choose Reset Essentials from the workspace switcher in the Application bar to reset the workspace.

● **Note:** If you don't see "Reset Essentials" in the workspace switcher menu, choose Window > Workspace > Essentials before choosing Window > Workspace > Reset Essentials.

Note: When dealing with embedded images and brushes, there is a direct impact on the performance of the document in Illustrator. There is a fixed limit to the size of the embedded image that can be used for a brush. You may see a dialog box telling you that the image needs to be resampled before you can make a brush from it.

3   Select the Selection tool (▶), and click the New Brush button (▤) at the bottom of the Brushes panel. This begins the process of creating a new brush from the selected raster artwork.

4   In the New Brush dialog box, select Art Brush and then click OK.

5   In the Art Brush Options dialog box, change the Name to **Palm tree**. Click OK.

6   Delete the image you placed off the right side of the artboard, since you don't need it anymore.

7   With the Selection tool selected, click to select the curved black line to the right of the ship.

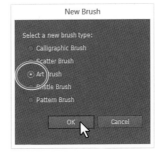

8   Click the brush named Palm tree in the Brushes panel to apply it.

Notice that the original tree image is stretched along the shape. This is the default behavior of an Art brush.

Editing an Art brush

Next, you will edit the Palm tree Art brush.

1   With the curved path still selected on the artboard, double-click the brush thumbnail to the left of the text "Palm tree" or to the right of the name in the Brushes panel to open the Art Brush Options dialog box.

▶ **Tip:** To learn more about the Art Brush Options dialog box, see "Art brush options" in Illustrator Help.

2 In the Art Brush Options dialog box, select Preview to see the changes as you make them and move the dialog box so you can see the curvy line with the brush applied. Make the following changes:

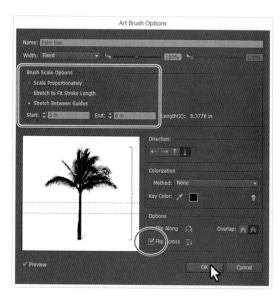

- Stretch Between Guides: **Selected**
- Start: **5 in**
- End: **6 in**
- Flip Across: **Selected**

Click OK.

3 In the dialog box that appears, click Apply To Strokes to apply the change to the curvy line that has the Palm tree brush applied.

4 Click the word "Opacity" in the Control panel, and choose Multiply from the Blend Mode menu. Press Enter or Return to close the Transparency panel.

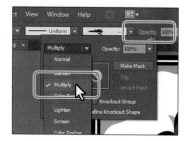

5 Choose Select > Deselect, and then choose File > Save.

Raster images in brushes

You can define Scatter, Art, and Pattern brushes using images, by dragging an embedded image into the Brushes panel (or using other creation methods).

Images in a brush will take the shape of the stroke (bend, scale, stretch) they are applied to. Also, such brushes behave and can be modified in the same way as other brushes, using the Brush Options dialog box.

Using large images in brushes will impact performance, though. When you choose such an image, Illustrator prompts you to allow it to re-rasterize the image to a lower resolution, before proceeding to create the brush.

—From Illustrator Help

Using Bristle brushes

Bristle brushes allow you to create strokes with the appearance of a natural brush with bristles. Painting with a Bristle brush, using the Paintbrush tool, creates vector paths with the Bristle brush applied, as you'll see in this section. You'll start by adjusting options for a brush, to change how it appears in the artwork, and then paint with the Paintbrush tool and Bristle brush to create smoke.

Bristle brush examples

Changing Bristle brush options

As you've seen, you can change the appearance of a brush by adjusting its settings in the Brush Options dialog box, either before or after brushes have been applied to artwork. In the case of Bristle brushes, it's usually best to adjust the brush settings prior to painting, since it can take some time to update the brush strokes.

1   In the Brushes panel, click the panel menu icon (▤), choose Show Bristle Brushes, and then deselect Show Art Brushes.

2   Double-click the thumbnail for the default Mop brush or directly to the right of the brush name to open the Bristle Brush Options dialog box for that brush. In the Bristle Brush Options dialog box, make the following changes:

- Shape: **Round Fan** (the default setting)

- Size: **7 mm** (The brush size is the diameter of the brush.)

- Bristle Length: **150%** (the default setting) (The bristle length starts from the point where the bristles meet the handle of the bristle tip.)

- Bristle Density: **20%** (The bristle density is the number of bristles in a specified area of the brush neck.)

- Bristle Thickness: **75%** (the default setting) (The bristle thickness can vary from fine to coarse [between 1% and 100%].)

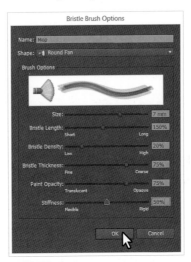

> **Tip:** Illustrator comes with a series of default Bristle brushes. Click the Brush Libraries Menu button (▣) at the bottom of the Brushes panel, and choose Bristle Brush > Bristle Brush Library.

> ● **Note:** To learn more about the Bristle Brush Options dialog box and its settings, see "Using the Bristle brush" in Illustrator Help (Help > Illustrator Help).

- Paint Opacity: **75%** (the default setting) (This option lets you set the opacity of the paint being used.)

- Stiffness: **50%** (the default setting) (Stiffness refers to the rigidness of the bristles).

Click OK.

Painting with a Bristle brush

Now, you'll use the Mop brush to draw some smoke above the ship. Painting with a Bristle brush can create a very organic, fluid path. In order to constrain the painting, you will paint inside a shape. This will mask (hide) part of the painting to be in the shape of smoke.

1 Select the Zoom tool ($\mathcal{Q}$) in the Tools panel, and click a few times, slowly, on the smoke shape above the ship (not the cloud), to zoom in on it.

2 Select the Selection tool ($\blacktriangleright$) in the Tools panel, and click to select the smoke shape. This selects the layer that the shape is on so that any artwork you paint will be on the same layer.

● **Note:** To learn more about the drawing modes, see Lesson 3, "Creating and Editing Shapes."

3 Click the Draw Inside button ($\boxed{\text{○}}$) at the bottom of the Tools panel.

● **Note:** If the Tools panel appears as one column, click the Drawing Modes button ($\boxed{\text{▣}}$) at the bottom of the Tools panel, and then choose Draw Inside from the menu that appears.

4 With the smoke shape still selected, change the Fill color to None ($\boxed{/}$) in the Control panel (press the Escape key to hide the Swatches panel). Leave the stroke as is. Choose Select > Deselect, to deselect the smoke shape.

The dotted lines on the corners of the shape indicate that any paths you paint will be masked by the smoke shape.

5 Select the Paintbrush tool ($\mathscr{I}$) in the Tools panel. Choose the Mop brush from the Brush Definition menu in the Control panel, if it's not already chosen.

6 Change the Fill color to None ($\boxed{/}$) and the Stroke color to white in the Control panel. Press the Escape key to hide the Swatches panel. Make sure that the Stroke weight is 1 pt in the Control panel.

▶ **Tip:** If you want to edit paths as you draw, you can select the Keep Selected option in the Paintbrush Tool Options for the Paintbrush tool or you can select paths with the Selection tool. You don't need to completely fill the shape.

7 Position the pointer at the top of the largest smokestack. (See the figure for the red X.) Drag up and then down and to the left, to loosely follow the edge of the smoke shape. Release the mouse button when you reach the end of the smoke shape.

When you release the mouse button, notice that the path you just painted is masked by the smoke shape.

▶ **Tip:** If you don't like what you just painted, you can choose Edit > Undo Bristle Stroke.

8 Use the Paintbrush tool () to paint more paths inside the smoke shape, using the Mop brush. Try drawing from each of the smokestacks, following the smoke shape. The idea is to fill up the smoke shape with the paths you paint.

Paint the first path.

Note the result.

9 Choose View > Outline to see all of the paths you just created when painting.

10 Choose Select > Object > Bristle Brush Strokes to select all of the paths created with the Paintbrush tool, using the Mop Bristle brush.

11 Choose Object > Group, and then choose View > Preview.

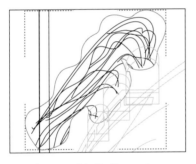

View the artwork in Outline mode.

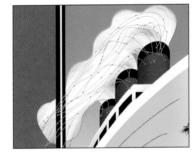

Note the result.

● **Note:** In the first part of the figure, we dimmed the shape paths so you could more easily see the smoke paths.

12 Click the Draw Normal button (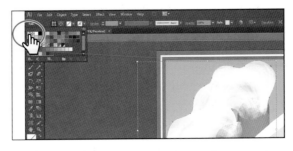) at the bottom of the Tools panel.

13 Select the Selection tool in the Tools panel. Choose Select > Deselect.

14 Double-click the edge of the smoke shape to enter Isolation mode. Click the dark gray stroke of the smoke shape. Change the Stroke color to None (☐) in the Control panel.

● **Note:** If the Tools panel appears as one column, click the Drawing Modes button () at the bottom of the Tools panel, and then choose Draw Normal from the menu that appears.

15 Press the Escape key several times to hide the panel and to exit Isolation mode.

16 Click the Layers panel icon () on the right side of the workspace to open the Layers panel. Click the eye icon (![eye]) to the left of the Spray/Tree layer name to hide the artwork on that layer. Click the Layers panel icon to collapse the panel.

17 Choose Select > Deselect, and then choose File > Save.

When saving, you may see a warning dialog box indicating that the document contains multiple Bristle brush paths with transparency. Painting with a Bristle brush, as was said earlier, creates a series of individual vector paths with the brush applied. This can lead to issues with printing or saving to EPS/PDF or legacy versions of Illustrator documents. In order to reduce the complexity and number of the Bristle Brush paths, you can rasterize paths with a Bristle brush applied. Select the path(s) with the Bristle brush applied, and choose Object > Rasterize.

The Bristle brush and graphic tablets

When you use Bristle brush with a graphic tablet, Illustrator interactively tracks the movements of the stylus over the tablet. It interprets all aspects of its orientation and pressure input at any point along a drawing path. Illustrator provides the output that is modeled on the stylus's x-axis position, y-axis position, pressure, tilt, bearing, and rotation. To learn more about Bristle brush and graphic tablets, search for "Bristle brush" in Illustrator Help (Help > Illustrator Help).

—From Illustrator Help

Using Pattern brushes

Pattern brushes paint a pattern made up of separate sections, or *tiles*. When you apply a Pattern brush to artwork, different tiles of the pattern are applied to different sections of the path, depending on where the section falls on the path—the end, middle, or corner. There are hundreds of interesting Pattern brushes that you can choose from when creating your own projects, from grass to cityscapes. Next, you'll apply an existing Pattern brush to a path to create windows on the ship.

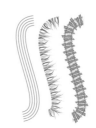

Pattern brush examples

1 Choose View > Fit Artboard In Window.

2 In the Brushes panel, click the panel menu icon (), choose Show Pattern Brushes, and then deselect Show Bristle Brushes.

3 Click to select the brush named Windows in the Brushes panel.

Next, you will apply the Pattern brush and then edit its properties.

4 Select the Selection tool (▶) in the Tools panel. Shift-click the two paths on the orange ship shape to select them both.

5 Choose the Windows Pattern brush from the Brush Definition menu in the Control panel to apply the Pattern brush.

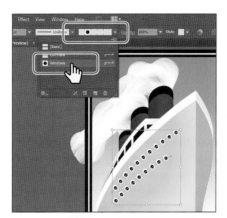

Next, you will edit the brush properties for the selected paths.

6 Choose Select > Deselect.

7 Click the bottommost path with the Windows brush applied to select it.

Tip: Just like other brush types, there is a series of default Pattern brush libraries that come with Illustrator. To access them, click the Brush Libraries Menu button (⊞) and choose a library from one of the menus (the Decorative menu, for example).

8 Click the Options Of Selected Object button (▦) at the bottom of the Brushes panel to edit the brush options for only the selected path on the artboard.

This opens the Stroke Options (Pattern Brush) dialog box.

9 Select Preview in the Stroke Options (Pattern Brush) dialog box. Change the Scale to **110%** either by dragging the Scale slider or by typing in the value. Click OK.

When you edit the brush options of the selected object, you only see some of the brush options. The Stroke Options (Pattern Brush) dialog box is used to edit the properties of the brushed path without updating the corresponding brush.

Tip: To change the size of the windows, you can also change the stroke of the lines on the artboard, with the brush applied.

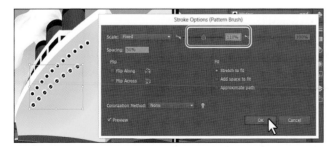

10 Choose Select > Deselect, and then choose File > Save.

Creating a Pattern brush

You can create a Pattern brush in several ways. For a simple pattern applied to a straight line, for instance, you can select the content that you're using for the pattern and click the New Brush button (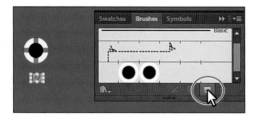) at the bottom of the Brushes panel.

To create a more complex pattern to apply to objects with curves and corners, you can select artwork in the Document window to be used in a pattern brush, create swatches in the Swatches panel from the artwork that you are using in the Pattern brush, and even have Illustrator auto-generate the Pattern brush corners. In Illustrator, only the side tile needs to be defined. Illustrator automatically generates four different types of corners based on the art used for the side tile. These four auto-generated options fit the corners perfectly.

Next, you'll create a Pattern brush for the border around the poster.

1 Choose View > Pattern objects. This should show you a zoomed-in view of the life preserver and the rope off the right edge of the artboard.

2 With the Selection tool (◤) selected, click to select the rope group.

3 Click the Brushes panel icon (▦) to expand the panel, if necessary, click the panel menu icon (▼≣), and choose Thumbnail View. In the Brushes panel, click the New Brush button (▤) to create a pattern out of the rope.

Notice that Pattern brushes in Thumbnail view are segmented in the Brushes panel. Each segment corresponds to a pattern tile. The side tile is repeated in the Brushes panel thumbnail preview.

4 In the New Brush dialog box, select Pattern Brush. Click OK.

A new Pattern brush can be made regardless of whether artwork is selected. If you create a Pattern brush *without* artwork selected, it is assumed that you will add artwork by dragging it into the Brushes panel later or by selecting the artwork from a pattern swatch you create as you edit the brush. You will see the latter method later in this section.

5 In the Pattern Brush Options dialog box, name the brush Border.

▶ **Tip:** Some brushes have no corner tiles because they are designed for curved paths.

Pattern brushes can have up to five tiles—the side, start, and end tiles, plus an outer corner tile and an inner corner tile to paint sharp corners on a path.

You can see all five tiles as buttons below the Spacing option in the dialog box. The tile buttons let you apply different artwork to different parts of the path. You can click a tile button for the tile you want to define, and then you select an auto-generated selection (if available) or a pattern swatch from the menu that appears.

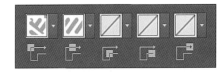

6 Under the Spacing option, click the Side Tile box (the second tile from the left). The artwork that was originally selected is in the menu that appears, along with None and any pattern swatches found in the Swatches panel. Choose Pompadour from the menu.

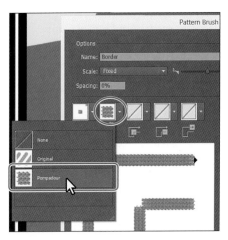

In the Preview area below the tiles, you will see how the new artwork effects a path.

7 Click the Side Tile box again, and choose the Original option.

8 Click the Outer Corner Tile box to reveal the menu.

The outer corner tile has been automatically generated by Illustrator, based on the original rope artwork. In the menu, you can choose from four types of corners that are automatically generated:

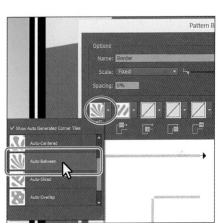

- **Auto-Centered**. The side tile is stretched around the corner and centered on it.

- **Auto-Between**. Copies of the side tile extend all the way into the corner, with one copy on each side. Folding elimination is used to stretch them into shape.

- **Auto-Sliced**. The side tile is sliced diagonally, and the pieces come together, similar to a miter joint in a wooden picture frame.

- **Auto-Overlap**. Copies of the tiles overlap at the corner.

Choose Auto-Between from the menu. This generates the outer corner of any path that the Pattern brush will be applied to from the rope.

9 Click OK. The Border brush appears in the Brushes panel.

▶ **Tip:** Position the pointer over the tile squares in the Pattern Brush Options dialog box to see a tool tip indicating which tile it is.

▶ **Tip:** Selected artwork becomes the side tile, by default, when creating a Pattern brush.

▶ **Tip:** To save a brush and reuse it in another file, you can create a brush library with the brushes you want to use. For more information, see "Work with brush libraries" in Illustrator Help.

Applying a Pattern brush

In this section, you'll apply the Border Pattern brush to a rectangular border around the artwork. As you've seen, when you use drawing tools to apply brushes to artwork, you first draw the path with the drawing tool and then select the brush in the Brushes panel to apply the brush to the path.

1   Choose View > Fit Artboard In Window.

2   With the Selection tool (▶) selected, click the white stroke of the rectangle on the border.

3   In the Tools panel, click the Fill box and make sure that None (◻) is selected. Then, click the Stroke box and select None (◻).

4   With the rectangle selected, click the Border brush in the Brushes panel.

5   Choose Select > Deselect.

The rectangle is painted with the Border brush, with the side tile on the sides and the outer corner tile on each corner.

Editing the Pattern Brush

▶ **Tip:** For more information on creating pattern swatches, see "About patterns" in Illustrator Help.

Now, you'll edit the Border brush using a pattern swatch that you create.

1   Click the Swatches panel icon (▦) to expand the Swatches panel, or choose Window > Swatches.

2   Choose View > Pattern objects to zoom in to the life preserver off the right edge of the artboard.

3   With the Selection tool (▶), drag the life preserver into the Swatches panel. The new pattern swatch appears in the Swatches panel.

After you create a pattern brush, you can delete the pattern swatches from the Swatches panel, if you don't plan to use them for additional artwork.

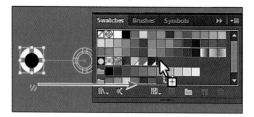

4   Choose Select > Deselect.

5 In the Swatches panel, double-click the pattern swatch that you just created. In the Pattern Options dialog box, name the swatch **Corner** and choose 1 x 1 from the Copies menu.

6 Click Done in the gray bar, along the top of the Document window, to finish editing the pattern.

7 Choose View > Fit Artboard In Window.

8 In the Brushes panel, double-click the Border Pattern brush to open the Pattern Brush Options dialog box.

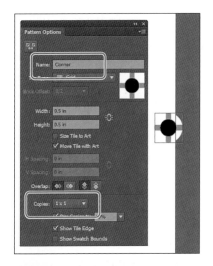

9 Click the Outer Corner Tile box, and choose the Corner pattern swatch from the menu that appears.

10 In the Pattern Brush Options dialog box, change the Scale to **70%** and click OK.

11 In the Brush Change Alert dialog box, click Apply To Strokes to update the border on the artboard.

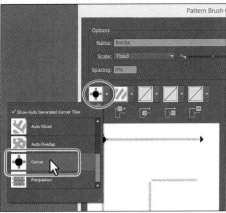

▶ **Tip:** You can also change the pattern tiles in a Pattern brush by pressing the Alt (Windows) or Option (Mac OS) key and dragging artwork from the artboard onto the tile of the Pattern brush you wish to change in the Brushes panel.

12 With the Selection tool selected, click to select one of the paths that contains a row of windows. Click the Border brush in the Brushes panel to apply it.

Notice that the life preservers are not applied to the path. The path is painted with the side tile from the Border brush. Because the path does not include sharp corners, outer corner and inner corner tiles are not applied to the path.

13 Choose Edit > Undo Apply Pattern Brush to remove the brush from the path.

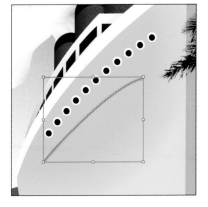

● **Note:** You may find that the palm tree path is being selected instead. If so, choose Object > Lock > Selection to prevent it from happening again.

● **Note:** Earlier in the lesson, you learned how to remove a brush from an object by clicking the Remove Brush Stroke button (⊠) in the Brushes panel. In this case, you chose Edit > Undo Apply Pattern Brush instead, because clicking the Remove Brush Stroke button would strip the previous formatting from the arch, leaving it with a default fill and stroke.

14 Choose Select > Deselect, and then choose File > Save.

Changing the color attributes of brushes

The colors that a Scatter, Art, or Pattern brush paints depend on the current stroke color and the colorization method of the brush. If you have not set a colorization method, the default color for that brush is used. For example, the Art brush applied to the water spray at the front of the boat (which was originally black) was applied with the current stroke of white because its colorization method was set to Tints.

To colorize Art, Pattern, and Scatter brushes, you can use three editing options in the Brush Options dialog box: Tints, Tints and Shades, and Hue Shift.

To learn more about each of these colorization methods, search for "Colorization options" in Illustrator Help (Help > Illustrator Help).

● **Note:** Brushes colorized with a stroke color of white may appear entirely white. Brushes colorized with a stroke color of black may appear entirely black. Results depend on which brush colors were originally chosen.

Working with the Blob Brush tool

You can use the Blob Brush tool to paint filled shapes that intersect and merge with other shapes of the same color. With the Blob Brush tool, you can draw with Paintbrush tool artistry. Unlike the Paintbrush tool, which lets you create open paths, the Blob Brush tool lets you create a closed shape with a fill only (no stroke) that you can then easily edit with the Eraser or Blob Brush tool. Shapes that have a stroke cannot be edited with the Blob Brush tool.

Path created with the
Paintbrush tool

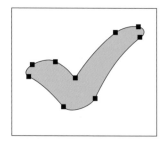

Shape created with the
Blob Brush tool

Editing and deleting effects

Effects are live, so they can be edited after they are applied to an object. You can edit the effect in the Appearance panel by selecting the object with the effect applied and then either clicking the name of the effect or double-clicking the attribute row in the Appearance panel. This displays the dialog box for that effect. Changes you make to the effect update in the artwork. In this section, you will edit the Drop Shadow effect applied to the barbells.

1   With the grouped barbell shapes still selected and the Appearance panel showing, click the orange text "Drop Shadow" in the Appearance panel.

2   In the Drop Shadow dialog box, change Opacity to **30%**. Select Preview to see the change, and then click OK.

3   Choose Object > Ungroup, to ungroup the barbell shapes.

Notice that the drop shadow is gone from the barbell group. When an effect is applied to a group, it affects the group as a whole. If the objects are no longer grouped together, the effect no longer applies. You will apply the shadow again later in the lesson.

4   Choose Object > Group, to regroup them.

Ensure that the drop shadow is no longer applied to the barbell group in the Appearance panel.

Next, you will remove an effect from the artwork.

5   With the Selection tool (▶), click the orange circle. The orange circle has a drop shadow applied to it.

6   In the Appearance panel, click to the right or left of the words "Drop Shadow" to highlight the attribute row for the Drop Shadow effect, if it's not already highlighted. After highlighting the attribute row, click the Delete Selected Item button (🗑) at the bottom of the panel.

● **Note:** Be careful not to click the underlined words "Drop Shadow," which will open the Drop Shadow dialog box.

▶ **Tip:** In the Appearance panel, you can also drag an attribute row, such as Drop Shadow, to the Delete Selected Item Button to delete it.

Styling text with effects

Text can have all sorts of effects applied, including a Warp effect, like you saw in Lesson 7, "Working With Type." Next, you will use a Warp effect to warp the text at the bottom of the label.

1   With the Selection tool (▶) selected, select the text "EST. 1973" at the bottom of the label.

2   Choose Effect > Warp > Arc Lower.

3   In the Warp Options dialog box, to create an arcing effect, set Bend to 21%. Select Preview to preview the changes. Try choosing other styles from the Style menu, and then return to Arc Lower. Try adjusting the Horizontal and Vertical Distortion sliders to see the effect. Make sure that the Distortion values are returned to 0, and then click OK.

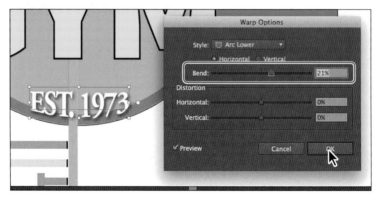

● **Note:** To learn more about the Appearance panel, see Lesson 13, "Applying Appearance Attributes and Graphic Styles."

4   With the warped text still selected, click the visibility icon (👁) to the left of the Warp: Arc Lower row in the Appearance panel to turn off visibility for the effect. Notice that the text is no longer warped on the artboard.

5   Select the Type tool (**T**) in the Tools panel, and select and change the text "1973" on the artboard to **1972**.

Toggle visibility of the effect.

Edit the text.

If the Appearance panel is still open and the cursor is in the text, notice that the effect isn't listed in the panel. That's because the effect was applied to the type area, not to the text.

6 Select the Selection tool, and then click the
   visibility column to the left of the Warp: Arc
   Lower row in the Appearance panel, to turn
   on visibility for the effect. Notice that the
   text is once again warped.

▶ **Tip:** It isn't necessary to turn the visibility off for the
Warp effect before editing the text on the artboard, but
doing so can make it easier.

7 Choose Select > Deselect, and then choose File > Save.

Editing shapes with a Pathfinder effect

Pathfinder effects are similar to working with Pathfinder commands in the
Pathfinder panel, except that they are applied as effects and do not change the
underlying content.

● **Note:** To learn more about the Pathfinder commands, see the "Working with Pathfinder effects"
section in Lesson 3, "Creating and Editing Shapes."

Next, you will apply a Pathfinder effect to several shapes.

1 With the Selection tool (▸), Shift-click to select the orange circle and yellow text
   "Joe's GYM."

2 Choose Object > Hide > Selection.

3 With the Selection tool, Shift-click to select the red circle and red rectangle.

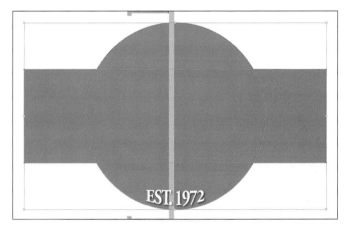

4 Choose Object > Group.

   You grouped the objects together because Pathfinder effects may only be
   applied to groups, layers, or type objects.

● **Note:** If you see a warning dialog box when you choose Effect > Pathfinder > Add, it's because you didn't group the objects first.

5   Choose Effect > Pathfinder > Add to combine the two shapes together.

Looking in the Appearance panel, notice that the Add effect appears beneath the word "Group," since the Add effect is applied to the Group. Beneath the Add effect attribute, the word "Contents" appears. If you were to double-click the word "Contents," you would see the appearance attributes of the individual items in the group. The Appearance panel lists the appearance attributes in stacking order—top to bottom in the panel correlates to front to back in the artwork.

● **Note:** To add shapes, you can also use the Pathfinder panel, which expands the shapes immediately, by default. Using the Effect menu lets you edit shapes independently.

Clicking the underlined word "Add" allows you to change the Pathfinder effect and to edit the more advanced features of the Add effect.

6   With the group still selected, choose View > Outline.

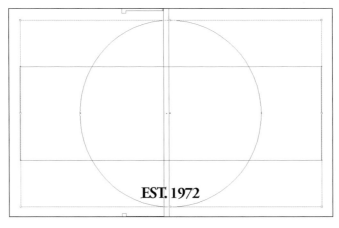

The two shapes are still there and completely editable, since the effect being applied is live.

7   Choose View > Preview, and then choose File > Save.

Applying an effect to convert a shape

Using an effect, you can convert an existing shape to a rectangle, a rounded rectangle, or an ellipse without having to redraw the shape. Next, you will convert a rectangle to a rounded rectangle.

1   With the Selection tool (▸), double-click the red rectangle group, to enter Isolation mode.

2 Click the red rectangle to select it.

3 Choose Effect > Convert To Shape > Rounded Rectangle. In the Shape Options dialog box, make the following changes:

- Size: **Relative** (the default setting)
- Extra Width: **0**
- Extra Height: **0**
- Corner Radius: **20 pt**

Select Preview to see the corners of the rectangle round. Click OK.

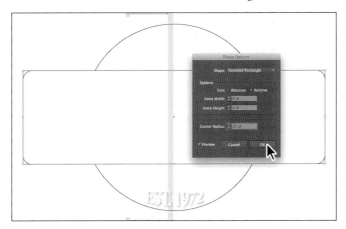

● **Note:** As of the writing of this book, selecting Preview on both platforms caused the artwork in the Document window to show a white fill with a black stroke.

4 Press the Escape key to exit Isolation mode. Choose Select > Deselect.

Applying a Stylize effect

Stylize effects are some of the more widely used since they contain effects like the Drop Shadow, Rounded Corners, Feathers, and Glows. Next, you'll apply a Rounded Corner effect to some shapes.

1 With the Selection tool (▶), click to select the combined shapes you previously had selected.

2 Click the Add New Fill button (▣) at the bottom of the Appearance panel. Drag the bottom of the panel down to make it taller so you can see all of the attributes listed.

When you add a new fill to content, such as the group, a new blank stroke is also added. Any fills or strokes that you apply to a group are applied on top of the strokes and fills of the objects within the group.

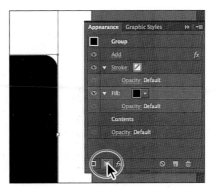

● **Note:** You will learn more about adding additional strokes and effects to artwork in Lesson 13, "Applying Appearance Attributes and Graphic Styles."

3 Click the Fill color box in the Appearance panel, and select the swatch named Dark Red. Press the Escape key to hide the Swatches panel.

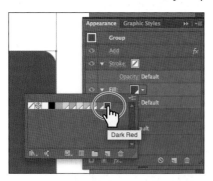

Note: If the Fill attribute row wasn't selected (highlighted), you could click to the right or left of the Fill box to select it.

4 With the Fill attribute row selected (highlighted) in the Appearance panel, choose Effect > Stylize > Inner Glow.

Selecting the Fill attribute row applies the effect to only the fill attribute.

5 In the Inner Glow dialog box, select Preview, and change the following values:

- Mode: **Screen** (the default setting)
- Color: Click the color box to open the Color Picker dialog box. Change the CMYK values to C=**0**, M=**84**, Y=**100**, K=**0**, and click OK.
- Opacity: **100%**
- Blur: **70 pt**
- Center: **Selected**

Click OK.

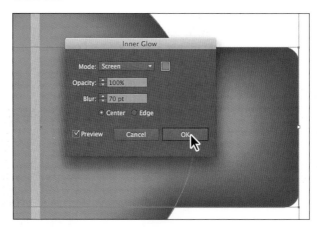

6 Choose File > Save, and leave the group selected.

Applying the Offset Path effect

Next, you will offset the stroke from the group. This process allows you to create the appearance of multiple stacked shapes.

1 With the group still selected, in the Appearance panel, click the underlined word "Stroke" to open the Stroke panel. Change the Stroke weight to **12 pt**. Press the Escape key to hide the Stroke panel.

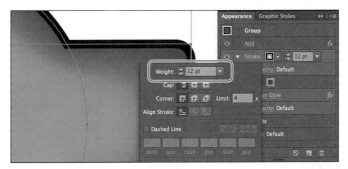

2 Click the Stroke Color in the Appearance panel, and make sure that the black swatch is selected in the Swatches panel. Press Enter or Return to close the Swatches panel, and return to the Appearance panel.

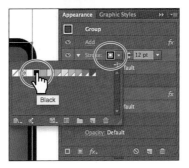

3 With the Stroke attribute row selected in the Appearance panel, choose Effect > Path > Offset Path.

4 In the Offset Path dialog box, make sure the Offset is 10 pt, and click OK.

5 In the Appearance panel, click the arrow to the left of the words "Stroke: 12 pt" to toggle it open (if it's not already open). Notice that Offset Path is a subset of Stroke. This indicates that the Offset Path effect is applied to only that Stroke.

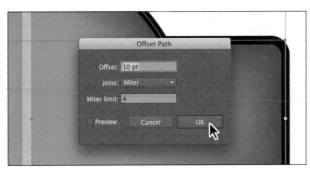

Apply the Offset Path filter.

Notice that the effect is a subset.

6 Choose Select > Deselect, and then choose File > Save.

Applying Distort & Transform

Next, you'll apply the Roughen effect to the orange circle in the background.

1 Choose Object > Show All to show the orange circle and yellow text.

2 Choose Select > Deselect, and then, with the Selection tool (▶), click to select the orange circle.

3 Choose Effect > Distort & Transform > Roughen.

4 In the Roughen dialog box, change the following options:

- Size: **30%**
- Relative: **Selected** (the default setting)
- Detail: **8** /in
- Smooth: **Selected**

Select Preview, and then click OK.

The Roughen effect applies the roughen randomly. That means that using the same settings on a copy of an object will most likely create a different outcome. Yours will look different than you see in the figure, and that's okay.

5 Choose Select > Deselect, and then choose File > Save.

Applying Photoshop effects

As described earlier in the lesson, Photoshop effects generate pixels rather than vector data. Photoshop effects include SVG Filters, all of the effects in the bottom portion of the Effect menu, and the Drop Shadow, Inner Glow, Outer Glow, and Feather commands in the Effect > Stylize submenu. You can apply them to either vector or bitmap objects.

Next, you will apply a Photoshop effect to the red shapes in the background.

1 With the Selection tool (▶), click to select the grouped red shapes in the background.

2 In the Appearance panel, select the Fill attribute row (click the word "Fill"), if it's not already highlighted.

3 Choose Effect > Artistic > Film Grain.

When you choose most of the Photoshop effects (not all), the Filter Gallery dialog box opens. Similar to working with filters in Adobe Photoshop, where you can also access a Filter Gallery, in the Illustrator Filter Gallery, you can try out different raster effects to see how they affect your artwork.

4   With the Filter Gallery open, choose Fit In View from the view menu in the lower-left corner of the dialog box (circled in the figure). That should fit the artwork in the preview area, so you can see how the effect alters the artwork.

The Filter Gallery dialog box, which is resizable, contains a preview area (labeled A), effect thumbnails that you can click to apply (labeled B), settings for the currently selected effect (labeled C), and the list of effects applied (labeled D). If you want to apply a different effect, expand a category in the middle panel of the dialog box, click a thumbnail, or choose an effect name from the menu in the upper-right corner of the dialog box.

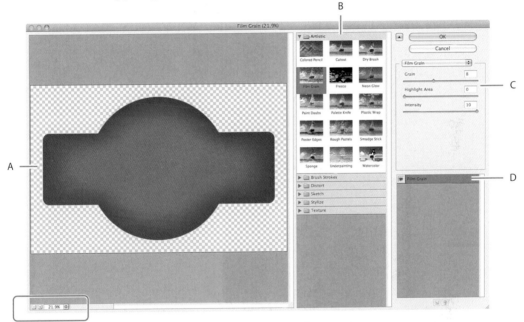

5   Change the Film Grain settings in the upper-right corner of the dialog box as follows (if necessary):

   •   Grain: **9**

   •   Highlight Area: **0**

   •   Intensity: **8**

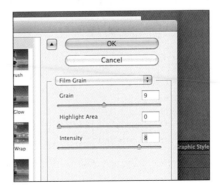

6 Click the eye icon (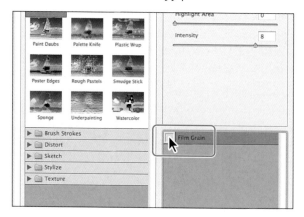) to the left of the name Film Grain to see the artwork without the effect applied. Click the same icon area again to preview the effect on the artwork. Click OK to apply the raster effect.

Document raster effects settings

Whenever you apply a raster effect, Illustrator uses the document's raster effects settings to determine the resolution of the resulting image. It's important to check the document raster effects settings before you start working with effects.

You set rasterization options for a document when creating a new document or by choosing Effect > Document Raster Effects Settings. In the Document Raster Effects Settings dialog box, for all raster effects in a document or when you rasterize a vector object, you can set Color Model, Resolution, Background, Anti-alias, Create Clipping Mask, and Add Around Object. To learn more about Document Raster Effects Settings, search for "About raster effects" in Help.

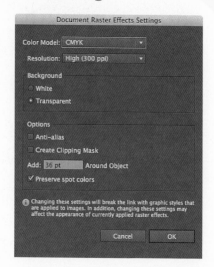

—From Illustrator Help

Review questions

1 Name two ways to apply an effect to an object.

2 When you apply a Photoshop (raster) effect to vector artwork, what happens to the artwork?

3 Where can the effects applied to an object be edited, once they are applied?

4 What three types of 3D effects are available? Give an example of why you would use each one.

5 How can you control lighting on a 3D object? Does the lighting of one 3D object affect other 3D objects?

Review answers

1 You can apply an effect to an object by selecting the object and then choosing the effect from the Effect menu. You can also apply an effect by selecting the object, clicking the Add New Effect button (fx) in the Appearance panel, and then choosing the effect from the menu that appears.

2 Applying a Photoshop effect to artwork generates pixels rather than vector data. Photoshop effects include SVG Filters, all of the effects in the bottom portion of the Effect menu, and the Drop Shadow, Inner Glow, Outer Glow, and Feather commands in the Effect > Stylize submenu. You can apply them to either vector or bitmap objects.

3 You can edit effects in the Appearance panel.

4 The types of 3D effects are Extrude & Bevel, Revolve, and Rotate.

   • **Extrude & Bevel:** Uses the z axis to give a 2D object depth by extruding the object. For example, a circle becomes a cylinder.

   • **Revolve:** Uses the y axis to revolve an object around an axis. For example, an arc becomes a circle.

   • **Rotate:** Uses the z axis to rotate 2D artwork in 3D space and to change the artwork's perspective.

5 By clicking the More Options button in any of the 3D dialog boxes, you can change the light, the direction of the light, and the shade color. Settings for the light of one 3D object do not affect the settings for other 3D objects.

13 APPLYING APPEARANCE ATTRIBUTES AND GRAPHIC STYLES

Lesson overview

In this lesson, you'll learn how to do the following:

- Edit and apply appearance attributes.
- Add a second stroke to an object.
- Reorder appearance attributes and apply them to layers.
- Copy, disable and enable, and remove appearance attributes.
- Save an appearance as a graphic style.
- Apply a graphic style to an object and a layer.
- Apply multiple graphic styles to an object or layer.
- Align content to the pixel grid.
- Work with the Slice and Slice Selection tools.
- Use the Save For Web command.
- Generate, export, and copy/paste Cascading Style Sheets (CSS) code.

 This lesson takes approximately an hour to complete.

Download the project files for this lesson from the Lesson & Update Files tab on your Account page at www.peachpit.com and store them on your computer in a convenient location, as described in the Getting Started section of this book.

Your Accounts page is also where you'll find any updates to the chapters or to the lesson files. Look on the Lesson & Update Files tab to access the most current content.

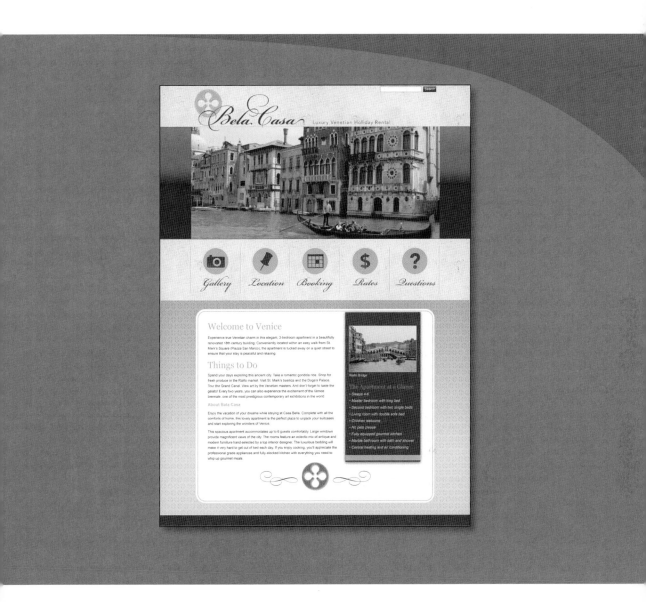

Without changing the structure of an object, you can change its look using appearance attributes, including fills, strokes, effects, and more. You can save appearance attributes as graphic styles and apply them to another object. You can also edit an object that has a graphic style applied to it and then edit the graphic style—an enormous time-saver!

Getting started

In this lesson, you'll enhance the design for a web page by applying appearance attributes and graphic styles to the type, background, and buttons. Before you begin, you'll restore the default preferences for Adobe Illustrator CC. Then, you will open the finished art file for this lesson to see what you'll create.

1   To ensure that the tools and panels function exactly as described in this lesson, delete or deactivate (by renaming) the Adobe Illustrator CC preferences file. See "Restoring default preferences," on page 3.

2   Start Adobe Illustrator CC.

● **Note:** If you have not already downloaded the project files for this lesson to your computer from your Account page, make sure to do so now. See "Getting Started" at the beginning of the book.

● **Note:** If a color profile warning dialog box appears, click OK.

3   Choose File > Open. Locate the L13end.ai file in the Lesson13 folder in the Lessons folder that you copied onto your hard disk, to view the finished artwork. Leave the file open for reference, or choose File > Close.

The design for the completed web page includes several graphic styles and effects, including gradients, drop shadows, and other graphics. This lesson contains a fictitious business name, made up for the purposes of the project.

● **Note:** In Mac OS, when opening lesson files, you may need to click the round, green button in the upper-left corner of the Document window to maximize the window's size.

4   Open the L13start.ai file in the Lesson13 folder, located in the Lessons folder on your hard disk.

5   Choose File > Save As. In the Save As dialog box, navigate to the Lesson13 folder and open it. Name the file **webdesign.ai**. Leave the Save As Type option set to Adobe Illustrator (*.AI) (Windows) or the Format option set to Adobe Illustrator (ai) (Mac OS), and click Save. In the Illustrator Options dialog box, leave the Illustrator options at their default settings and then click OK.

6   Choose View > Fit Artboard In Window.

7   Choose Window > Workspace > Reset Essentials.

● **Note:** If you don't see "Reset Essentials" in the Workspace menu, choose Window > Workspace > Essentials before choosing Window > Workspace > Reset Essentials.

Using the Appearance panel

You can apply appearance attributes to any object, group, or layer by using effects, the Appearance panel, and the Graphic Styles panel. An *appearance attribute* is an aesthetic property—such as a fill, stroke, transparency, or effect—that affects the look of an object but does not affect its basic structure. An advantage of using appearance attributes is that they can be changed or removed at any time without affecting the underlying object or any other attributes applied to the object in the Appearance panel (Window > Appearance).

1 Click the Appearance panel icon (▣) on the right side of the workspace to see the Appearance panel.

2 Select the Selection tool (▶), and click to select the bright green rectangle behind the image. The Appearance panel shows appearance attributes applied.

Note: Depending on your operating system, the selection color of objects (the bounding box) may be different and that's okay.

The different options available in the Appearance panel are described below:

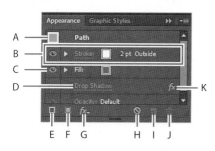

A. Selected object and thumbnail

B. Attribute row

C. Visibility column

D. Link to options

E. Add New Stroke

F. Add New Fill

G. Add New Effect

H. Clear Appearance

I. Duplicate Selected Item

J. Delete Selected Item

K. Indicates an effect applied

Editing appearance attributes

You'll start by changing the basic appearance of the green rectangle.

1 With the green rectangle still selected (see steps above), in the Appearance panel, click the green Fill color box in the Fill attribute row until the Swatches panel appears. Click the swatch named Black. Press the Escape key to hide the Swatches panel. You will find that you can change appearance attributes, like Fill color, in the Appearance panel or elsewhere in the workspace.

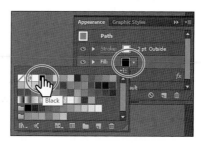

Note: You may need to click the Fill box twice to open the Swatches panel.

2 Click the words "2 pt Outside" in the Stroke row. The Stroke Weight option appears. Change the Stroke weight to **1 pt**.

3 Click the underlined word "Stroke" to reveal the Stroke panel. Click the Align Stroke To Inside button (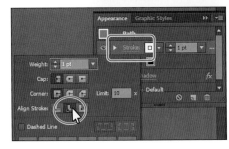), and press the Escape key to hide the Stroke panel.

Clicking underlined words in the Appearance panel, as in the Control panel, shows more formatting options—usually in a panel like the Swatches or Stroke panels.

Appearance attributes, like Fill or Stroke, can have other options, like Opacity or an effect applied to only that attribute. These additional options are listed as a subset under the attribute row and can be shown or hidden by clicking the toggle triangle icon (▶) on the left end of the attribute row.

4 Click the toggle triangle icon (▶) to the left of the word "Fill" in the Appearance panel to reveal the Opacity option. Click the word "Opacity" to reveal the Transparency panel. Choose 100% from the Opacity menu. Press the Escape key to hide the Transparency panel and to return to the Appearance panel.

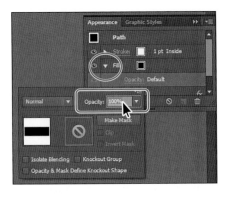

▶ **Tip:** You can view all hidden attributes by choosing Show All Hidden Attributes from the Appearance panel menu.

5 In the Appearance panel, click the visibility column to the left of the words "Drop Shadow" to see the effect applied to the rectangle (you may need to scroll down in the panel).

Adding another stroke

Artwork in Illustrator can have more than one stroke and fill applied to it to add interesting design elements. You'll now add another stroke to an object, using the Appearance panel.

1　Select the Zoom tool (🔍), and drag a marquee across the "Welcome to Venice" heading text underneath the row of buttons.

2　Select the Selection tool (▶), and click to select the large, white, rounded rectangle with the gray stroke, behind the text.

3　In the Appearance panel, click the Add New Stroke button (▣) at the bottom of the panel.

　A stroke is added above the original stroke row. It has the same color and stroke weight as the first stroke.

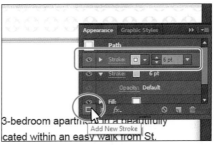

● **Note:** Depending on your operating system, the selection color of objects (the bounding box) may be different and that's okay.

4　For the new stroke row, leave Stroke weight at 6 pt. Click the Stroke color box in the new appearance row to open the Swatches panel. Select the white swatch. Press the Escape key to close the Swatches panel.

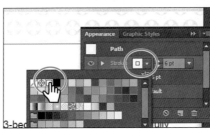

▶ **Tip:** Other ways to close panels that appear when clicking an underlined word, like "Stroke," include pressing the Escape key or clicking the Stroke attribute row.

　Notice in the artwork that the white stroke is now covering the original gray stroke. The order of the attribute rows is important in the Appearance panel. The bottom attribute listed is applied first, and the top attribute row is applied last.

5　Click the word "Stroke" in the new stroke row and, in the Stroke panel that appears, click the Align Stroke To Outside button (▣). You should now see both strokes (although the white stroke will be harder to see).

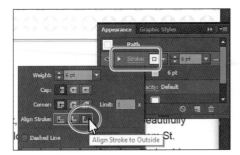

6　Choose Select > Deselect, and then choose File > Save.

Adding another fill

You'll now add another fill to an object, using the Appearance panel. This can be a great way to achieve interesting design effects with just one object.

1   Choose View > Fit Artboard In Window.

2   With the Selection tool (▶), click the pattern-filled shape behind the rounded rectangle that was previously selected.

3   In the Appearance panel, click the Fill attribute row to select it.

If you select an attribute row before adding a new stroke or new fill, the new stroke or fill row will be added directly above the selected row.

4   Click the Add New Fill button (▢) at the bottom of the Appearance panel. A new fill is added above the existing fill in the Appearance panel and is selected.

Tip: You can drag the bottom edge of the Appearance panel down to make it taller, like you see in the figure.

5   With the new fill attribute row selected, click the Fill color box and select the background gradient swatch. This new fill will cover the existing orange/yellow gradient fill. Press the Escape key to hide the swatches.

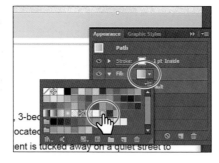

Tip: Depending on which attribute row is selected in the Attributes panel, the options in panels, like the Control panel, Gradient panel, and others, will affect the attribute selected.

6   Click the Gradient panel icon (▨), and choose 90 from the Angle menu. Leave the shape selected.

Reordering appearance attributes

The ordering of the appearance attribute rows can greatly change how your artwork looks. In the Appearance panel, fills and strokes are listed in stacking order—top to bottom in the panel correlates to front to back in the artwork. You can reorder attribute rows in a way similar to dragging layers in the Layers panel, to rearrange the stacking order. Now, you'll change the appearance of the artwork by reordering attributes in the Appearance panel.

1   Click the Appearance panel icon (◉), and drag the bottom of the Appearance panel down so that you can view all its contents. Click the toggle triangle icon (▶) to the left of all of the appearance rows to hide their properties.

2   Drag the new Fill attribute row (with the background gradient swatch applied) to below the original Fill attribute row.

Moving the new Fill attribute below the original Fill attribute changes the look of the artwork. The original pattern fill is now covering the new fill. Since the pattern has transparent areas, you can see the gradient fill beneath it.

▶ **Tip:** You can also apply blending modes and opacity changes to each Fill row to achieve different results.

3   Choose Select > Deselect, and then choose File > Save.

Applying an appearance attribute to a layer

You can also apply appearance attributes to layers or sublayers. For example, to make everything on a layer 50% opaque, you can target that layer and change the opacity. Every object on that layer will have the 50% opacity applied (even if you add the object to the layer later).

Next, you'll target a layer that is part of the navigation and add a drop shadow.

1   Select the Zoom tool (🔍), and drag a marquee across the line to the left of the orange Gallery button.

2   Click the Layers panel icon (▨) to open the panel. In the Layers panel, click the triangle icon (▶) to the left of the Nav layer to view its content, if necessary.

● **Note:** You may need to drag the left edge of the Layers panel to the left to see the names of objects in the panel.

Note: The layer colors you see may be different, depending on your operating system, and that's okay.

3   Click the target icon (⊙) to the right of the Nav-lines sublayer.

After clicking, notice that the target icon is now a double-ring (⊙). A hollow double-ring means that the layer is targeted (selected) but has no appearance attributes beyond a single fill and stroke. Any appearance attributes you add in the Appearance panel will be applied to that layer (and any objects on the layer).

4   Open the Appearance panel, and notice the word "Layer" at the top.

The word "Layer" indicates that any attributes applied will be applied to all content on that layer. When you select items that contain other items, such as a layer or group, the Appearance panel displays a Contents item. You could double-click to edit the appearance attributes of the individual objects, but don't.

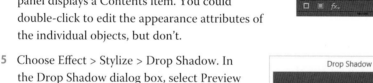

5   Choose Effect > Stylize > Drop Shadow. In the Drop Shadow dialog box, select Preview and change the following options:

- Mode: **Screen**
- Opacity: **80%**
- X Offset: **2 px**
- Y Offset: **1 px**
- Blur: **0 px**
- Click the Color box, and change the CMYK values to C=0, M=0, Y=0, K=0 (white) in the Color Picker. Click OK in the Color Picker to close the dialog box.

Click OK, and notice that the lines now have a subtle white drop shadow.

Tip: You can also copy attributes from one layer to another by Alt-dragging (Windows) or Option-dragging (Mac OS) the target icon (⊙) from one layer to another.

6   Click the Layers panel icon (◈), and notice that the target icon now has a shaded center (◉), indicating that the layer has appearance attributes applied to it.

7   Choose Select > Deselect, and then choose File > Save.

Using graphic styles

A *graphic style* is a saved set of appearance attributes that you can reuse. By applying graphic styles, you can quickly and globally change the appearance of objects and text.

The Graphic Styles panel (Window > Graphic Styles) lets you create, name, save, apply, and remove effects and attributes for objects, layers, and groups. You can also break the link between an object and an applied graphic style to edit that object's attributes without affecting other objects that use the same graphic style.

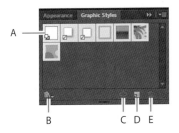

A

B   C D E

A. Graphic style thumbnail

B. Graphic Styles Libraries Menu

C. Break Link To Graphic Style

D. New Graphic Style

E. Delete Graphic Style

For example, if you have a map that uses a shape to represent a city, you can create a graphic style that paints the shape green and adds a drop shadow. You can then use that graphic style to paint all the city shapes on the map. If you decide to use a different color, you can change the fill color of the graphic style to blue. All the objects that use that graphic style are then updated to blue.

Applying an existing graphic style

You can also apply graphic styles to your artwork from graphic style libraries that come with Illustrator. Now, you'll add a graphic style to a button in the design.

1 Choose View > Search button, to zoom in to a button off of the upper-right corner of the artboard.

2 Choose Window > Workspace > Reset Essentials.

3 Click the Graphic Styles panel tab. Click the Graphic Styles Libraries Menu button (▨) at the bottom of the panel, and choose Illuminate Styles.

4 Click the Black Highlight graphic style. Clicking that style adds it to the Graphic Styles panel for the active document. Close the Illuminate Styles panel.

5 With the Selection tool (▸), click the edge of the white rectangle off of the upper-right corner of the artboard to select it. Be careful not to select the white text that is on top of it.

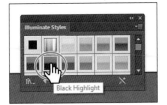

Tip: Use the arrows at the bottom of the Illuminate Styles library panel to load the previous or next Graphic Styles library in the panel.

6 Right-click (Windows) or Control-click (Mac OS), and hold down the mouse button on the Black Highlight graphic style thumbnail in the Graphic Styles panel to preview the graphic style on the shape. When finished, release the mouse button, and then release the Control key on Mac OS.

Previewing a graphic style is a great way to see how it will affect the selected object, without actually applying it.

7 Click the Black Highlight graphic style in the Graphic Styles panel to apply it to the shape. Click the Graphic Styles panel tab to collapse the panel group.

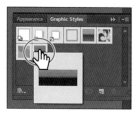
Preview the graphic style.

Apply the graphic style.

8 Choose Select > Deselect, and then choose File > Save.

● **Note:** You may see a warning icon appear on the left end of the Control panel. That's okay. This is a helpful indicator that the topmost fill/stroke is not active in the Appearance panel.

Creating and applying a graphic style

▶ **Tip:** To create a graphic style, you can also click to select the object that you are using to make the graphic style. In the Appearance panel, drag the appearance thumbnail at the top of the listing into the Graphic Styles panel.

Now, you'll save and name a new graphic style using the appearance attributes applied to one of the orange buttons. You will then apply the same appearance attributes to another button.

1 Choose View > Nav, to zoom in to the navigation buttons.

2 With the Selection tool (▶), click to select the orange Gallery button shape (the circle).

● **Note:** Depending on your operating system, the bounding box and edges (the aqua outlines in the figure) of some selected objects may be a different color, and that's okay.

3 Click the Graphic Styles panel icon (▣) on the right side of the workspace to open the Graphic Styles panel. Click the New Graphic Style button (▣) at the bottom of the panel.

The appearance attributes from the orange button are saved as a graphic style.

4 In the Graphic Styles panel, double-click the new graphic style thumbnail. In the Graphic Style Options dialog box, name the new style **Buttons**. Click OK.

Create a new Graphic Style.   Name the style.

5   Click the Appearance panel tab and, at the top of the Appearance panel, you will see Path: Buttons. This indicates that a graphic style named Buttons is applied to the selected artwork (a path).

6   With the Selection tool, click to select the white circle behind the Location icon (to the right of the button you just used to create the graphic style).

7   Click the Graphic Styles panel tab, and then click the Buttons graphic style thumbnail to apply the style to the circle.

▶ **Tip:** In the Graphic Styles panel, graphic style thumbnails that show a small box with a red slash (☒) indicate that the graphic style does not contain a stroke or fill. It may just be a drop shadow or outer glow, for instance.

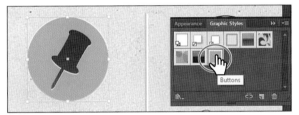

Notice Path: Buttons.   Apply the Buttons graphic style.

8   Choose Select > Deselect, and then choose File > Save.

Updating a graphic style

Once you create a graphic style, you can still edit the object that the style is applied to. You can also update a graphic style, and all artwork with that style applied will update its appearance, as well.

1   With the Selection tool (▶), click to select either of the orange button shapes. In the Graphic Styles panel, you will see that the Buttons graphic style thumbnail is highlighted (has a border around it), indicating that it is applied.

2   Click the Appearance panel tab. Click the Path: Buttons row to select it. This applies the next appearance attribute to the object as a whole (not to just the stroke or the fill, for instance).

3 Choose Effect > Distort & Transform > Pucker & Bloat. In the Pucker & Bloat dialog box, change the value to **13%** and click OK.

4 Click the Graphic Styles panel tab to see that the graphic style is no longer highlighted, which means that the graphic style is no longer applied.

5 Press the Alt (Windows) or Option (Mac OS) key, and drag the selected orange button shape on top of the Buttons graphic style thumbnail in the Graphic Styles panel. Release the mouse button, and then release the modifier key when the thumbnail is highlighted. Both orange button shapes now look the same.

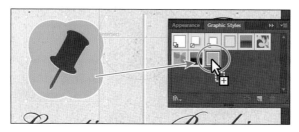

6 Choose Select > Deselect.

7 Click the Appearance panel tab. You will see No Selection: Buttons at the top of the panel (you may need to scroll up).

When you apply appearance settings, graphic styles, and more to artwork, the next shape you draw will have the appearance settings listed in the Appearance panel.

8 Click the Clear Appearance button (⊘) at the bottom of the Appearance panel.

By clicking the Clear Appearance button with nothing selected, you are setting the default appearance for new artwork. If artwork had been selected, the Clear Appearance button removes all appearance attributes applied to selected artwork, including any stroke or fill.

9 Choose File > Save.

Applying a graphic style to a layer

When a graphic style is applied to a layer, everything added to that layer has that same style applied to it. Now, you'll apply the Buttons graphic style to the layer with the button shapes to apply the style to them all at once.

1   Choose View > Fit Artboard In Window.

If you apply a graphic style to artwork and then apply a graphic style to the layer (or sublayer) that it's on, the graphic style formatting is added to the appearance of the artwork—it's cumulative. This means that, in order for the buttons to have only the appearance attributes from the graphic style applied, you need to remove the formatting from the button shapes before applying the graphic style.

2   Click the Layers panel icon (⬗). In the Layers panel, click the toggle triangle icon (▶) to the left of the Nav layer to expand the layer, if it isn't already. Click in the selection column of the Buttons sublayer (the blank space *to the right of* the target icon [◉]) to select all of the content on the layer.

3   At the bottom of the Appearance panel, click the Clear Appearance button (⊘). All of the button shapes now have no stroke, no fill, and no other appearance attributes applied.

4   In the Layers panel, click the target icon (◉) for the Buttons sublayer. This selects the layer content (it was already selected) and targets the layer for any appearance attributes.

5   Click the Graphic Styles panel icon (⬚), and then click the Buttons graphic style thumbnail to apply the style to the layer and all its contents.

6   Choose Select > Deselect, and then choose File > Save.

> **Tip:** In the Layers panel, you can drag a target icon to the Trash button (🗑) at the bottom of the Layers panel to remove the appearance attributes.

Editing the layer's graphic style formatting

Next, you will edit the Buttons graphic style applied to the layer.

1 With the Selection tool (⬆), click to select any of the orange button shapes.

2 Click the Appearance panel tab to open the Appearance panel.

In the Appearance panel, notice the name Layer: Buttons at the top of the panel. The Appearance panel shows that the button shape is on a layer with a graphic style called Buttons applied to it.

▶ **Tip:** You can also select the Buttons sublayer target icon in the Layers panel and then edit the effect in the Appearance panel.

3 Click the words "Layer: Buttons" to access the appearance attributes from the graphic style applied to the layer. This also selects all of the shapes on the layer.

4 Click the eye icon (👁) to the left of the Pucker & Bloat effect row to remove the effect from the shapes. Click the visibility column to the left of the Stroke 2 pt row to apply the stroke to the button shapes. Leave the Appearance panel showing.

5 Choose Select > Deselect, and then choose File > Save.

Applying multiple graphic styles

You can apply a graphic style to an object that already has a graphic style applied. This can be useful if you want to add properties to an object from another graphic style.

1 Choose View > Search button, to zoom in to the button off of the upper-right corner of the artboard.

● **Note:** If the Style menu doesn't appear in the Control panel, open the Graphic Styles panel by clicking its icon on the right side of the workspace.

2 With the Selection tool (⬆), click the rectangle behind the text "Search." Click the Style menu in the Control panel. In the Graphic Styles panel that appears, click the Buttons graphic style to apply it to the button shape. Leave the menu open.

Notice that the fills and the strokes from the Black Highlight graphic style you applied earlier are no longer visible. Graphic styles replace the formatting on selected objects, by default.

3 Click the Chrome Highlight graphic style thumbnail to apply it.

4 Alt-click (Windows) or Option-click (Mac OS) the Outer Glow 5 pt graphic style thumbnail.

Notice that the fills and stroke are preserved and that the there is a glow (shadow). Alt-clicking (Windows) or Option-clicking (Mac OS) adds the graphic style formatting to the existing formatting, rather than replacing it.

5 With the Selection tool, Shift-click the text "Search" and choose Object > Group. Leave the button group selected.

Scaling strokes and effects

In Illustrator, when scaling (resizing) content, any strokes and effects that are applied do not change. For instance, suppose you scale a circle with a 2-pt. stroke from small to the size of the artboard. The shape may change size, but the stroke will remain 2 pt. by default. That can change the appearance of scaled artwork in a way that you didn't intend, so you'll need to watch out for that when transforming artwork.

1 Click the X, Y, W, or H link in the Control panel to reveal the Transform panel (Window > Transform). Select Scale Strokes & Effects at the bottom of the Transform panel. Click the Constrain Width And Height Proportions button (⬚). Change the height (H) to **20 px**. Press Enter or Return to change the width, as well, and hide the Transform panel.

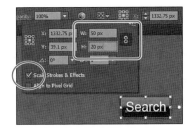

● **Note:** If you choose Window > Transform to open the Transform panel, you will need to choose Show Options from the panel menu.

2 Drag the button group to the left, onto the artboard. Make sure it's just to the right of the search field (the white box at the top of the artboard), using the Smart Guides to align it.

3 Choose Select > Deselect, and then choose File > Save.

Applying a graphic style to text

Next, you'll apply an existing graphic style to some text.

1   Choose View > Fit Artboard In Window.

2   With the Selection tool (▶), click the "Welcome to Venice" heading text.

3   Select the Zoom tool (🔍), and drag a marquee around the text to zoom in.

4   Click the Graphic Styles panel icon (▦) to expand the panel, if necessary. Click the panel menu icon (▤), and ensure that Override Character Color is chosen in the Graphic Styles panel menu.

When you apply a graphic style to type, the fill color of the text overrides the fill color of the graphic style, by default. If you deselect Override Character Color, the fill color (if there is one) in the graphic style will override the color of the text.

5   Choose Use Text For Preview from the Graphic Styles panel menu (▤).

6   In the Graphic Styles panel, right-click (Windows) or Control-click (Mac OS) and hold down the mouse button on the Blue Neon graphic style to preview the graphic style on the text. Release the mouse button or the Control key, and then click the Blue Neon graphic style to apply it.

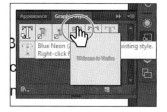

If the Override Character Color option had been deselected, the fill would still be black (although you most likely wouldn't be able to see it).

7   Choose Edit > Undo Graphic Styles to remove the graphic style formatting from the text.

8   Choose View > Fit Artboard In Window.

9   Choose Select > Deselect. Leave the webdesign.ai file open.

Saving content for the web

Using Illustrator CC, you can save your artwork for the web using a variety of methods and formats. If you need web images for use in a website or an on-screen presentation, you can use the Save For Web command. Images can be saved in several file formats, such as GIF, JPEG, and PNG. These three formats are optimized for use on the web and are compatible with most browsers, yet they each have different capabilities.

Tip: To learn more about working with web graphics, search for "File formats for exporting artwork" in Illustrator Help (Help > Illustrator Help).

If you are building a website or wish to hand off content to a developer, you can transform the visual designs in Illustrator to CSS styles using the CSS Properties panel (Window > CSS Properties) or File > Export command. Illustrator allows you to easily export CSS or copy and paste CSS from Illustrator into your HTML editor. You can also export Scalable Vector Graphics (SVG) using a variety of methods.

In the first part of the section on creating web content, you will focus on the pixel grid and on slicing content for export using the Save For Web command. Then you will translate your design into CSS for use in a website.

Aligning content to the pixel grid

Before you save content for the web, it's important to understand the pixel grid in Illustrator. It's critical that raster images look sharp, especially standard web graphics at 72 pixels per inch (ppi) resolution. To enable web designers to create pixel-accurate designs, you can align artwork to the pixel grid. The *pixel grid* is a grid of 72 squares per inch, vertically and horizontally, that is viewable when you zoom to 600% or higher with Pixel Preview mode enabled (View > Pixel Preview).

Tip: To learn about working with text and anti-aliasing, see the PDF named TextAntiAliasing.pdf in the Lesson_extras folder in the Lessons folder.

When the pixel-aligned property is enabled for an object, all the horizontal and vertical segments in the object get aligned to the pixel grid, which provides a crisp appearance to strokes. When you create a new document, you can set the Align New Objects To Pixel Grid option at the document level by choosing Web from the Profile menu in the New Document dialog box. This makes all artwork (that is able to be aligned to the pixel grid) align to it automatically. You can also align content to the pixel grid later, as you will do in this section.

1 Choose File > New. In the New Document dialog box, choose Web from the Profile menu. Click the triangle to the left of the Advanced content, toward the bottom of the dialog box.

    In the Advanced settings, you can see that the Color Mode is RGB for all artwork you create, the Raster Effects are 72 ppi, and Align New Objects To Pixel Grid is selected.

2 Click Cancel.

3 In the webdesign.ai file, choose File > Document Color Mode and you will see that RGB is selected.

After you create a document, you can change the document color mode. This sets the default color mode for all *new* colors you create. RGB is the correct color mode to use when creating content for the web or for on-screen presentations.

4 Select the Zoom tool (🔍), and drag a marquee around the orange Gallery button (the first on the left), to zoom in very closely.

▶ **Tip:** You can turn off the pixel grid by choosing Edit > Preferences > Guides & Grid (Windows) or Illustrator > Preferences > Guides & Grid (Mac OS) and deselecting Show Pixel Grid (Above 600% Zoom).

5 Choose View > Pixel Preview, to preview a rasterized version of the design.

The artwork in Preview mode

The artwork in Pixel Preview mode

6 Choose 600% from the View menu in the lower-left corner of the Document window (in the Status bar).

By zooming in to at least 600%, and with Pixel Preview turned on, you can see a pixel grid appear, as in the figure. The pixel grid divides the artboard into 1-pt. (1/72-inch) increments.

7 With the Selection tool (▶), click to select the camera shape on the button. Scroll in the Document window using the scroll bars, if necessary, to see the entire camera shape.

8 Choose View > Hide Edges so you can see the edge of the camera more easily. Notice how certain edges of the camera look a little "fuzzy."

9 Click the word "Transform" (or X, Y, W, or H) in the Control panel, and select Align To Pixel Grid at the bottom of the Transform panel.

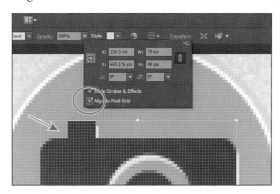

● **Note:** Objects that are pixel-aligned, but do not have any straight vertical or horizontal segments, are not modified to align to the pixel grid. For example, because a rotated rectangle does not have straight vertical or horizontal segments, it is not nudged to produce crisp paths when the pixel-aligned property is set for it.

10 Choose View > Fit Artboard In Window, and then choose View > Show Edges.

11 Choose Select > Object > Not Aligned To Pixel Grid to select all artwork in the document that is eligible to be, but is not currently, aligned to the pixel grid.

12 Click the word "Transform" in the Control panel, and select Align To Pixel Grid. Leave the Transform panel showing.

You do need to look at how aligning to the pixel grid affects artwork. For instance, text converted to outlines may change appearance.

13 Click the Transform panel menu icon (▼☰). Notice that Align New Objects To Pixel Grid is selected. If this document were created using a Print profile, it would *not* be selected. Press the Escape key to hide the Transform panel.

This option sets all new artwork to be aligned to the pixel grid automatically.

14 Choose Select > Deselect (if available), and then choose File > Save.

Slicing content

If you create artwork on an artboard and choose File > Save For Web, Illustrator creates a single image file the size of the artboard. You can create multiple artboards for artwork, each containing a piece of the web page, like a button, and save each artboard as a separate image file.

● **Note:** To learn more about creating slices, search for "Create slices" in Adobe Illustrator Help (Help > Illustrator Help).

You can also design your artwork on an artboard and slice the content. In Illustrator, you can create *slices* to define the boundaries of different web elements in your artwork. For example, if you design an entire web page on an artboard and there is a vector shape that you want to save as a button for your website, that artwork can be optimized in GIF or PNG format, while the rest of the image is optimized as a JPEG file. You can isolate the button image by creating a slice. When you save the artwork as a web page using the Save For Web command, you can choose to save each slice as an independent file with its own format and settings.

Next, you will create a new layer that will contain the slices and then you will create slices for different parts of the artwork.

● **Note:** To learn more about creating layers, see the section "Creating layers" in Lesson 8, "Working With Layers."

● **Note:** The new layer you create may have a different layer color, and that's okay.

1 Click the Layers panel icon ( ) to open the Layers panel. Click to select the Header layer. Alt-click (Windows) or Option-click (Mac OS) the Create New Layer button ( ) at the bottom of the Layers panel. In the Layer Options dialog box that appears, change the name of the layer to **Slices** and click OK. Make sure that the new layer named Slices is selected.

When you create slices, they are listed in the Layers panel and can be selected, deleted, resized, and more. It helps to keep them on their own layer so that you can more easily manage them, but this isn't necessary.

2 Select the Zoom tool ( ), and drag a marquee around the Bela Casa logo in the upper-left corner of the artboard. The text in the logo has been converted to outlines (paths).

3 Select the Slice tool ( ) in the Tools panel. Click and drag a slice around the circle and "Bela Casa" text shapes, stopping the bottom of the slice at the top of the image. See the figure for help. Don't worry about it fitting perfectly right now; you will edit it later.

When you create a slice, Illustrator divides the surrounding artwork into automatic slices to maintain the layout of the page. Auto slices account for the areas of your artwork that you did not define as a slice. Illustrator regenerates auto slices every time you add or edit your own slices. Also, notice the number 3 in the corner of the slice you created. Illustrator numbers slices from left to right and from top to bottom, beginning in the upper-left corner of the artwork.

Next, you will create a slice based on selected content.

4 Choose View > Nav, to zoom in to the orange navigation buttons.

5 Choose Select > Deselect.

6 Select the Selection tool ( ), and Shift-click the Gallery text shapes, the camera shape, and the orange circle to select all three objects.

7 Select the Slices layer in the Layers panel to place the new slice on that layer.

8 Choose Object > Slice > Create From Selection.

   Illustrator can create slices based on guides
   you create or on content that you select in the
   Document window.

9 Choose Select > Deselect, and then choose
   File > Save.

Tip: Use the Object > Slice > Make command when you want the slice dimensions to match the boundary of an element in your artwork. Using the Make command, If you move or modify the element, the slice area automatically adjusts to encompass the new artwork.

Selecting and editing slices

Editing user slices is necessary, for instance, when sliced content changes or when what is included in the slice needs to change.

1 Choose View > Fit Artboard In Window, select the Zoom tool (🔍), and then drag a marquee around the Bela Casa logo in the upper-left corner of the artboard.

2 Select the Slice Selection tool (✐) from the Slice tool group in the Tools panel by clicking and holding down on the Slice tool (✐).

3 Click in the center of the first slice you created over the Bela Casa logo. The selected slice is highlighted, and four corner bounding points appear.

   The Slice Selection tool allows you to edit slices you've created using the different methods. You can also select a user slice with the Selection or Direct Selection tools by clicking the stroke (edge) of the slice or from within the Layers panel.

4 Position the pointer over the bottom edge of the selected slice. When a double arrow appears, click and drag down until it goes beyond the curve of the "B" in "Bela."

   When slicing content, you should contain all appearance attributes, like drop shadows, in the slice area. This can be difficult if the shadow is very blurry. Using the Object > Slice > Create From Selection command creates a slice that surrounds all appearance properties, like effects, if those effects are applied directly to the artwork and not to the layer the artwork is on. Using the Slice Selection tool, you can click and drag a slice, copy and paste it, delete it, and much more.

5 Choose Select > Deselect, and then choose View > Lock Slices so that you cannot select them. Choose File > Save.

Using the Save For Web command

After slicing your artwork, if necessary, you can then optimize that artwork for use on the web. You can use the File > Save For Web command to select optimization options and to preview optimized artwork. The key to the effective use of images on a website is finding the balance of resolution, size, and color to achieve optimal quality.

1   Choose View > Fit Artboard In Window, and then choose View > Hide Slices.

    While working on your artwork, you don't have to have the slices showing. This can make it so that you can concentrate on selecting artwork without selecting slices. You can also hide the layer that the slices are on if you created a layer for them in the Layers panel.

2   Select the Selection tool (▶), and Shift-click the shape with the gray pattern background (behind the buttons), the black rectangle, and the large image on top of the black rectangle. Choose Object > Hide > Selection.

    When you save sliced content using the Save For Web command, all content that is showing in a slice will be flattened into a raster image. If you want to have transparency in the selected artwork (part of the image will be see-through), you need to first hide what you don't want to save. The areas where you see the artboard in a slice can be transparent, depending on the type of image you choose.

3   Choose Select > Deselect, if necessary.

● **Note:** To resize the slices, you need to make sure that they are unlocked. Choose View > Lock Slices. (If a check mark appears to the left of the menu item, they are locked.)

4   Choose View > Show Slices, and ensure that the artwork and drop shadows are contained within the slices. If not, you can resize either slice.

5   Choose File > Save For Web.

6   In the Save For Web dialog box, click the 2-Up tab at the top of the dialog box to select that display option, if it's not already selected.

    This shows a split window with the original artwork on the left and the optimized artwork on the right.

7   With the Slice Selection tool (✄) selected, click in the optimized area on the right. Click to select the slice that covers the Bela Casa logo at the top of the artboard, if it isn't selected already. You can tell when a slice is selected because of the light brown border around it.

8 In the Preset area on the right side of the dialog box, choose PNG-24 from the Optimized File Format menu (below Name).

You can choose from four file formats, including GIF, JPEG, PNG-8, and PNG-24, as well as set the options for each in the Preset area. The available options change depending on the file format you select. If your image contains multiple slices that you are going to save, be sure to select each separately and to optimize all the slices.

9 Choose Selected Slices from the Export menu.

Any slices that you select in the Save For Web dialog box will be exported. You can select multiple slices, after you've assigned optimization settings to them, by Shift-clicking the desired slices. By choosing All User Slices from the Export menu, all slices that you created will be exported.

10 Click the Preview button in the lower-left corner of the dialog box to launch the default web browser on your computer and to preview the sliced content. After viewing the content, close the browser and return to Illustrator.

● **Note:** If nothing happens after clicking the Preview button, try clicking again. You may also need to click the Select Browser Menu button to the right of the Preview button and choose Edit List to add a new browser.

11 In the Save For Web dialog box, click Save. In the Save Optimized As dialog box, navigate to the Lesson13 folder in the Lessons folder and open it. Change the name to **logo**, and click Save.

In your Lesson13 folder is an images folder that Illustrator generated. In that folder, you can see the single image that is labeled according to the name entered in the Save Optimized dialog box, with the slice number appended to the end.

12 Choose View > Hide Slices.

13 Choose Object > Show All.

14 Choose Select > Deselect, and then choose File > Save.

Creating CSS code

● **Note:** Exporting or copying CSS from Illustrator CC does not create HTML for a web page. It is intended to create CSS that is applied to HTML you create elsewhere, such as in Adobe Dreamweaver®.

As was mentioned earlier, you can also transform the visual designs in Illustrator to CSS styles using the CSS Properties panel (Window > CSS Properties) or the File > Export command. This is a great way to move the styling from your web design in Illustrator straight to your HTML editor or to hand it off to a web developer.

Cascading Style Sheets are a collection of formatting rules, much like paragraph and character styles in Illustrator that control the appearance of content in a web page. Unlike paragraph and character styles in Illustrator, CSS can control the look and feel of text, as well as the formatting and positioning of page elements found in HTML.

● **Note:** To learn more about what CSS is, visit the "Understanding Cascading Style Sheets" section of Adobe Dreamweaver Help (http://helpx.adobe.com/dreamweaver/using/cascading-style-sheets.html). You can also check out the CSS video series on Adobe Dreamweaver Developer Center: http://www.adobe.com/devnet/dreamweaver/articles/understanding_css_basics.html.

The great thing about generating CSS from your Illustrator artwork is that it allows for flexible web workflows. You can export all of the styling from a document, or you can just copy the styling code for a single object or a series of objects and paste it into an external web editor, like Adobe Dreamweaver. But creating CSS styling and using it effectively requires a bit of setup in your Illustrator CC document, and that's what you'll learn about first.

Setting up your design for generating CSS

If you intend to export or copy and paste CSS from Illustrator CC, slicing is not a necessary part of that process, but setting up the Illustrator CC file properly before creating CSS allows you to name the CSS styles that are generated. In this next section, you'll look at the CSS Properties panel and see how you can set up the content for style export using *named* or *unnamed* content.

1 Choose Window > Workspace > Reset Essentials.

2 Choose Window > CSS Properties, to open the CSS Properties panel.

   Using the CSS Properties panel, you can do the following:

   • Preview CSS code for selected objects.

   • Copy CSS code for selected objects.

   • Export generated styling for selected objects to a CSS file (along with any images used).

   • Change options for the CSS code exported.

   • Export the CSS for all objects to a CSS file.

The different options available in the panel are described here:

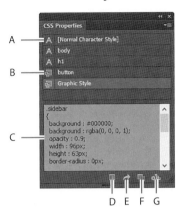

A ──
B ──
C ──

A. Character style

B. Graphic style

C. Styling of selected content

D. Export options

E. Export selected CSS

F. Copy selected style

G. Generate CSS

D E F G

3   Select the Selection tool (↖), and click to select the very dark gray rectangle shape (see the figure).

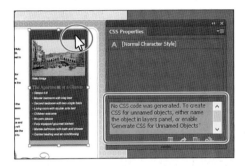

Take a look in the CSS Properties panel, and you will see that a message appears in the preview area. Instead of CSS code (which is what the preview area typically shows), the message states that the object needs to be named in the Layers panel or you need to allow Illustrator to create styling from unnamed objects.

4   Open the Layers panel and click the Locate Object button (🔍) at the bottom of the panel, to easily find the selected object in the panel. Double-click directly on the name of the selected <Path> object, and change the name to **sidebar** (lowercase). Press Enter or Return to make the change.

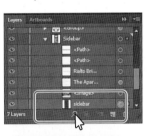

● **Note:** You may need to drag the left edge of the Layers panel to the left to see the entire name of the object.

5   Look in the CSS Properties panel again, and you should see a style named .sidebar.

When content is unnamed, a CSS style is not created for it, by default. If you name the object in the Layers panel, the CSS is generated and the name of the style created matches the object name in the Layers panel. Illustrator creates styles called *classes* for most content.

▶ **Tip:** You can tell a style is a class in CSS because the name has a period (.) before it.

● **Note:** You may wish to drag the bottom edge of the CSS Properties panel down to see the entire style.

● **Note:** If you see a style named ".sidebar_1_" it's usually because there is an extra space after the name "sidebar" in the Layers panel.

▶ **Tip:** If you are using HTML5 markup in your HTML editor, any objects in the Layers panel that you name according to the standard HTML5 markup tags, like "header," "footer," "section," or "aside," for instance, will not become a class style when the CSS code is generated. Rather, the style will be named according to the HTML5 markup tag.

For objects in the design (not including text objects, as you will see), the name you give them in the Layers panel should match the class name in the HTML that is created in a separate HTML editor, like Dreamweaver. But, you can also forgo naming the objects in the Layers panel and simply create generic styles that you can then export or paste into an HTML editor and name there. You will see how to do that next.

6 With the Selection tool (⬆), click to select the white rounded rectangle behind the sidebar rectangle. In the CSS Properties panel, a style will not appear since the object is unnamed in the Layers panel (it just has the generic <Path> name).

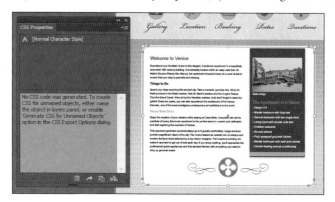

7 Click the Export Options button (▤) at the bottom of the CSS Properties panel.

The CSS Export Options dialog box that appears contains export options that you can set, such as which units to use, which properties to include in the styles, and other options, like which Vendor pre-fixes to include.

8 Select Generate CSS For Unnamed Objects, and click OK.

9 Look in the CSS Properties panel again. With the rounded rectangle still selected, a style called .st0 appears in the preview area of the CSS Properties panel.

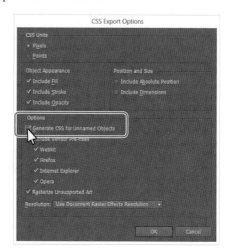

.st0 is short for style 0 and is a generic name for the formatting that is generated. Every object that you don't name in the Layers panel will now be named .st1, .st2, and so on, after turning on Generate CSS For Unnamed Objects. This type of style-naming can be useful if, for instance, you are creating the web page yourself and you are going to paste or export the CSS from Illustrator and name it in your HTML editor, or if you simply needed some of the CSS formatting for a style you already have in your HTML editor.

10 Choose Select > Deselect, and then choose File > Save.

Working with character styles and CSS code

Illustrator will create CSS styles based on text formatting, as well. Formatting, such as font family, font size, leading (called *line-height* in CSS), color, kerning and tracking (collectively called *letter-spacing* in CSS), and more, can be captured in the CSS code. In order for you to create styles that are named, for text, you create and apply Character styles to the text in your design. Any Character styles that you use in your design are listed in the CSS Properties panel and are generated with the same name as the character style.

● **Note:** Currently, paragraph styles are not taken into account when naming styles in the CSS code that is generated.

Next, you will apply a Character style to text.

1 In the CSS Properties panel, notice the style named [Normal Character Style], toward the top of the panel.

In the CSS Properties panel, only Character styles that are applied to text appear. The Normal Character Style is applied to text by default, so it appears in the panel.

2 Choose Window > Type > Character Styles to open the Character Styles panel.

3 Select the Type tool (**T**) in the Tools panel. Select the heading text "Welcome to Venice."

4 Alt-click (Windows) or Option-click (Mac OS) to apply the character style named h1 in the Character style panel. The text should now be orange and larger in size.

In the CSS Properties panel, the character style named h1 should appear in the list. This indicates that it is applied to text in the design.

5   Select the Selection tool (⬦), and with the "Welcome to Venice" text object still selected, you will see CSS code in the preview area of the CSS Properties panel.

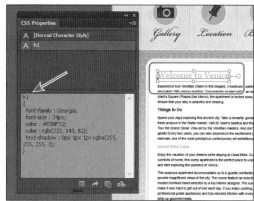

Selecting a text object will show all of the generated CSS code for the styling used in the entire text area.

You can also use the Character styles listed in the CSS Properties panel as a way to apply the styles to text.

6   With the Type tool selected, select the black text "Things to Do," below the heading with h1 applied.

7   Click the h1 style name in the CSS Properties list to apply the formatting to the selected text.

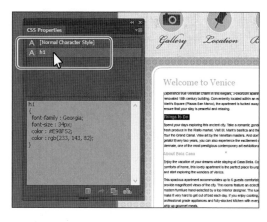

This applies the h1 character style, but it may not apply all of the formatting. If you look in the Character Styles panel, you may see a plus sign (+) next to the h1 style name, indicating local formatting that is overriding the h1 style formatting.

● **Note:** Selecting a type area gives you the ability to see all of the CSS code generated from the styling. It is also a great way to be able to copy or export all of the text formatting from a selected type area.

8   Click again on the h1 style name in the CSS Properties panel to remove the local formatting. The text should now look like the "Welcome to Venice" text.

9   Select the Selection tool, and make sure that the type object that contains the "Things to Do" heading is selected. Look in the CSS Properties panel, and you will see a series of CSS styles listed. These are the styles applied to all of the text in the type area.

Working with graphic styles and CSS code

CSS code can also be copied or exported for any graphic styles that are applied to content. Next, you'll apply a graphic style and see the CSS code for it.

1   With the Selection tool (➤), click to select the black rectangle behind the large image above the buttons. Click the Graphic Styles menu in the Control panel, and click to apply the Black Highlight style thumbnail.

► **Tip:** Like selecting a Character style in the CSS Properties panel to apply the formatting, you can also select content and select an Object style listed in the CSS Properties panel to apply it.

Looking in the CSS Properties panel, you will see the object style named Black Highlight listed, because it is applied to content in your document. You will also see CSS code for a style named .st0. The CSS code is the same as for the Black Highlight graphic style you just saw, since that graphic style is applied. But it's not naming the style with the Black Highlight name since the graphic style is just a way to apply formatting and the CSS code is being generated for that particular object. Remember, this is an unnamed style, since we didn't rename the black rectangle object in the Layers panel.

● **Note:** The unnamed style is being generated because you selected Generate CSS For Unnamed Objects in the CSS Export options earlier.

2   Leave the black rectangle selected, and then choose File > Save.

Copying CSS

At times, you may only need to capture a bit of CSS code from part of your design to paste into your HTML editor or to send to a web developer. Illustrator lets you copy and paste CSS code easily. Next, you will copy the CSS for a few objects and learn about how grouping can change the way CSS code is generated.

1   Click the Copy Selected Style button (🖼) at the bottom of the CSS Properties panel. This copies the CSS code currently showing in the panel.

Next, you will see that you can select multiple objects and copy the generated CSS code at one time.

● **Note:** Notice the yield sign icon (⚠) that appears at the bottom of the panel. It indicates that not all of the Illustrator appearance attributes (like the multiple strokes applied to the shape) can be written in the CSS code for the selected content.

2 With the Selection tool (⬉), click to select the rounded white rectangle behind the text and then Shift-click the dark gray (almost black) sidebar rectangle on top of it (not the image and text).

In the CSS Properties panel, you will not see any CSS code since you need to have Illustrator generate the code for more than one selected object.

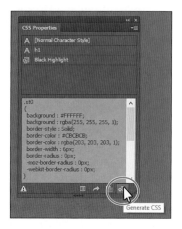

3 Click the Generate CSS button (▦) at the bottom of the panel.

The code for two CSS styles, .st0 and .sidebar, now appears in the bottom half of the CSS Properties panel. To see both styles, you may need to scroll down in the panel. Yours may be in a different order and that's okay.

▶ **Tip:** When CSS code appears in the CSS Properties panel for selected content, you can also select a part of the code and right-click (Windows) or Ctrl-click (Mac OS) the selected code and choose Copy to copy just that selection.

With both styles showing in the CSS Properties panel, you could copy the styles and paste them into your HTML editor code or paste them into an email to send to a web developer, for instance.

Next, you will discover how Illustrator makes PNG images out of artwork that is considered unsupported art (CSS code can't be generated).

4 With the Selection tool, click to select the orange circle shape just above the bottom of the artboard.

In the CSS Properties panel, you will see CSS code for a style named .image. That code contains a background-image property. When Illustrator encounters artwork (or raster images) that it can't make CSS code from, it rasterizes the exported content (*not* the artwork on the artboard)

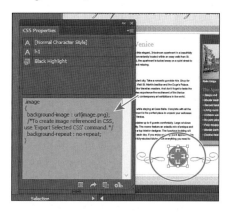

when you export the CSS code. The CSS code that is generated can be applied to an HTML object, like a div, and the PNG image will be applied as a background image in the HTML object.

With the symbol instance still selected on the artboard, notice that, in the Control panel, you see the word "Symbol" and symbol-related options.

Next, you will edit the Rest Area symbol so that both instances are affected. There are several ways to edit a symbol, and in this section we will focus on one.

8 With the Selection tool (▶), double-click the Rest Area symbol instance in the CENTRAL PARK area on the artboard. A warning dialog box appears, stating that you are about to edit the original symbol and that all instances will update. Click OK to continue. This takes you into Symbol Editing mode, so you can't edit any other objects on the page.

▶ **Tip:** Another way to edit a symbol is to select the symbol instance on the artboard and then click the Edit Symbol button in the Control panel.

The Rest Area symbol instance you double-clicked appears to change in size. That's because you are looking at the original symbol, not at the resized symbol instance on the page. You can now edit the shapes that make up the symbol.

9 Select the Zoom tool (🔍), and draw a marquee around the symbol instance in the CENTRAL PARK area to zoom in to it.

10 Select the Selection tool, and click to select any of the red shapes that make up the picnic bench.

11 In the Control panel, change the Fill color to the swatch named Local Green.

12 With the Selection tool, double-click away from the symbol content or click the Exit Symbol Editing Mode button (◀) in the upper-left corner of the artboard until you exit Symbol Editing mode so that you can edit the rest of the content.

13 Choose View > Fit Artboard In Window, and notice that both Rest Area instances on the artboard now have a green fill.

14 Choose File > Save, and leave the document open.

Creating symbols

Illustrator also lets you create your own symbols. You can make symbols from objects, including paths, compound paths, text, embedded (not linked) raster images, mesh objects, and groups of objects. Symbols can even include active objects, such as brush strokes, blends, effects, or other symbol instances. Now, you will create your own symbol from existing artwork.

1 Choose View > symbol content (at the very bottom of the View menu). This takes you to a zoomed in view off of the right side of the artboard.

2 With the Selection tool (▸), drag a marquee across the yellow fork content to select it. Drag the selected content into a blank area of the Symbols panel.

▶ **Tip:** By default, the selected artwork becomes an instance of the new symbol. If you don't want the artwork to become an instance of the symbol, press the Shift key as you create the new symbol.

3 In the Symbol Options dialog box, change the name to **Food** and select Graphic as the Type. Click OK to create the symbol.

In the Symbol Options dialog box, you will see a note that explains that there is no difference between a Movie Clip and a Graphic Type in Illustrator, so if you do not plan on exporting this content to Adobe Flash, you don't need to worry about choosing a Type.

● **Note:** To learn about Align To Pixel Grid and artwork for use on the web or for screen display, see Lesson 13, "Applying Appearance Attributes and Graphic Styles."

After creating the Food symbol, the original fork group off the right edge of the artboard is converted to an instance of the Food symbol. You can leave it there or delete it—it's up to you.

4 If it isn't already there, drag the Food symbol thumbnail (◯) to the right of the Rest Area to change the order of the symbols in the panel.

Reordering symbols in the Symbols panel has no effect on the artwork. It can simply be a way to organize your symbols.

5 Choose File > Save.

Symbol Options

Editing a symbol

In this next section, you will add several instances of the Food symbol to the artwork. Then, you will edit the symbol in the Symbols panel and all instances will be updated.

1 Choose View > Fit Artboard In Window.

2 Using the Selection tool (▶), drag an instance of the Food symbol (◉) from the Symbols panel to just to the right of the MARKET ST label in the middle of the artboard.

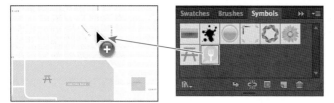

3 Drag another instance of the Food symbol from the Symbols panel just to the right of the EMERALD AVE label. See the figure for placement.

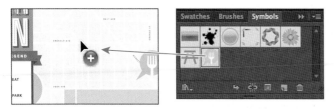

Next, you will learn how to add more instances of a symbol that's already on the artboard, using a modifier key.

4   With the Selection tool (➤), press the Alt key (Windows) or Option key (Mac OS) and drag one of the Food symbol instances already on the artboard to create a copy of the instance. Drag it to the right of the WALNUT ST label. When the new instance is in position, release the mouse button and then release the modifier key.

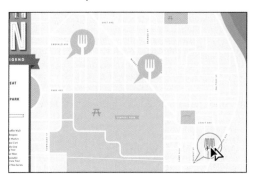

5   Create four more copies by pressing the Alt (Windows) or Option (Mac OS) key and dragging one of the Food symbol instances. Drag them to the right of the EAST AVE, PARK AVE, COAST AVE, and FACTORY ST labels.

You should now have a total of seven Food symbol instances on the artboard.

6   In the Symbols panel, double-click the Food symbol to edit it.

A temporary instance of the symbol appears in the center of the Document window. Editing a symbol by double-clicking the symbol in the Symbols panel hides all artboard content except the symbol. This is just another way to edit a symbol.

7   Press Ctrl++ (Windows) or Command++ (Mac OS) several times to zoom in.

8   With the Selection tool, click to select the yellow shape. Change the Fill color to the swatch named New Local Blue in the Control panel.

9   Choose Select > All, or drag across the shapes with the Selection tool.

● **Note:** There is also a white fork shape that needs to be selected. That's why you choose Select > All.

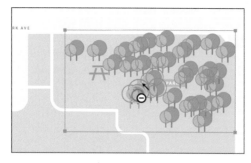

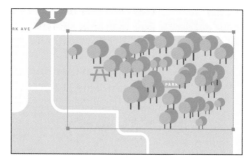

Resize some of the trees.   Notice the result.

Now, you will reposition some of the trees in the symbol set.

5   Select the Symbol Shifter tool (icon) from the Symbol Sizer tool group.

6   Double-click the Symbol Shifter tool. In the Symbolism Tools Options dialog box, change the Intensity to **8**, and then click OK.

    The higher the Intensity, the further you can move the symbol instances.

7   Position the pointer over a tree in the selected symbol set, and then drag left or right to move it. Drag the trees away from the CENTRAL PARK label so that you can see the whole thing.

    The more you move the pointer, the further you can drag instances. The trees you see in your symbol set may be arranged differently than in the figures, and that's okay.

▶ **Tip:** The circle (diameter setting) around the Symbolism tools pointers indicates that any symbol instances within that circle will be affected. Press the left bracket key ([) or the right bracket key (]) to change the brush diameter.

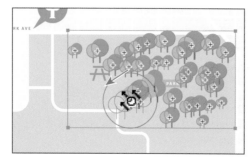

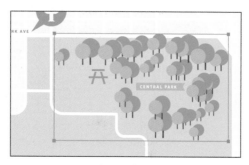

Drag the trees.   Notice the result.

You may notice that, as you drag, some of the trees that should be behind other trees are actually in front of them.

Next, you will fix this with the Symbol Shifter tool.

You may want to zoom in to the symbol set for the next steps.

8 With the Symbol Shifter tool selected, press the left bracket key ([) a few times to decrease the diameter. Make sure that the circle surrounding the pointer (that indicates the diameter) isn't much bigger than a tree. Shift-click one of the trees that should be in front, to bring it to the front.

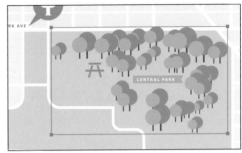

Change the stacking order of instances.   Notice the final result.

9 Select the Symbol Stainer tool (🖋) from the Symbol Shifter tool group in the Tools panel. With the symbol set still selected, position the pointer over the symbol set. Press the right bracket key (]) several times to increase the size of the brush.

10 Change the Fill color to the New Local Yellow swatch in the Control panel, and begin clicking trees in the symbol set to change their color.

You can always choose Edit > Undo Staining, if you don't like how it's affecting the trees, or Alt-click (Windows) or Option-click (Mac OS) to decrease the amount of colorization.

▶ **Tip:** There are lots of Symbolism tools for you to experiment with, including the Symbol Styler tool (☺), which allows you to apply graphic styles to symbol instances in the symbol set. To learn more about the different types of Symbolism tools available, search for "symbolism tool gallery" in Illustrator Help (Help > Illustrator Help).

11 Choose Select > Deselect, and then choose File > Save.

Copying and editing symbol sets

A symbol set is treated as a single object. In order to edit the instances in it, you use the Symbolism tools in the Tools panel, as you've already seen. You can, however, duplicate symbol instances and use the Symbolism tools to make the duplicates look different.

Next, you will duplicate the Trees symbol set.

1   Select the Selection tool (▶), and click to select the Trees symbol set.

2   Press the Alt (Windows) or Option (Mac OS) key, and drag a copy of the instances down and to the left, into the lower-left part of the CENTRAL PARK green area. When it is in position (see the figure), release the mouse button and then release the modifier key.

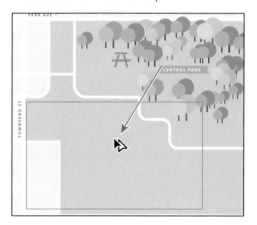 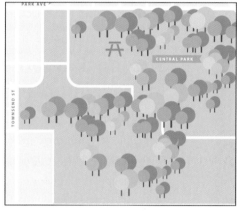

● **Note:** There are many transformations that you can make to a symbol set. You can also drag a point in the bounding box of a symbol set with the Selection tool to resize it.

3   Select the Symbol Shifter tool (🔀) from the Symbol Stainer tool group. Double-click the Symbol Shifter tool, and change the Intensity to **9**. Click OK. Drag the trees in the symbol set so that they fit within the green park area, as you see in the figure.

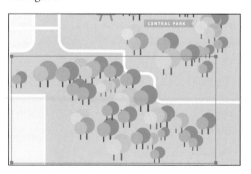

▶ **Tip:** You can change the diameter by pressing the left bracket ([) key or the right bracket (]) key. This will help you move more or fewer trees.

4   With the Symbol shifter tool, Shift-click the trees that should be in front, to bring them to the front. Shift+Alt-click (Windows) or Shift+Option-click (Mac OS) to send a tree behind.

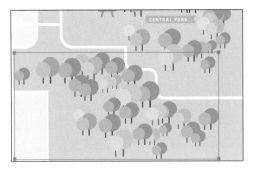

5   Choose Select > Deselect, and then choose File > Save.

Storing and retrieving artwork in the Symbols panel

Saving frequently used logos or other artwork as symbols lets you access them quickly. Unfortunately, symbols you create in one document are not accessible by default in another document.

In this next part of the lesson, you will take symbols that you've created and save them as a new symbol library that you can share with other documents or users.

1   In the Symbols panel, click the Symbol Libraries Menu button (⬛) at the bottom and then choose Save Symbols.

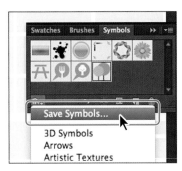

● **Note:** When saving symbols as a separate library, the document that contains the symbols that you want to save should be open and active in the Document window.

● **Note:** You'll probably notice that symbol libraries are simply saved as Adobe Illustrator (.ai) files.

2   In the Save Symbols As Library dialog box, choose a location, such as your Desktop, where you will place the symbol library file. Name the library file **map_symbols.ai**. Click Save.

● **Note:** When you first open the Save Symbols As Library dialog box, Illustrator takes you to the default Symbols folder, where you can store the libraries that you create. Illustrator recognizes any libraries stored here and lets you choose them from the Symbol Libraries menu later.

▶ **Tip:** If you save the library in the default folder, you can make subfolders and create a folder structure that suits you. You can then easily access them using the Symbol Libraries Menu button or by choosing Window > Symbol Libraries > User Defined > *your symbol library*.

3 Without closing the map.ai file, create a new document by choosing File > New. Leave the default settings, and then click OK.

4 In the Symbols panel, click the Symbol Libraries Menu button (▥) and choose Other Library at the bottom of the menu. Navigate to the folder where you saved the map_symbols.ai library, select it, and then click Open.

The map_symbols library appears as a free-floating panel in the workspace. You can dock it or leave it where it is. It stays open as long as Illustrator is open. When you close Illustrator and then relaunch it, this panel does not reopen.

5 Drag any of the Symbols from the map_symbols library panel onto the artboard.

6 Choose File > Close, and do not save the new file.

7 Close the map_symbols library.

8 With the map.ai file open, choose File > Save, if necessary, and then choose File > Close.

▶ **Tip:** When you work on multiple machines, managing and syncing preferences, presets, and libraries among them can be time-consuming and complex, and it can lead to errors. The Sync Settings feature enables individual users to sync their preferences, presets, and libraries (such as symbols libraries) to the Creative Cloud. To learn more, see "Sync settings using Adobe Creative Cloud," in the "Getting started" section, on page 6.

Mapping a symbol to 3D artwork

You can apply 2D artwork stored as a symbol in the Symbols panel to selected surfaces on a 3D object. To learn about mapping symbols to 3D artwork, see the PDF file, in the Lesson_extras folder, called 3DArtwork.pdf.

Working with symbols and Adobe Flash® integration

Illustrator CC also provides excellent support for SWF file type export. When you export to Flash, you can set the symbol type to Movie Clip. In Adobe Flash, you can choose another type, if necessary. You can also specify 9-slice scaling in Illustrator so that the movie clips scale appropriately when needed for user interface components.

To learn more about working with symbols and Adobe Flash, see the PDF file in the Lesson_extras folder, FlashSymbols.pdf.

Review questions

1 What are three benefits of using symbols?

2 How do you update an existing symbol?

3 Name something that cannot be used as a symbol.

4 Name the Symbolism tool that is used for shifting symbol instances in a symbol set.

5 If you are using a Symbolism tool on an area that has two different symbols applied, which one is affected?

6 How can you access symbols from other documents?

Review answers

1 Three benefits of using symbols are:

- You can edit one symbol, and all instances are updated.

- You can map artwork to 3D objects (see the PDF called 3DArtwork.pdf, in Lesson_extras folder).

- Using symbols reduces file size.

2 To update an existing symbol, double-click the symbol icon in the Symbols panel, double-click an instance of the symbol on the artboard, or select the instance on the artboard and then click the Edit Symbol button in the Control panel. Then, you can make edits in Isolation mode.

3 A linked image cannot be used as a symbol.

4 The Symbol Shifter tool (🔧) allows you to shift symbol instances in a symbol set.

5 If you are using a Symbolism tool over an area that has two different symbol instances, the symbol active in the Symbols panel is the only instance affected.

6 You can access symbols from saved documents either by clicking the Symbol Libraries Menu button (▦) at the bottom of the Symbols panel and by choosing Other Library from the menu that appears; by choosing Open Symbol Library > Other Library from the Symbols panel menu; or by choosing Window > Symbol Libraries > Other Library.

15 COMBINING ILLUSTRATOR CC GRAPHICS WITH OTHER ADOBE APPLICATIONS

Lesson overview

In this lesson, you'll learn how to do the following:

- Work with Adobe Bridge CC.
- Place linked and embedded graphics in an Illustrator file.
- Place multiple images at once.
- Apply color edits to images.
- Create and edit clipping masks.
- Create a clipping mask from a compound path.
- Make and edit an opacity mask.
- Sample color in a placed image.
- Work with the Links panel.
- Embed and unembed images.
- Replace a placed image with another and update the document.
- Package a document.

This lesson takes approximately an hour to complete.

Download the project files for this lesson from the Lesson & Update Files tab on your Account page at www.peachpit.com and store them on your computer in a convenient location, as described in the Getting Started section of this book.

Your Accounts page is also where you'll find any updates to the chapters or to the lesson files. Look on the Lesson & Update Files tab to access the most current content.

You can easily add an image created in an image-editing program to an Adobe Illustrator file. This is an effective method for incorporating images into your vector artwork or for trying out Illustrator special effects on bitmap images.

Getting started

Before you begin, you'll need to restore the default preferences for Adobe Illustrator CC. Then, you'll open the finished art file for this lesson to see what you'll create.

1   To ensure that the tools and panels function exactly as described in this lesson, delete or deactivate (by renaming) the Adobe Illustrator CC preferences file. See "Restoring default preferences," on page 3.

2   Start Adobe Illustrator CC.

● **Note:** If you have not already downloaded the project files for this lesson to your computer from your Account page, make sure to do so now. See "Getting Started" at the beginning of the book.

3   Choose File > Open. Locate the file named L15end.ai in the Lesson15 folder in the Lessons folder that you copied onto your hard disk. This is a poster for a farmers market, and you will add and edit graphics in this lesson. Leave it open for reference, or choose File > Close.

Now, you'll open the start file from Adobe Bridge CC.

Working with Adobe Bridge CC

Adobe Bridge CC is an application available with your Adobe Creative Cloud subscription. It allows you to browse content visually, manage metadata, and more.

● **Note:** The first time Adobe Bridge launches, a dialog box may appear asking if you want Bridge to start at login. Click Yes if you want it to launch at startup. Click No to manually launch Bridge when you need it.

1   Choose File > Browse In Bridge to open Adobe Bridge.

2   In the Favorites pane on the left, click Desktop and navigate to the L15start.ai file in the Lesson15 folder. Click the thumbnail in the Content (center) pane.

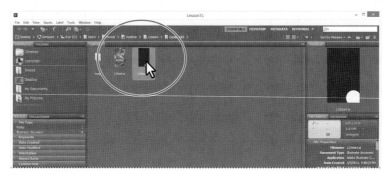

3   At the bottom of the Content pane, drag the slider to the right to increase the size of the thumbnails in the Content pane.

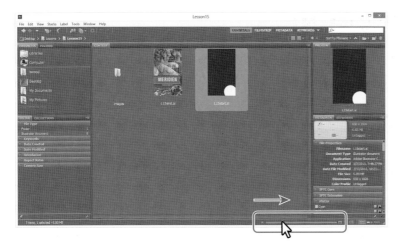

4　At the top of Bridge, click Filmstrip (or choose Window > Workspace > Filmstrip). This changes the appearance of the workspace to a filmstrip view that provides a larger preview of the selected object. Click Essentials to return to the original workspace.

5　At the bottom of the Content pane, drag the slider to the left until you see all the thumbnails in the Content pane (if necessary).

There are many features available in Adobe Bridge CC, including previewing files, working with metadata and keywords, and many more. To learn more about working with Bridge, search for "Adobe Bridge" in Illustrator Help (Help > Illustrator Help).

6　Double-click the file L15start.ai in the Content pane to open the file in Illustrator. You may close Bridge at any time.

7　Choose View > Fit Artboard In Window.

8　Choose Window > Workspace > Reset Essentials to reset the Essentials workspace.

9　Choose File > Save As. In the Save As dialog box, navigate to the Lesson15 folder and open it. Name the file **marketposter.ai**. Leave the Save As Type option set to Adobe Illustrator (*.AI) (Windows) or the Format option set to Adobe Illustrator (ai) (Mac OS), and then click Save. In the Illustrator Options dialog box, leave the Illustrator options at their default settings. Click OK.

● **Note:** In Mac OS, when opening lesson files, you may need to click the round, green button in the upper-left corner of the Document window to maximize the window's size.

Combining artwork

You can combine Illustrator artwork with images from other graphics applications in a variety of ways for a wide range of creative results. Sharing artwork between applications lets you combine continuous-tone paintings and photographs with vector art. Illustrator lets you create certain types of raster images, and Adobe Photoshop excels at many additional image-editing tasks. The images edited or created in Photoshop can then be inserted into Illustrator.

This lesson steps you through the process of creating a composite image, including combining bitmap images with vector art and working between applications. You will add photographic images created in Photoshop to a poster created in Illustrator. Then, you'll adjust the color of an image, mask an image, and sample color from an image to use in the Illustrator artwork. You'll update a placed image and then export your poster to Photoshop.

Understanding vector versus bitmap graphics

▶ **Tip:** To learn more about bitmap graphics, search for "Importing bitmap images" in Illustrator Help (Help > Illustrator Help).

Illustrator creates *vector graphics*, also called *draw graphics*, which contain shapes based on mathematical expressions.

This logo is drawn as vector art, which retains its crispness when scaled to a larger size.

Bitmap images—technically called *raster images*—use a rectangular grid of picture elements (pixels) to represent images. Each pixel is assigned a specific location and color value. It's important to understand the differences between these two and how they can work together.

This logo is rasterized as bitmap art and loses its definition when enlarged.

Placing image files

You can bring raster artwork from Photoshop or other applications into Illustrator using the Open command, the Place command, the Paste command, and drag-and-drop. Illustrator supports most Adobe Photoshop data, including layer comps, layers, editable text, and paths. This means that you can transfer files between Photoshop and Illustrator without losing the ability to edit the artwork.

When placing files using the File > Place command, no matter what type of image file it is (JPG, GIF, PSD, etc.), it can either be embedded or linked. *Embedding* files stores a copy of the image in the Illustrator file, and the Illustrator file size increases to reflect the addition of the placed file. *Linked* files remain separate external files, and a link to the external file is placed in the Illustrator file. Linking to files can be a great way to ensure that image updates are reflected in the Illustrator file. The linked file must always accompany the Illustrator file, or the link will break and the placed file will not appear in the Illustrator artwork.

● **Note:** Illustrator includes support for Device N rasters. For instance, if you create a Duotone image in Photoshop and place it in Illustrator, it separates properly and prints the spot colors.

Placing an image

First, you will place a JPEG (jpg) image into your document.

1   Click the Layers panel icon (■) to open the Layers panel. In the Layers panel, select the Woman layer.

When you place an image, it is added to the selected layer. The layer already includes the white circle you see on the artboard.

2   Choose File > Place.

3   Navigate to the carrots.jpg file in the images folder inside the Lesson15 folder, and select it. Make sure that Link is *selected* in the Place dialog box. Click Place.

By default, placed image files are linked to their source file. So, if the source file is edited (outside of Illustrator), the placed image in Illustrator is updated. Deselecting the Link option while placing embeds the image file in the Illustrator file.

The pointer should now show the loaded graphics cursor. You can see a number (1) next to the pointer, indicating how many images are being placed, and a thumbnail, so you can see what image you are placing.

4 Position the loaded graphics cursor near the upper-left corner of the artboard, and click to place the image.

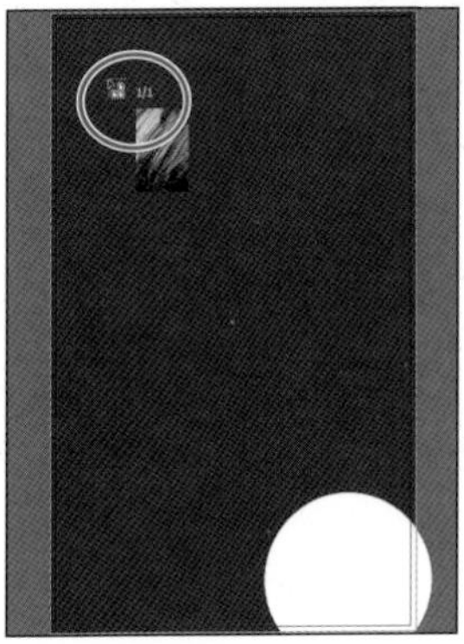

Position the graphics cursor

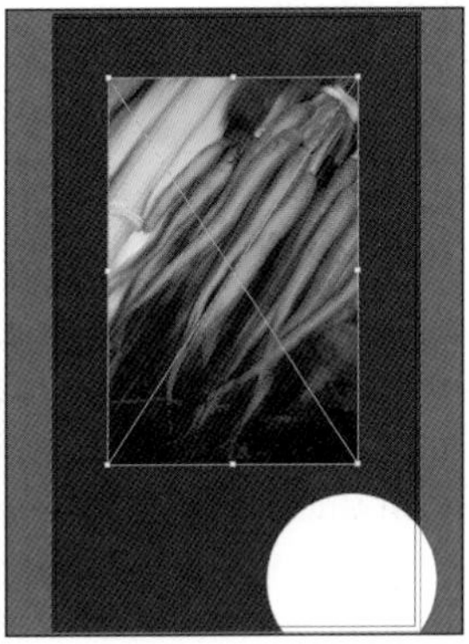

Click to place the image.

▶ **Tip:** The X on a selected image indicates that the image is linked (with edges showing, View > Show Edges).

The image appears on the artboard, with the upper-left corner of the image where you clicked. The image is 100% of its original size. You could also have dragged with the loaded graphics cursor to size the image as you placed it. Notice in the Control panel that, with the image selected, you see the words "Linked File," indicating that the image is linked to its source file, together with other information about the image.

Transforming a placed image

You can duplicate and transform placed images just as you do other objects in an Illustrator file. Unlike vector artwork, you need to consider the resolution of the raster image content in your document, since raster images without enough resolution may not print correctly. Working in Illustrator, if you make an image smaller, the resolution of the image increases. If you make an image larger, the resolution decreases. Next, you will move, resize, and rotate the carrots.jpg image.

● **Note:** Transformations performed on a linked image in Illustrator, and any resulting resolution changes, do not change the original image. The changes apply only to the image within Illustrator.

1 With the Selection tool (↖) selected and the carrots image already selected, drag the image down and to the right so that it is positioned over the top of the white circle in the lower-right corner of the artboard. You may need to scroll down in the Document window.

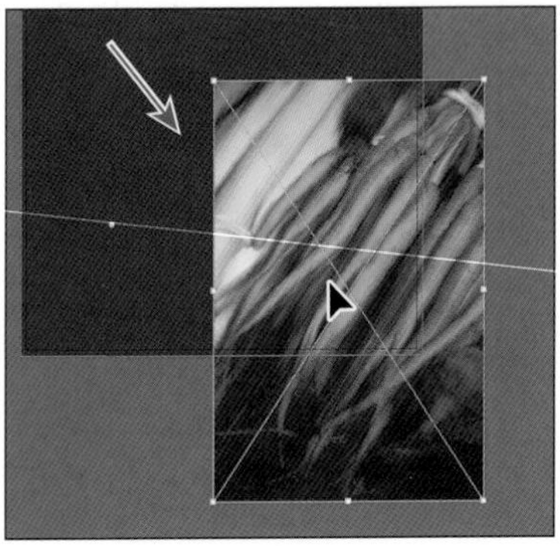

2 Holding down the Alt+Shift (Windows) or Option+Shift (Mac OS) keys, use the Selection tool to drag the upper-right bounding point toward the center of the image until the width is approximately 4.5 in. Release the mouse button, and then release the keys.

After resizing the image, notice that the PPI (Pixels Per Inch) value in the Control panel is approximately 157. PPI refers to the resolution of the image.

▶ **Tip:** To transform a placed image, you can also open the Transform panel (Window > Transform) and change settings there.

3 With the Selection tool, position the pointer just off the upper-right bounding point. The rotate arrows should appear. Drag up and to the left to rotate the image about 13 degrees (it doesn't have to be exact).

With Smart Guides on (View > Smart Guides), you'll see a measurement label. Make sure that the image completely covers the circle.

4 Choose Select > Deselect, and then choose File > Save.

Placing a Photoshop image with Show Import Options

When you place image files in Illustrator, you have the ability to change options on how the file is imported for assets with import settings in Illustrator. For instance, if you place a Photoshop file (.psd), you can choose to flatten the image or even to preserve the layers in the file. Next, you will place a Photoshop file, set import options, and embed it in the Illustrator file.

1 In the Layers panel, click the eye icon (👁) for the Woman layer to hide the contents and then select the Background layer.

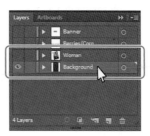

2 Choose View > Fit Artboard In Window.

3 Choose File > Place.

4 In the Place dialog box, navigate to the market.psd file in the images folder inside of the Lesson15 folder. In the Place dialog box, set the following options:

- Link: **Deselected** (Deselecting the Link option embeds an image file in the Illustrator file. Embedding the Photoshop file allows for more options when it is placed, as you'll see.)

- Show Import Options: **Selected**

Click Place.

The Photoshop Import Options dialog box appears because you selected Show Import Options in the Place dialog box.

Note: Even though you select Show Import Options in the Place dialog box, the Import Options dialog box will not appear if the image doesn't have any options to change.

5 In the Photoshop Import Options dialog box, set the following options:

- Layer Comp: **All** (A *layer comp* is a snapshot of a state of the Layers panel that you create in Photoshop. In Photoshop, you can create, manage, and view multiple versions of a layout in a single Photoshop file.)

- Show Preview: **Selected** (Preview displays a preview of the selected layer comp.)

- Convert Layers To Objects: **Selected** (This option and the next are only available because you deselected the Link option and chose to embed the Photoshop image.)

- Import Hidden Layers: **Selected** (to import layers hidden in Photoshop)

Click OK.

Note: A color mode warning may appear in the Photoshop Import Options dialog box. This indicates that the image you are placing may not be the same color mode as the Illustrator document. For this image (and going forward), if a color warning dialog box appears, click OK to dismiss it.

6   Position the loaded graphics cursor in the upper-left corner of the red bleed guides (off the upper-right corner of the artboard), and click to place the image.

Rather than flatten the file, you have converted the market.psd Photoshop layers to layers that you can show and hide in Illustrator. When placing a Photoshop file, in particular, if you had left the Link option selected (to link to the original PSD file), the only option in the Options section of the Photoshop Import Options dialog box would have been to flatten the content.

7   In the Layers panel, click the triangle (▶) to the left of the Background layer to expand it. Drag the bottom of the panel down, if necessary, so that you can see more of the layers. Click the triangle to the left of the market.psd sublayer to expand it.

● **Note:** We dragged the left edge of the Layers panel to the left to see the more of the sublayer names.

Notice the sublayers of market.psd. These sublayers were Photoshop layers in Photoshop and appear in the Layers panel in Illustrator because you chose not to flatten the image when you placed it. Also notice that, with the image still selected on the page, the Control panel shows the word "Group" on the left side and includes an underlined link to Multiple Images. When you place a Photoshop file with layers and you choose to convert the layers to objects in the Photoshop Import Options dialog box, Illustrator treats the layers as separate images in a group.

8   Click the eye icon (👁) to the left of the Color Fill 1 sublayer to hide it.

9   With the Selection tool (▶), drag the market image down so that the bottom edge of the image snaps to the lower, red bleed guide.

Hide the Color Fill 1 sublayer.

Position the image.

10 Choose Select > Deselect, and then choose File > Save.

Placing multiple images

In Illustrator you can also place multiple files in a single action. Next, you'll place two images at once and then position them.

1   In the Layers panel, click the eye icon () to the left of the Background layer to hide it. Click the triangle (▼) to the left of the Background layer to collapse it. Click the visibility column in the Berries/Corn layer to show the contents, and then select the Berries/Corn layer.

2   Choose File > Place.

▶ **Tip:** You could also select a series of files in the Place dialog box by pressing the Shift key.

3   In the Place dialog box, select the berries.psd file in the images folder inside the Lesson15 folder. Ctrl-click (Windows) or Command-click (Mac OS) the image named corn.tif to select both image files. Deselect the Show Import Options option and make sure that the Link option is *not* selected. Click Place.

● **Note:** By default, our Windows OS is showing the images as icons. Yours may be in a different view, like a List view, and that's okay.

▶ **Tip:** To discard an asset that is loaded and ready to be placed, use the arrow keys to navigate to the asset, and then press the Escape key.

4   Position the loaded graphics cursor in the upper-left corner of the artboard, where the red bleed guides meet. Press the right or left arrow key (or up and down arrow keys) a few times to see that you can cycle between the image thumbnails. Whichever thumbnail is showing when you click in the Document window is placed. Make sure that you see the berries image thumbnail, and click to place.

5   Choose Object > Arrange > Send To Back.

6   Position the loaded graphics cursor on the left bleed guide (off the left side of the artboard), just above the text "LOCAL." When the word "edge" appears, click and drag down and to the right, stopping at the red bleed guide off the right side of the artboard when the word "edge" appears. Release the mouse button.

on the artboard. Also, notice that the document tab shows (<Opacity Mask>/Opacity Mask), indicating that you are now editing the mask.

5 Click the Layers panel icon () on the right side of the workspace to reveal the Layers panel.

In the Layers panel, notice that the layer <Opacity Mask> appears, indicating that the mask—rather than the artwork that is being masked—is selected.

6 With the mask selected in the Transparency panel and on the artboard, in the Control panel, click the Fill color and select a white-to-black linear gradient, called White, Black.

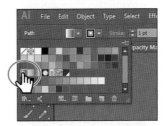

You will now see that, where there is white in the mask, the market.psd image is showing, and where there is black, it is hidden. The gradient gradually reveals the image from black to white.

7 Choose View > Hide Gradient Annotator.

8 Make sure that the Fill box (toward the bottom of the Tools panel) is selected.

9 Select the Gradient tool (■) in the Tools panel. Holding down the Shift key, position the pointer in the center of the mask (horizontally and vertically) and then click and drag up to the top of the mask shape, as shown in the figure. Release the mouse button, and then release the Shift key.

Drag to edit the opacity mask.

Notice the result.

10 Click the Transparency panel icon (●), and notice how the mask has changed appearance in the Transparency panel.

11 Choose View > Show Gradient Annotator.

Next, you'll move the image but not the opacity mask. With the image thumbnail selected in the Transparency panel, both the image and the mask are linked together, by default, so that if you move the image, the mask moves, as well.

● **Note:** You only have access to the link icon when the image thumbnail, not the mask thumbnail, is selected in the Transparency panel.

12 In the Transparency panel, click the image thumbnail so that you are no longer editing the mask. Click the link icon (🔗) between the image thumbnail and the mask thumbnail. This allows you to move just the image or the mask, but not both.

● **Note:** The position of the market.psd does not have to match the figure exactly.

13 With the Selection tool, begin dragging the market.psd image down. As you drag, press and hold the Shift key to constrain the movement vertically. Release the mouse button, and then release the key to see where it is positioned. Drag until it

looks approximately like the figure, always releasing the mouse button and then releasing the key.

14 In the Transparency panel, click the broken link icon (🔗) between the image thumbnail and the mask thumbnail to link the two together again.

15 Choose Select > Deselect, and then choose File > Save.

Sampling colors in placed images

You can *sample*, or *copy*, the colors in placed images to apply the colors to other objects in the artwork. Sampling colors enables you to easily make colors consistent in a file that combines images and Illustrator artwork.

1 In the Layers panel, make sure that all of the layers are collapsed, and then click the visibility column to the left of the Banner, Berries/Corn, and Woman layers to show their contents on the artboard.

2 With the Selection tool (▶) selected, click the white banner shape behind the "MERIDIEN" text.

● **Note:** Using the Shift key with the Eyedropper tool allows you to apply only the sampled color to the selected object. If you don't use the Shift key, you apply all appearance attributes to the selected object.

3 Make sure that the Fill box (toward the bottom of the Tools panel) is selected.

4 Select the Eyedropper tool (🖋) in the Tools panel, and Shift-click the top green area in the top of the "C" in "LOCAL," to sample and apply a green color from the corn image. You can try sampling the color of different images and content, if you want. The color you sample is applied to the selected shape.

5   Choose Select > Deselect, and then choose File > Save.

Working with image links

When you place images in Illustrator and either link to them or embed them, you can see a listing of these images in the Links panel. You use the Links panel to see and manage all linked or embedded artwork. The Links panel displays a small thumbnail of the artwork and uses icons to indicate the artwork's status. From the Links panel, you can view the images that are linked to and embedded, replace a placed image, update a linked image that has been edited outside of Illustrator, or edit a linked image in the original application, such as Photoshop.

Finding link information

When you place images, it can be helpful to see where the original image is located, what transformations have been applied to the image (such as rotation and scale), and more information. Next, you will explore the Links panel to discover image information.

1   Choose Window > Links, to open the Links panel.

Looking in the Links panel, you will see a listing of all of the images you've placed. Images with a name to the right of the image thumbnail are linked, and those images without a name are embedded. You can also tell if an image has been embedded, by the embedded icon (▣).

2   Scroll down in the panel, and double-click the carrots.jpg image (which shows the name to the right of the thumbnail) to reveal the link information at the bottom of the panel.

You will see information, such as the name, original location of the image, the file format, resolution, modification and creation dates, transformation information, and more.

● **Note:** You can also select the image in the list, and then click the toggle arrow in the lower-left corner of the panel to see the image information.

3 Click the Go To Link button () below the list of images. The carrots.jpg image will be selected and centered in the Document window.

4 Click the orange text "Linked File" in the Control panel to open the Links panel.

This is another way to access the Links panel. If you select a linked image or the image content of a Clip Group, you will see the text "Linked File."

5 In the Control panel, click the filename carrots.jpg to reveal a menu of options.

The menu of options that appears mirrors those options found in the Links panel. If you were to select an embedded image, you would instead see the link named Embedded in the Control panel. Clicking that orange link would show the same menu options but some of them would be inaccessible.

6 Press the Escape key to hide the menu and leave the carrots image selected.

Embedding and unembedding images

● **Note:** Neither 1-bit images nor images that are either locked or hidden can be unembedded.

As was mentioned previously, if you choose not to link to an image when placing it, the image is embedded in the Illustrator file. That means that the image data is stored within the Illustrator document. You can choose to embed an image later, after placing and linking to it, if you choose. Also, you might want to use embedded images outside of Illustrator or to edit them in an image editing application like Photoshop. Illustrator allows you to unembed images, which saves the embedded artwork to your file system as a PSD or TIFF file (you can choose) and automatically links it to the Illustrator file. Next, you will embed an image in the document.

● **Note:** Certain file formats, like PSD, show an Import Options dialog box when you embed the image, allowing you to select placement options.

1 With the carrots image still selected, click the Embed button in the Control panel to embed the image.

The link to the original carrot.jpg file is removed, and the image data is embedded in the Illustrator document. Visually, you can tell the image is embedded because it no longer has the X going through the middle of it (with the image selected and edges showing [View > Show Edges]).

With an image embedded, you may realize that you need to make an edit to that image in a program like Adobe Photoshop. You can just as easily unembed an image, which is what you'll do next to the carrots image.

2   With the carrots image still selected on the artboard, click the Unembed button in the Control panel. You can also choose Unembed from the Links panel menu.

3   In the Unembed dialog box, navigate to the Lesson15 > images folder (if you are not already there). Choose TIFF (*.TIF) from the Save As Type (Windows) or File Format (Mac OS) menu and, click Save.

● **Note:** The embedded carrots image data is unembedded from the file and saved as a TIFF file in the images folder. The carrots image on the artboard is now linked to the TIFF file.

Replacing a linked image

You can easily replace a linked or embedded image with another image to update the artwork. The replacement image is positioned exactly where the original image was, so no adjustment should be necessary if the new image is of the same dimensions. If you scaled the image that you are replacing, you may need to resize the replacement image to match the original. Next, you will replace the selected carrots.tif image with another image.

1   In the Links panel, with carrots.tif selected, click the Relink button () below the list of images.

2   In the Place dialog box, navigate to the Lesson15 > images folder and select woman.psd. *Make sure that the Link option is selected.* Click Place to replace the carrots image with the image of the woman.

The replacement image (woman.psd) appears on the artboard in place of the carrots.tif image. When you replace an image, any color adjustments made to the original image are not applied to the replacement. However, masks applied to the original image are preserved. Any layer modes and transparency adjustments that you've made to other layers also may affect the image's appearance.

3   With the Selection tool (▶) selected, click the Edit Contents button (◉) in the Control panel (if it's not already selected). Drag the new woman.psd image until it is positioned as you see in the figure.

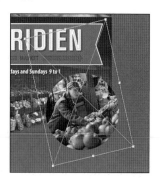

▶ **Tip:** You can also press the arrow keys on the keyboard to reposition the image.

4   Click the Edit Clipping Path button (▣) in the Control panel.

5   In the Control panel, change the Stroke color to white and the Stroke weight to **3 pt**.

6   Choose Select > Deselect, and then choose File > Save.

Packaging a file

When you *package* a file, you create a folder that contains a copy of the Illustrator document, any necessary fonts, copies of the linked graphics, and a report that contains information about the packaged files. This is an easy way to hand off all necessary files for an Illustrator project. Next, you will package the poster files.

● **Note:** If the file needs to be saved, a dialog box will appear to notify you.

1 Choose File > Package. In the Package dialog box, set the following options:

- Click the folder icon (■) and navigate to the Lesson15 folder, if you are not already there. Click Select Folder (Windows) or Choose (Mac OS) to return to the Package dialog box.

- Folder name: **marketposter** (remove _Folder from the name)

- Options: Leave at default settings.

Click Package.

The Copy Links option *copies* all of the linked files to the new folder it creates. The Collect Links In A Separate Folder option creates a folder called Links and copies the links into there. The Relink Linked Files To Document option updates the links within the Illustrator document to link to the new copies.

2 In the next dialog box that discusses font licensing restrictions, click OK. Clicking Back would allow you to deselect Copy Fonts Used In Document (Except CJK).

3 Click Show Package to see the package folder.

In the package folder should be a folder called Links which contains all of the linked images. The marketposter Report (.txt file) contains information about the document contents.

4 Return to Illustrator, and choose File > Close.

Exploring Adobe Illustrator and Adobe Photoshop, Adobe InDesign, Adobe Muse™, Adobe Fireworks®, and Adobe Flash

To learn more about working with Illustrator artwork and other Adobe applications, see the PDF file, Adobeapps.pdf, in the Lesson_extras folder (in the Lessons folder).

Review questions

1 Describe the difference between *linking* and *embedding* in Illustrator.

2 What kinds of objects can be used as masks?

3 How do you create an opacity mask for a placed image?

4 What color modifications can you apply to a selected object using effects?

5 Describe how to replace a placed image with another image in a document.

6 Describe what *packaging* does.

Review answers

1 A *linked file* is a separate, external file connected to the Illustrator file by an electronic link. A linked file does not add significantly to the size of the Illustrator file. The linked file must accompany the Illustrator file to preserve the link and to ensure that the placed file appears when you open the Illustrator file. An *embedded file* is included in the Illustrator file. The Illustrator file size reflects the addition of the embedded file. Because the embedded file is part of the Illustrator file, no link can be broken. You can update linked and embedded files using the Relink button (⊜) in the Links panel.

2 A mask can be a simple or compound path. You can use type as a mask. You can import opacity masks with placed Photoshop files. You can also create layer clipping masks with any shape that is the topmost object of a group or layer.

3 You create an opacity mask by placing the object to be used as a mask on top of the object to be masked. Then, you select the mask and the objects to be masked and either click the Make Mask button in the Transparency panel or choose Make Opacity Mask from the Transparency panel menu.

4 You can use effects to change the color mode (RGB, CMYK, or grayscale) or to adjust individual colors in a selected object. You can also saturate or desaturate colors or invert colors in a selected object. You can apply color modifications to placed images, as well as to artwork created in Illustrator.

5 To replace a placed image, select the image in the Links panel. Then, click the Relink button (⊜) and locate and select the replacement image. Click Place.

6 *Packaging* is used to gather all of the necessary pieces for an Illustrator document. Packaging creates a copy of the Illustrator file, the linked images, and the necessary fonts (if desired), and gathers them all into a folder.

INDEX

brushes. *See also specific types of brushes*
  adding fill color with, 326
  applying Pattern, 338
  auto corners for pattern, 11, 336, 337
  changing color attributes for, 340
  creating Pattern, 336–337
  drawing with Paintbrush tool, 322–323, 345
  editing Art, 329–330
  editing Paintbrush tool paths, 324–325, 332, 345
  lesson files for, 320
  libraries of, 323, 331, 335, 337
  made from raster images, 9, 328–329, 330, 345
  modifying, 325–326
  painting on existing art, 321–322
  quick tour of, 26
  removing brush strokes, 326–327, 340
  types of, 321
  using existing Art, 327–328, 345
Brushes panel
  check mark in, 322, 327
  illustrated, 321
  removing brush strokes in, 326–327, 340
  selecting brush tools from, 345

C

Calligraphic brushes
  applying to existing art, 321–322
  drawing with, 322–323
  editing paths drawn with, 324–325
  illustrated, 321
  modifying, 325–326
  removing strokes of, 326–327
canvas, 37, 55
cascading documents, 58, 61
Cascading Style Sheets. *See* CSS
certification programs, 4
Character panel, 224–226
Character Style Options dialog box, 236

characters. *See also* CSS
  creating and applying styles, 235–237, 245
  CSS styling for, 393–394
  glyphs, 230–231
  modifying text attributes, 224–226
Classroom in a Book lessons. *See* lesson files
clipping masks
  applying, 435
  creating and adding, 25–26
  defined, 25, 260, 435
  editing, 436–437
  hiding art with, 260–261, 267
  importing Photoshop, 435
  masking complex objects, 438–439, 447
  opacity masks vs., 439
  using shape for, 437
clipping sets, 435
closed paths
  adding text on, 241–242
  creating, 168–169, 172
  open vs., 98
closing panels, 44
CMYK color mode, 177, 189
collapsing panels, 42–43, 44–45
color. *See also* color groups; color modes; sampling
  adding to gradient, 317
  adjusting, 189
  applying, 16, 180
  assigned to layers, 251, 267
  assigning to artwork, 198–200
  changing brush, 340
  choosing in Color Guide panel, 191–192
  Color Picker for choosing, 185–186
  copying swatch, 182
  creating smooth blends of, 314–315, 316
  customizing color swatch, 181–182
  editing placed image, 434–435, 447
  global, 183–184, 209
  groups of, 190
  harmonizing, 191, 196
  Illustrator swatch libraries, 186

  lesson files for, 176
  main controls for, 178–179
  modifying artwork, 195–196
  process, 186
  radial gradient, 303–304, 307–308
  sampling, 189, 308, 316, 442–443
  spot, 186, 187
  stroke, 16–17
  swatch, 183
  tint, 188–189
  transparencies with gradient, 309–310
  working with Kuler, 197
color groups
  creating, 190
  editing, 192–195
  renaming, 193
  showing name of, 206
Color Guide panel, 179, 191–192
color management resources, 364
color modes
  about, 177
  changing for placed images, 430, 447
  choosing, 178
  converting, 189, 434–435, 447
Color panel, 178, 296
Color Picker, 16, 185–186
color stops
  defined, 295
  deleting, 301
  editing color of, 317
  radial gradient, 302, 303–304
colorization with Symbol Stainer tool, 416
compound paths, 438
computer platforms
  adjusting user interface brightness, 37
  conflicts when syncing, 7
  instructions for different platforms, 1
  syncing Illustrator CC on multiple, 6–7
constraining
  Eraser tool, 111
  lines, 147–148
  transformations with Shift key, 139

Fill box (Tools panel), 178
fills. *See also* gradient fills
    adding to objects, 24–25
    appearance attributes for adding, 372
    applying to path, 97
    brushing on color, 326
    color of, 16
    defined, 69
    modifying color of font, 223–224
    objects selected without, 79, 115
    paths without, 98
    patterns using, 201
    selecting objects by, 69
Filter Gallery dialog box, 359, 360
Fireworks, 446
Flash, 419, 446
flattening layers, 266
flipping objects, 129–130
floating panels, 39–40, 44
fonts
    available Illustrator, 2
    changing family and style of, 220–222
    color of, 223–224
    finding glyphs, 230
    improvements in, 9
    outlining, 244, 245
    resizing, 222–223
    selecting, 221–222
formatting
    Character panel options for, 224–226
    character styles, 235–237, 245
    editing layer's graphic style, 380
    font family and style, 220–222
    keeping for placed Word documents, 234
    paragraphs, 233–235, 245
    retaining for imported text, 216
    sampling text, 237
    text with CSS, 393–394
    using graphic styles for, 382
    using Touch Type tool for, 226–228
forums, 4
Free Distort option, 140
Free Transform tool, 11, 138–140, 141

G

GIF files, 389, 399
global rulers, 125, 141
global swatches, 183–184
glyphs, 230–231
gradient annotator, 298, 299
gradient color stop, 295
gradient fills. *See also* linear gradient fills; radial gradient fills
    adding color to, 317
    applying, 316
    creating and editing, 19
    defined, 19, 293, 295, 316
    direction and angle of, 298–299, 317
    lesson files for, 294
    linear, 295–297
    radial, 295, 302–310
    sampling color of, 308, 316
    saving in Swatches panel, 297
    transparency added to, 309–310
Gradient panel, 295, 317
Gradient tool, 298–299, 316, 317
graphic styles
    about, 276
    applying existing, 375–376
    copying CSS for, 395–397
    creating and applying, 376–377
    defined, 375
    exporting CSS for, 397–398
    layers using, 379, 399
    lesson files for, 368
    scaling strokes and effects, 381
    styling symbol sets with, 416
    text with applied, 382
    updating, 377–378
    using, 367, 380–381, 399
Graphic Styles panel, 375
graphics. *See* images; raster graphics; vector graphics
grid. *See also* perspective grid
    pixel, 383–385
    working with, 88
gripper bar, 41
Group Selection tool, 79
groups. *See also* color groups
    applying effects to, 350, 353–354
    dragging and copying target icon to, 265

grouping content on perspective grid, 289
    Live Paint, 206, 208
    nested, 75–76
    panel, 44, 45–46
    putting objects in, 74
    selecting objects within, 74–75, 79
guides
    adding bleed, 122–123
    creating, 125
    snapping points to, 128

H

Hand tool
    fitting artboard in window with, 50
    scrolling documents with, 50–51
Harmony Rules menu, 191
help resources, 4–5
hidden panels, 43
hidden red circle, 77
hidden tools, 39
Hide Color Group Storage icon, 195
hiding/showing
    all panels, 44
    appearance attributes, 370
    gradient annotator, 298
    grid, 88
    layers, 256–257, 267
    objects, 78, 79
    perspective grid, 276, 291
highlighting anchor points, 67
horizontal scale of text, 226–227

I

icons
    eye, 256, 267
    Eyeglass, 222
    selected-art indicator, 254
    Show Color Group Storage, 196
    spot-color, 188
    target, 264, 265, 267
    turning into crosshairs for tools, 145, 171
    Type tool, 241, 242
    yield sign, 395

Illustrator CC. *See* Adobe
     Illustrator CC
Illustrator Options dialog box, 35
Image Trace
     converting photos to vector
          graphics, 31
     tracing pictures with, 112–114,
          115
images. *See also* embedded images;
     placed images; raster graphics;
     vector graphics
     adding and removing embedded,
          444–445
     applying clipping mask to, 435
     applying effects to, 31
     brushes made from, 9, 328–329,
          330, 345
     converting photos to vector
          graphics, 31
     enhancements to, 10
     file formats for web, 383
     painting with embedded, 328–
          329, 330, 345
     placing, 30
     tracing, 31, 112–114, 115
     working with linked, 443–444,
          445, 447
Import Options dialog box, 430
importing
     masks created in Photoshop, 435
     multiple files into layout, 10
     Photoshop placed images,
          429–431
     symbols into documents, 404
     text files, 216–217
InDesign, 215–216, 446
Inner Glow effect, 356
instances. *See also* symbol instances
     defined, 403
     stacking order of, 416
isolating layers, 266
Isolation mode
     editing text in perspective
          using, 285
     isolating layers, 266
     selecting objects in, 74–75

J

joining open paths, 97–98
JPEG files, 427–428

K

kerning, 227, 230–231, 393
key objects, 71–72
keyboard shortcuts
     adjusting objects in perpendicular
          direction, 280
     adjusting symbol instances with,
          415, 417
     available for perspective
          drawing, 275
     changing stacking order with, 416
     constraining transformations
          using, 139
     Hand tool, 51
     kerning adjustments using, 227
     Mac OS Zoom tool, 50
     nudging points with arrow
          keys, 161
     Pen tool constraints using Shift
          key and Smart Guides, 147
     preventing art from becoming
          symbol instances, 406
     repositioning images, 445
     repositioning path text, 242
     resizing fonts with, 222
     selecting active plane with,
          283, 291
     shape adjustments with, 94
     switching planes with, 280
     tool selection with, 39
     Zoom command, 48, 61
Knife tool, 168–169
Kuler, 11, 197

L

launching
     Bridge at startup, 424
     Illustrator CC first time, 6
layer comps, 430
Layer Options dialog box, 250, 251
layers
     about, 248–249, 267
     applying appearance attributes to,
          263–265, 373–374
     benefits of, 247, 267
     clipping masks on, 260–261, 267
     colors assigned to, 251, 267
     creating, 250–251
     deleting, 250
     duplicating content on, 253

editing graphic style formatting
     for, 380
flattening, 266
graphic styles applied to, 379, 399
hiding/showing, 256–257, 267
isolating, 266
lesson files for, 248, 249
locating, 263
locking, 255–256
merging, 261–262
navigating closed, 252
options for imported Photoshop,
     429, 430–431
organizing artwork in, 20
pasting, 259–260, 267
placing type on separate, 250
rearranging objects on, 251–252
reordering, 253–254, 267
symbol, 403, 411
viewing, 256–258
Layers panel
     illustrated, 249
     location of clipping masks in, 260
     locking layers from, 255–256
leading
     adjusting, 232–233
     CSS styling for, 393
     defined, 225
lesson files
     appearance attributes and
          graphic styles, 368
     blending colors and shapes, 294
     brushes, 320
     color and painting, 176
     downloading, 2
     effects, 348
     layer, 248, 249
     pen and pencil drawings, 144
     perspective drawing, 270
     preference files for, 3–4
     quick tour, 14
     selection techniques, 64
     shapes, 82
     symbols, 402
     transformation operations, 118
     type, 212
     work area, 34–35
     working with other
          applications, 424
letter-spacing, 393

Shift key
  constraining transformations with, 139
  Pen tool constraints using Smart Guide and, 147
Show Color Group Storage icon, 196
Show Import Options (Place dialog box), 430
showing. *See* hiding/showing
slicing artwork
  creating slices, 385–387
  editing sliced content, 387
  optimizing for web use, 388–389
  selecting and editing slices, 387
Smart Guides
  changing color of, 89
  constraining tools using Shift key with, 147
  defined, 65
  enabling/disabling, 90, 147
  positioning objects with, 137
  unavailable with Snap To Grid enabled, 88
smooth color blend, 314–315, 316, 317
smooth points
  converting to corner, 152–153, 156–157, 164–165
  illustrated, 148
Smooth tool, 324
Snap to Grid, 88
Snap to Point, 128
snapping to perspective grid, 275
spine of blended object, 313–314, 317
spirals, 94
spot color, 186, 187
spot-color icon, 188
spraying symbol instances, 412–414
squares, 115
stacking order
  arranging for objects, 76–77
  effect on objects, 76
  keyboard shortcuts for, 416
  selecting objects below others, 77–78, 79
stars, 93, 94
status bar, 36
steps for blends, 311, 317

stroke
  adding as appearance attribute, 371, 399
  adding color to, 16
  adjusting width of, 98–101
  aligning objects by, 95
  applying Art brush to, 345
  applying brush to, 26
  applying gradient to, 299–300
  dashed lines added to, 167–168
  defined, 69
  editing color of, 17
  editing gradient on, 300–301
  gradient, 316
  modifying color of font, 223–224
  outlining, 101–102
  removing brush, 326–327, 340
  saving width profiles of, 101
  scaling, 127–129, 141, 381
  selecting objects with similar, 69
  weight of, 69
  width of, 94–95
Stroke box (Tools panel), 178
Stroke Options (Pattern Brush) dialog box, 335
styling. *See also* CSS; graphic styles; text
  text with effects, 352–353
  using Stylize effects, 264, 355–356
Stylize commands, 264
sublayers. *See also* layers
  creating, 251
  deleting, 250
  dragging and copying target icon to, 265
  merging, 261–262
  navigating closed, 252
SVG (Scalable Vector Graphics), 398
Swatch Options dialog box, 297
swatches
  copying, 182
  customizing color, 181–182
  editing, 183
  global, 183–184
  pattern, 21–23, 209
  saving color groups to, 192, 209
  using Illustrator libraries of, 186
  viewing on Swatches panel, 179

Swatches panel
  creating color group, 190
  creating patterns for, 21–23
  saving gradient in, 297
  using, 179
symbol instances
  adjusting with bracket keys, 415, 417
  breaking link to, 411
  copying and pasting, 404, 405
  defined, 403
  editing, 405, 411, 414–416
  preventing artwork from becoming, 406
  spraying, 412–414
  transforming, 405, 409
Symbol Options dialog box, 406, 407, 412
symbol sets
  applying graphic styles to, 416
  copying and editing, 417–418
  defined, 412
Symbol Shifter tool, 415, 417, 418, 420, 421
Symbol Sizer tool, 414
Symbol Sprayer tool, 412–413
Symbol Stainer tool, 416, 417
Symbol Styler tool, 416
Symbolism tools
  editing symbol instances with, 414–416
  selecting symbol instance affected by, 420, 421
  spraying symbol instances, 412–414
symbols. *See also* symbol instances; symbol sets
  about, 401
  accessing from saved documents, 420, 421
  adding to perspective grid, 288
  breaking link between instance and, 411
  creating, 23–24, 406
  defined, 23, 403
  editing, 405, 407–409, 412
  editing in perspective, 288–289
  exporting for Flash, 419
  layers for, 403, 411
  lesson files for, 402

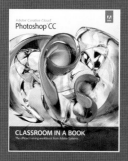

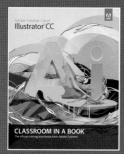

The fastest, easiest, most comprehensive way to learn

Adobe® Creative Cloud™

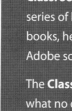

Classroom in a Book®, the best-selling series of hands-on software training books, helps you learn the features of Adobe software quickly and easily.

The **Classroom in a Book** series offers what no other book or training program does—an official training series from Adobe Systems, developed with the support of Adobe product experts.

To see a complete list of our Adobe Creative Cloud titles go to:
www.adobepress.com/adobecc

Adobe Photoshop CC Classroom in a Book
ISBN: 9780321928078

Adobe Illustrator CC Classroom in a Book
ISBN: 9780321929495

Adobe InDesign CC Classroom in a Book
ISBN: 9780321926975

Adobe Dreamweaver CC Classroom in a Book
ISBN: 9780321919410

Adobe Flash Professional CC Classroom in a Book
ISBN: 9780321927859

Adobe Premiere Pro CC Classroom in a Book
ISBN: 9780321919380

Adobe After Effects CC Classroom in a Book
ISBN: 9780321929600

Adobe Audition CC Classroom in a Book
ISBN: 9780321929532

Adobe SpeedGrade CC Classroom in a Book
ISBN: 9780321927002

Digital Video with Adobe Creative Cloud Classroom in a Book
ISBN: 9780321934024

Design with the Adobe Creative Cloud Classroom in a Book
ISBN: 9780321940513

AdobePress